Outsourcing, Downsizing, and Reengineering: Internal Control Implications

By
Albert J. Marcella Jr.,
COAP, CQA, CSP, CDP, CISA

The Institute of Internal Auditors

Disclosure

ISBN 0-89413-331-4
94448 1/95w
95447 12/95w

Dedication

Albert J. Marcella, Sr.
(10/31/28 - 6/4/94)

This work is dedicated
to the memory of my Dad.
To all who knew him
(which, at times when I was growing up,
seemed like everyone),
he was always, and will forever be,
"Big Al."

His tenacious approach to life helped him to endure the
Depression, ill health, and later in his professional career,
times of economic downsizing and fiscal belt-tightening.
It was his uncanny ability to find the least costly supplier
for some of the most arcane items during his career
as a senior purchasing agent that made him
a most valued employee.

His commitment to succeed and to the conviction
of doing a job well the first time are lessons
I am grateful he taught me,
and which I will teach my children.

A lifetime of love and learning
can hardly be summed up in a single page —
his words and my memories of him
will be with me always.

Contents

About the Author

Albert J. Marcella Jr., COAP, CQA, CSP, CDP, CISA, is a tenured Associate Professor of Management Information Systems at the Tabor School of Business at Millikin University in Decatur, Illinois. Mr. Marcella remains the president of Business Automation Consultants, a data processing management consulting firm specializing in the design, implementation and performance of quality audits in such areas as ISO 9000 Gap Analysis, Outsourcing/Downsizing Impact Analysis, Disaster Contingency Planning, System Development Life Cycle Reviews, Electronic Data Interchange, and Systems Programming. Prior to the formation of his own firm in 1984, Mr. Marcella was employed by the Dun & Bradstreet Corporation where he established and formalized the EDP audit function.

Mr. Marcella's additional professional experiences include providing internal systems consulting services to the Hartford Insurance Group, and the design and execution of operational, financial, and data processing audits for the Uniroyal Corporation, both in the United States and abroad. He has contributed numerous articles to audit-related publications and has authored and co-authored eight audit-related textbooks, including *Auditing IBM's Customer Information Control System; End-User and Departmental Computing; Auditing Disaster Contingency Planning;* and *EDI: Security, Control and Audit.*

Mr. Marcella holds a bachelor of science degree in business administration with a dual major in management information systems and management from Bryant College in Rhode Island and a master of business administration in finance from The University of New Haven in Connecticut. Mr. Marcella is currently completing his doctoral studies in management and MIS at Walden University. The focus of his dissertation research is titled *Ethics and Auditor Judgment.* He has been designated a Certified Systems Professional (CSP) by the Association for Systems Management, a Certified Quality Assurance Analyst (CQA) by the Quality Assurance Institute, a Certified Office Automation Professional (COAP) by the Office Automation Society International, a Certified Information Systems Auditor (CISA) by the Information Systems Audit and Control Association, and holds a Certificate in Data Processing (CDP) conferred by the Data Processing Management Association. Mr. Marcella has also been recognized as a Distinguished Adjunct Faculty Member by The Institute of Internal Auditors (IIA).

Mr. Marcella, is a member of the following professional societies: Information Systems Audit and Control Association; The Institute of Internal Auditors; Information Systems Security Association; and the International Information Management Association.

Acknowledgments

Looking back at the time, effort, and energy which has been spent in creating this work, I realize that its completion would not have been possible if left solely to my own resources. Many individuals have lent their support, encouragement, insight, and convictions into the work you are about to read. I have benefited greatly from their sage advice, insightful comments, gentle (and at times not-so-gentle) proddings, and always meaningful analysis.

I am deeply grateful to the faculty of Walden University, with whom I have worked over the past three years. Special thanks goes to Dr. Thomas Sawyer, Dr. Margaret Vaughan, Dr. Robert O'Reilly, and Dr. Earl Joseph who have always held high standards for the research work they would accept, and by doing so, have challenged me to raise my own standards; Richard A. Mannweiler, Dean of the Tabor School of Business at Millikin University, for his support, patience, and commitment to a higher level of professionalism; my colleagues at Millikin University and the staff of the Tabor School, for their support and assistance throughout this project; Jennifer E. Bird, internal auditor with Bunzl USA, Inc. for her suggestions on topical coverage and her continued encouragement; Edward L. Morrisey, CIA, Education Specialist with The Institute of Internal Auditors (IIA) for his excellent critique of my original work and suggestions for improvement in this final piece; Barbara J. Davison, CIA, Assistant Vice President for Investments with The Security Benefit Group; Belden Menkus, friend, colleague, and Editor of *EDPACS*, for his timely and insightful contribution on outsourcing's impact on the internal auditing function; and the reviewers provided by the publisher, including IIA administrators, IIA education committee members, and the external reviewers, who will for eternity remain anonymous.

To each of these special individuals — my thanks. This work is a better product as a result of your involvement.

Kristina and Andy, thank you for your love, patience, and understanding, especially of the time we spent apart as I toiled to complete this work. You are always a source of strength and motivation.

Preface

> "...there is nothing more difficult to plan, more doubtful of success, nor more dangerous to manage than the creation of a new system. For the initiator has the enmity of all who would profit by the preservation of the old institutions and merely the lukewarm defenders in those who would gain by the new ones. The hesitation of the latter arises in part from the fear of their adversaries, who have the laws on their side, and in part from the general skepticism of mankind which does not really believe in an innovation until experience proves its value. So it happens that whenever his enemies have occasion to attack the innovator they do so with the passion of partisans while the others defend him sluggishly so that the innovator and his party are alike vulnerable."
>
> *Niccolo Machiavelli,*
> *The Prince*

The Wall Street Journal has reported that top business consultants are now "selling" a go-slow approach to downsizing. Peter Drucker, management guru and professor at the Claremont Graduate School, states, "We are seeing too many amputations before the diagnosis." A recent study conducted by Arthur D. Little showed that two-thirds of the 700 organizations surveyed encountered "unexpected problems" as they implemented changes in their staffing structures

According to Peter Scott-Morgan, a director at Arthur D. Little, there is a little troubling link between reengineering and downsizing. "If people are worried about their jobs, the unwritten rules change and the people fight to save their jobs," notes Scott-Morgan. Perhaps the best explanation for the limited reengineering success revealed in this survey is expressed in the following finding: Some 64 percent of the respondents said their organization's most daunting barrier to implementing change was a lack of buy-in among managers and employees that change was necessary in the first place (Hoard, 1994).

These findings are scary. They have a direct effect and a direct link to internal auditing and internal auditors. The ramification of a wholesale shift in management philosophy from Theory Y/Theory Z/personnel focused to a "slash and burn" outsourcing/downsizing approach (in times of an economic crunch) can spell potential disaster for an auditing function.

The primary objective of this book is *not* to dwell upon the pros and cons of outsourcing the internal auditing function. The reader is directed to Part 3, A Question of Independence: Outsourcing Internal Auditing; the End Note to this text; and Appendix XXXII, The IIA's Perspective on Outsourcing Internal Auditing, for a further treatment and discussion of this timely topic. The objective of this book *is*, however, to present an overview of managing an organization into the 21st century under the rubric of outsourcing, downsizing, reengineering, etc. What are the potential problems, pitfalls, exposures, and weaknesses in a shift of management philosophy toward outsourcing, downsizing, etc., and how is the resulting "organization" to be controlled?

This work is divided into three separate parts. This approach lends itself to a greater flexibility in presentation and an ability for the reader to choose between perusing a section solely by topic or reading the text in its entirety. Part 1 addresses managing the "new" organization. Primary here is the presentation of traditional and emerging organizational "models" and the impact that outsourcing, downsizing, etc. will have on an organization's management "style." The auditor should be concerned here because a change in corporate direction/philosophy *may* compromise existing internal controls and render others ineffective.

Part 2 provides the reader with a detailed examination into the organizational "shifts" of outsourcing, downsizing, rightsizing, reengineering, and partnering. The reader is presented with an answer to the question: What exactly is outsourcing, downsizing, etc., and why should I (as a professional auditor) be concerned?

Part 3 contributes toward a better understanding and examination of third-party service organizations. The impact on in-house operations is addressed through the use of audit programs specifically developed for this book and designed to be used by practicing auditors.

> Information technology is a means to a business end. We have learned over the past decade that it is not the technology that creates a competitive edge, but the management process that exploits that technology.
>
> — *Peter G. W. Keen*
> *(author of* Shaping the Future: Business Design Through Information Technology*)*

The audit "programs" to be found in Part 3 are divided into four categories:

1. General Overview Questions.
2. Management Questions.
3. Security Questions.
4. Third-party Contract Questions.

These "programs" or checklists have been designed to serve as a basis for the audit of management's decision to outsource, downsize, reengineer, etc., and the impact upon an organization's ability to maintain a high level of internal controls as a result of this management decision.

There are no magic formulas for organizational change, no quick fixes to avoid destructive behavior. However, there is an integrated process for shifting culture which, when supported by senior executives, has proven to be effective. This process consists of six stages:

1. Who are "we" the firm? (Analyze and understand the current culture.)
2. Who do "we" want to be? (Determine the desired elements of the new culture.)
3. Begin at the top.
4. Unfreeze the culture with team training.
5. Revise the old systems and structures to reinforce the new culture.
6. Monitor the process.

A wealth of information is presented in the Appendices to this text. The reader is encouraged to refer to them often as a basis for enhancing the audit checklists in Part 3, or in developing additional, customized audit programs.

There is also a detailed glossary of key terms used in outsourcing, downsizing, reengineering, etc. Additionally, the reader will find an extensive list of recommended readings sorted by appropriate category. These readings are included here for two reasons. First of all, they are a value-added benefit to the reader. Having access to such an extensive reference listing will become increasingly valuable over time. Secondly, they demonstrate to the reader the importance and the interest within the industry concerning almost any movement toward outsourcing, downsizing, etc.

I wish you well in your efforts to tame these emerging management philosophies. Should you have any further questions I invite you to contact me through the publisher.

Part 1
Managing the "New" Organization

> Accept any reasonable technology risk that has significant business payoff, but that will not compromise the firm's name in the industry.

Introduction

The challenges of doing business in markets that are increasingly competitive, fast-moving, and global are enough to test the skills of even the most business-savvy manager. The challenges range from redesigning business processes to streamlining technical infrastructures. Organizations intent on shaping the marketplace rather than merely reacting to it must prepare by marshaling and reevaluating their technical and human resources with an eye toward long-term business goals.

From a management perspective, the buzzwords abound: reengineering, downsizing, outsourcing, and so forth. They sound simple and effective, but creating a new corporate paradigm requires that managers move to the next level above their departmental goals. They must commit to being business people first by working directly from the corporate business plan.

Organizations that want to enter new markets face a different set of problems in getting up to speed on the business plan. As president and CEO of Fireman's Fund Insurance of New Jersey, Chris Bluemer relied on outsourcing to help him start a separate automobile insurance company and pick up 20,000 new policyholders in a matter of six months.

"The worst thing to do," says Bluemer, "is to start incorporating the parent-company systems, the parent-company payroll, and bureaucracy into the new system, no matter how advanced the parent-system. We have basically outsourced almost every service here — medical benefits, policy issue, customer information systems. It's better to rent a company than to start your own." Bluemer's decision to outsource allowed him to further support the business plan by putting his money into hiring an exceptional business staff rather than programmers.

It is no secret that information technology (IT) — computer, communications, and the like — is enabling and, in some cases, driving drastic changes in the structure and operation of organizations. While research may raise many questions about the exact form of changes (Huff, 1986), movements such as downsizing and de-layering, team-based organizational structures, dominance of knowledge workers, and global communication networks are reflections of these changes that are becoming reality.

Bluemer's Rules
Advice on dealing with outsourcing vendors

1. Ask only those questions that need answers.
2. Insist on getting answers to the questions you ask.
3. Ask for short follow-up times. These lead to positive reactions.
4. Make every answer a 10-second answer.
5. Keep data honest.
6. Forgive mistakes. When someone errs, give him or her a can of Coca-Cola. It serves as a reminder that even though a mistake was made, the fix can be unexpectedly great.
7. Use the "Art Linkletter Approach." Ask outsourcing vendors, "What would you ask if you were me?"
8. Don't guess when you can avoid it.

— *Chris Bluemer,*
President and CEO, Fireman's Fund of New Jersey

Peter Drucker referred to this future organization as an information-based organization (Drucker, 1992). He argued that, rather than the traditional pyramidal form with its numerous bureaucratic layers and its command-and-control mentality, the future successful organization will resemble a university, hospital, or large symphony orchestra.

> Firms that stick with outmoded but "safe" technology will fail.
>
> — *Raphael Needleman*
> *Editor,* Corporate Computing

However, as one sage put it, "Prediction is hard, especially prediction about the future." The best predictions concerning organizations of the future, and the role of IT in shaping them, should derive from people who are actually leading the changes.

Geoff Ralph, CIO for General Electric Canada, in a speech to students of the School of Business Administration at the University of Western Ontario, addressed the broad social, economic, and technological changes currently underway and the need for corporations to confront these changes. He asserted that corporations are facing:

- **A new economy** (a major shift from an industrial to a service economy).
- **New competitors** (e.g., as a result of globalization and strategic alliances).
- **New rules of competition** (e.g., as a result of deregulation).
- **New technologies** (often IT-based).
- **A changing workforce** (knowledge worker-based).

According to Ralph, in order to survive these organizations will undergo radical changes. They will need to downsize, delayer, and develop new management forms. They will have to think and act globally, focus clearly on customers, and develop greater flexibility and responsiveness.

While he sees the changes as radical and necessary, Ralph does not see information technology as forcing the changes, but rather as enabling them. He argues that new technology does not determine anything, but simply makes possible things that were previously infeasible.

> The ethical dimension of IT will also grow in importance; just because IT makes something possible that was previously impossible, does not make it right.
>
> — *Geoff Ralph*
> *Chief Information Officer,*
> *General Electric Canada*

A key variable in the change process will be the ability of senior executives to develop and communicate a consistent and compelling vision of the role of IT in defining and supporting the organization (Huff, 1986).

Paul Starita, Senior Vice President, Royal Trust (Canada), argues that traditional organizations follow a "divide and conquer" approach to management. The overall task faced by the firm is broken up into a multitude of tiny subtasks and farmed out to various units. This mentality tends to produce what he terms "mushroom management"; organizational workers are largely kept in the dark and operate in a "manure-rich medium." Furthermore, expertise is presumed, under this view, to reside at the top and to be passed downward as necessary.

All this is in stark contrast to what Starita sees as the future of successful organizations. Driving the changes is the shrinking "information float" of modern firms. Decision processes were lengthy in the past, in large part because information and decisions had to pass through numerous intermediate layers before anything actually happened. Today's information technology makes it possible to eliminate many of those layers and many of the intermediate processes as well, shrinking the information float (Huff, 1986).

Management must do more than create the vision. Managers will need to serve as facilitators of change, delegators of authority, entrepreneurs, and superb communicators.

> In the management of business, it is not what you think but what you know that counts. And it is not just what you know that is important, but in making effective use of what you know.

Effective Organizational Behavior: The 1990s and Beyond

> Today, computer services is an idea whose time has come. More and more [companies] don't want to be distracted by areas that are not directly related to their core businesses, their customers, and their markets. The best analogy I can give is if you could have an electrical power generator plant for every company. It's more cost effective to buy electricity from a public utility. I don't think [outsouring] is a criticism at all of IS management. We're reducing the costs of producing the information and improving the quality. So you get higher quality at a lower cost.
>
> — *H. Ross Perot*

What are the new skills demanded of effective managers in the 1990s and beyond? Competence and comfort in handling IT will be high on the list. IT — computers plus telecommunications plus workstations plus information stores — is one of the forces reshaping and structuring the new organizational theory for the 21st century. Since IT commands nearly 50 percent of most large firms' annual capital expenditures, it is essential that it become a part of top business managers' responsibilities.

The next year or two will add even more urgency to most firms' IT strategies, because it is now so integrally linked to their business planning.

> Information is the responsibility of everyone in a company. Those companies that service and thrive have leaders who understand the nature of information — their information requirements, the form it should take, and who else needs to have it.
>
> — *Peter Drucker*

According to Keen (1991), the business realities of the 1990s speak for themselves:

- Between 25 and 80 percent of an organization's cash flow is processed on-line.
- Electronic data interchange is the norm in operations (see Marcella and Chan, *EDI Security, Audit, and Control,* Artech House Publishers, for more on EDI and controls).
- Point-of-sale and electronic payments are an element in every electronic transaction processing system.
- Image technology is a necessity.
- Organizations are directly linked to major suppliers and customers in electronic partnerships.
- Reorganization is frequent, not exceptional.
- Work is location-independent.

Globalization of business demands globalization of organization. A multinational firm is composed of relatively independent national and regional units upon which corporate management imposes only limited requirements for worldwide commonality in key processes and operations. Coordination of IT strategies and corporate business strategies are pivotal to success in the 1990s and into the 21st century.

You would think someone had just invented the word "change" the way it is being flung about by corporate America. As industry players are aware, there is nothing *really* new about it.

What is new, however, is how much change is taking place. For many reasons — not the least of which are new technology, over-expansion in the 1980s, and an inevitable shrinking of the economy — almost every company and industry will undergo what has been fondly referred to as reengineering: bottom-up, no holds-barred change, all in the name of better business.

> Most of us fear change. Even when our minds say change, it is normal for our stomachs to quiver at the prospect. But for leaders and managers today, there is no choice but to change.
>
> — *Robert H. Waterman Jr.*

In terms of an evolving organizational behavior for the 1990s, now is the time for management to question everything, dare to rethink and restructure individual departments/divisions, the way the organization does business, and even with whom the firm does its business. There is no looking back; the answers to today's problems lie in future choices (outsourcing, downsizing, rightsizing), some of which are just starting to get underway, (reengineering) and some of which may never have been tried (partnering, insourcing, upsizing).

Organizational Behavior Management and Information Technologies

Corporate management (managers in general) can ill afford to avoid the process of making decisions about IT. It affects the entire business — from organizational structure to product market strategies. The technical experts just do not have a deep enough understanding of where the overall business is going (Davenport, 1989).

Clearly, many companies headed into the second half of the 1990s and the 21st century will need a revised strategy, a proactive plan focused toward IT decision making that melds the technical knowledge of the computer expert with the vision of senior management.

> Leadership throughout the developed world no longer rests on financial control or traditional cost advantages. It rests on control of brainpower.
>
> — *Peter F. Drucker*

In "How Executives Can Shape Their Company's Information Systems," (Davenport, et al., 1989), the authors relate findings of their research which indicates successful organizations had articulated (through written principles) their basic philosophies about IT. These organizations appeared to be using technology more effectively.

Principles guiding organizational behaviors, therefore, are simple, direct statements of an organization's basic beliefs about how the company wants to use IT over the long term. By translating the main aspects of an organization's business strategy into the language of technology managers, these principles bridge the communications gap between top managers and technical experts. This way, an organization's business strategy drives its technical strategy, as conventional wisdom says it should.

Collins and Devanna (1990) postulate that the strategic use of information technology is primarily concerned with the likely impact of IT on the practice of strategic management. One could theorize then that a basis for such a postulation reflects a fundamental belief that IT can potentially influence the core of an organization's activities. Activities such as decisions pertaining to products, markets, and technologies (the corporate strategy level), as well as competitive methods within each of the product-market segments (the business strategy level) are all influenced by the evolving changes within IT.

Over the past several years new and powerful forces in the technological and market environment compel one to recognize the link between strategic management and information technology in terms of the fundamental role played by IT in influencing the formulation of an organization's strategy rather than merely supporting its implementation. The radical transformation of this link can be viewed as a combination of technology push and competitive pull. In addition, an organization's proactive behavior to introduce innovative deployments of IT-based systems and mechanisms designed to gain a strategic advantage plays a key role in this linkage.

Organizational Behavior: The Future — Where Are We Going From Here?

More and more people working in and for organizations will actually be on the payroll of an independent outside contractor. Drucker commented that the 1990s will bring far-reaching changes in the social and economic environment, and in the strategies, structure, and management of business.

> A corporation has responsibilities both to the society of which it is a part, and to its parts, its members. The principal social function is the production and distribution of wealth. Its principal means of distributing wealth is through...employment.

Businesses will undergo more and more radical restructuring in the 1990s than at any time since the modern corporate organization first evolved in the 1920s. Businesses of tomorrow will follow two new rules: One — to move work to where the people are, rather than people to where the work is [as so echoed by Keen (1991)], and Two — to farm out to an outside contractor those activities that do not offer opportunities for advancement into fairly senior management and professional positions. The corporation, in stock market jargon, will be unbundled.

Of course there is a price for this unbundling. If large numbers of people cease to be employees of the organization for which they actually work, there are bound to be substantial social repercussions. And yet, so far there is no other option in sight for giving us a chance to tackle what is fast becoming a central productivity problem of developed societies (Drucker, 1992).

A further gaze into Drucker's crystal ball provides us with several insights into the future of organizational structure and behavior. In light of changing world economies, the advent of the information-based organization, and the need to systemize innovation and entrepreneurship, Drucker (1988) provided us with an insight into what skills and abilities an executive will need in order to be effective within a newly "designed," reorganized corporate structure.

1. Manage by going outside. . .Learn to be outside where the results of the business take place.

2. Find out the information you need to do your job . . . People must learn to take responsibility for their own information needs.

3. Build learning into the system. . . Learning must be continuous. (Drucker, 1992)

The productivity of the newly dominant groups in the workforce — knowledge workers and service workers — will be the biggest and toughest challenge facing managers in the developed countries for decades to come. Serious work on this daunting task has only begun.

> "Empowerment" is the mantra of the 1990s. Government officials, academics, consultants, and corporate chieftains are singing the praises of giving each employee the authority and responsibility to make his or her company more successful, and in the process, upgrade their jobs from drone to dynamo.
>
> — *Bill Eaton*
> *Chief Information Officer,*
> *Levi Strauss & Company*

Toffler (1990), another visionary keen on the view of organizational behavior in the years to come, states that there is a "new system for wealth creation, which is transforming work, capital, and money itself."

That new system is information. Now more than ever, Toffler (1990) indicates, it is not violence nor wealth that will determine the future, but knowledge. He is referring to information and all it entails — electronically transferred information, information wars, and the increasing value of information.

Toffler (1990) points out that in the infrastructure of the 21st century, information will run instantly from customer to distributor to manufacturer. Of course, anyone who has purchased anything in the last decade is aware of this already. By the simple act of ringing up a retail sale, the cash register electronically notifies the warehouse or purchasing office of the depletion of that item.

The race is to the swiftest, particularly when it comes to information exchange and access.

> Information is the ultimate weapon.

Organization behavior is changing, and as a result, management has to change its strategies. Computer technologies are evolving and affecting the way businesses operate. If organizations want to move ahead, and stay ahead, management must pay attention to these changes and adapt to them. The competition certainly will be!

Summary

Plans to centralize and consolidate IS operations are being implemented across corporate America. A new organizational model is emerging which combines both centralization and decentralization, resulting in an operation that is flexible enough to adapt to changing business conditions. Of the 1990 Computerworld Premier 100 Companies, 56 of the 100 companies say their IS organizations are already a mix of centralized and decentralized functions. A consensus has emerged that centrally managed functions should include setting technology and architecture standards, approving major purchases, and identifying cross-functional systems opportunities. Conversely, there is agreement that business applications development should be in the business units, where IS and line managers can quickly respond to customers and market demands. According to Dudley Cooke of the Executive Insight Group, the most important thing is to continue to be flexible — a practice called "rightsizing."

According to a recent study (Bradley, 1992) the worldwide market for business and personal productivity software is expected to grow to $101 billion by 1996, up from $45.1 billion in 1991. One observation which was also presented from this study is that by the end of the 1990s, it is estimated that one-third of existing data center operations will be outsourced.

Clearly, the financial difficulties being experienced by several of the large software and hardware vendors — downsizing, rightsizing, outsourcing (consolidations of data center operations by corporations seeking a better return on their IS investment) — have created an environment of uncertainty and change.

> Change is the issue because it alters the power bases and comfort zones of people. Effective CIOs keep people uncomfortable because they are constantly initiating change.
>
> — *Doug Nagan*
> *Senior Vice President and CIO*
> *John Wiley & Sons, Inc.*

It is within this environment that the remainder of this text will focus. The material that follows in Part 2 examines in significant depth the contribution that changes in economies and IT have made to organizational behavior.

Specifically, each of the "newly empowered" organizational "styles" or behaviors (outsourcing, downsizing, rightsizing, partnering, and reengineering) will be analyzed with respect to its role in reshaping organizational theory, and ultimately its impact upon internal controls.

Due to increasing information demands and changes in technology, organizations must redevelop new, proactive management styles. Outsourcing, downsizing, rightsizing, partnering, and reengineering are all responses to this shift of organizational philosophy.

> The pursuit of corporate ethical/moral and aesthetic objectives requires providing employees at all levels with opportunities to participate in making decisions that affect them directly, and in exercising collective control over those who control them separately.
>
> — *Russell L. Ackoff*
> *Chairman of the Board and CEO,*
> *INTERACT: The Institute for*
> *Interactive Management*

Part 2
Audit and Control of the "New" Organization

Introduction

The winds of change are sweeping across corporate America, altering the long-held beliefs of organizational behavior. This introductory material will examine the five primary shifts in organizational behavior brought about by changes in American as well as global economies and information technologies. These new (and some not so new) behaviors or restructures of the traditional organizational philosophy are sweeping American industry. Downsizing, rightsizing, partnering and reengineering are the industry buzzwords currently receiving extensive press coverage. Each "behavior" requires a different management style and corporate philosophy. Outsourcing, which is not so much a behavior as it is a style, is receiving the same level of notoriety but has been a method of operation within American firms for many years. It had, however, operated under its previous name — third-party vendor. "Services are more sophisticated, but I don't think it's substantially changed in 30 years. We called it time-sharing, we called it remote processing. Now we call it outsourcing." (Don Seiden, President of Computer Reserves, Inc.) Admittedly these terms are not as flashy or as trendy as outsourcing. Thus, "You gotta write what sells!" Therefore, outsourcing joins the industry's lexicon for the 1990s, replacing third-party vendor of the 1980s, and remote processing and time-sharing of the 1970s.

The approach that will be followed to analyze these organizational "behavioral styles" will entail a review of each "style."

The following questions serve as a basis for the analysis.

1. How does an industry define outsourcing, partnering, reengineering, etc.?
2. What are the benefits of this organizational approach?
3. What are the costs/risks of this organizational approach?
4. What has been (or is expected to be) the impact of outsourcing, downsizing, reengineering, etc. upon the internal controls within an organization?

Each of the organizational "behaviors" will be examined; however, the order of analysis does not indicate, nor is it meant to indicate, any priority, greater acceptance within or by an industry, popularity, or effectiveness over any other behavior. The order of review is purely random. It would be best to define here why these "behaviors" represent new organizational approaches.

As previously stated, changes in economics and great forward strides in IT have forced organizations to rethink their core business(es) and how best to succeed at the business(es). As a result, changes in organizational theory, behavior, and design were inevitable.

"If you can't grow the business the way you thought, you have to find a way to reduce expenses."

— *David MacPherson,*
CIO, Del Monte Foods,
commenting on the impact of
a poor U.S. economy forcing
the company to farm out
its IS function,
*(*Computerworld,
November 9, 1992, pg. 12.)

A firm cannot decide to pursue a course of outsourcing, reengineering, or downsizing, for example, and expect not to affect the corporation as a whole. Decisions such as these are far-reaching and impact all facets of the organization. Theories, policies, and procedures that worked under one methodology may no longer prove to be valid nor effective. They will require change. Purchasing, marketing, personnel, production control, finance, and all departments having a stake in the successful functioning of an organization will feel the impact of a major shift in organizational philosophy (behavior).

Therefore, the five primary "shifts" in organizational design which are to be examined in this text represent a milestone in the continual, progressive state of organizational development. The impact of these organizational "shifts" on corporate America will be felt for years to come.

> Information technology's role in commercial life is changing against a backdrop of economic, social, fiscal, and even geographical instability.
>
> — *Joseph McCarthy,*
> *Vice President, BAC Systems, Inc.*

Analysis of Organizational "Shifts"
Outsourcing

Outsourcing Defined

Thanks to new technologies, executives can divide up their organizations' value chains, handle the key strategic elements internally, outsource others advantageously anywhere in the world with minimal transaction costs, and yet coordinate all essential activities more effectively to meet customers' needs. Under these circumstances, moving to a less integrated but more focused organization is not just feasible, but imperative for competitive success.

Organizations that understand this philosophy build their strategies not around products, but around deep knowledge of a few highly developed core service skills. Organizations are kept as lean as possible. They strip down to the essentials necessary to deliver customers the greatest possible value from its core skills — and outsource as much of the rest as possible.

As a result, management focuses on what it does best, avoids distractions, and leverages its organizational and financial resources far beyond what traditional strategies allow (Quinn 1990).

By establishing true strategic focus, an organization can concentrate more power in its chosen markets than anyone else can. Recognizing this, smart strategists no longer analyze market shares and their associated cost positions ad infinitum, nor do they build integrated organizations to exploit them. Instead, they concentrate on identifying those few core service activities where their organization has — or can develop — unique capabilities. Then they aggressively seek ways to reduce, limit, or outright outsource activities where the organization cannot attain superiority, unless those activities are essential to its chosen areas of strategic focus.

> Outsourcing of some kind is now a foregone conclusion for most IS operations. These days, the relevant question for the majority of companies is not whether to outsource IS functions, but how much to outsource and to whom.
>
> — *Max D. Hopper,*
> *Senior Vice President of IS, AMR Corp.*

An excellent example of this is E & J Gallo Wineries. The company turned to outsourcing an activity that many traditionalists consider to be the heart of the winery business — growing the specialized grapes for its wines. Gallo instead devotes its resources and management attention to maintaining the world-renowned marketing and sales strength that give the company its volume advantages and to using the deep knowledge base its 31 percent market share can provide to purchase grapes with the precise qualities its wines require. A significant strategic benefit from this organizational approach is that Gallo has avoided the investments and risks inherent in growing grapes.

As organizations modify their behaviors to accommodate this new "style," management will be afforded an opportunity to view each and every corporate function, operation, and task for necessity and efficiency. Management should now ask, are we really the best in the world's market for what we do? If not, can intelligent (strategic) use of outsourcing or other organizational behaviors improve our productivity and strengthen our long-term competitive position?

By avoiding investments in vertical integration and by managing "intellectual systems" instead of workers and machines, organizations decrease their investment and leverage resources substantially. They also are better able to minimize certain unavoidable risks.

> Most companies will move to large-scale outsourcing only if they believe that they will increase operating income or reduce capital needs in the process.
>
> — *Howard Frank,*
> *Editor,* Networking Management

What are the Benefits of Outsourcing?

Outsourcing provides management with the following benefits:

- Better "response time" due to more powerful mainframes used by outsource vendors than are available in-house currently. Faster response time leads to lower costs and increased productivity in personnel.

- More time and opportunity to concentrate on the facilities, applications-management, and development side of the business.

> Nearly 25 percent of firms with sales between $1 million and $50 million are either outsourcing or considering outsourcing. About 37 percent of companies with sales less than $2.5 billion are now using or considering outsourcing.
>
> — *Mike Corbett,*
> *President, Frost & Sullivan's*
> *Computer Services Assessment Group*

- Access by the client to greater levels of security, reliability, and higher processing standards maintained by the outsource vendor than previously available to the client within its own operations.

- Access to the latest technology which the client could not have afforded on its own.

- An effective way to expand the organization's network internationally without having to add bilingual staff familiar with foreign regulations and carriers.

- An avenue to make the transition to client/server, open systems computing environment.

- An exercise that forces IS users to examine every facet of their operation. The result, optimally, is a more efficient IS enterprise — whether self-managed or run by an outsider.

- Opportunities for up to a 20 percent increase in productivity from outsourcing, while stiff cuts anywhere else may save only three percent to five percent.

- An opportunity to assist firms in keeping up with advancing technology while maintaining steady budgets and avoiding the periodic surges caused by upgrades or shifts to new types of systems.

- The ability for an organization that hires an outsource vendor for IT operations to sell much of its expensive computer hardware. Instead of depreciating those computers over several years, the organization can deduct its outsourcing costs as a business expense.

- Outsourcers offer economies of scale that may translate into 15 percent to 20 percent savings over in-house operations.

- Benefits from outsourcing can include:
  - Altering network loads or imbalances.
  - Improve network management/uptime.
  - Filling in missing skills.
  - Better response to user dissatisfaction.
  - Upgrade systems or add technologies.
  - Fill an information strategy vacuum.
  - Move employees to strategic tasks.
  - Migrate between technologies.
  - Off-load software development.

  - Gain an outsourcer's efficiencies.
  - Stabilize or reduce network costs.

- An opportunity to obtain stable pricing, eliminating the need to shop around while worrying about distribution and consistency of quality.

- By outsourcing, organizations can reduce the overhead of employees and personnel support staff. They can increase their return on assets by having fewer assets invested in ancillary services and muster them into the main line of the business.

- According to a survey of federal agencies by the Input Organization, lack of in-house staff and the desire to improve services are the biggest reasons federal agencies employ outsourcing firms.

> By the mid-1990s, more than 20 percent of the Fortune 500 will be outsourcing in some fashion.
>
> — *Computer Security Newsletter #93*
>
> Five years ago, 70 percent of computer support operations were handled internally. Today that's down to 45 percent.
>
> — Digital Update, *July 1991*

- Provide career opportunities for employees of the outsourced organization which may never have been possible prior to the outsource deal.

- Establish cost predictability in the client's operational expenses.

- Reduce the time management spends on IS operations, allowing managers to redirect their energies into the organization's core business.

- Allow for the sharing of risk between client and outsource vendor.

What are the Risks of Outsourcing?

> Outsourcing is very much like a marriage. It takes a long leap of faith, and then you have to live with the consequences, good or bad.

For all of the benefits to organizations provided by outsourcing, there are many inherent risks associated with this strategy:

- Incomplete, uncontrolled data links between client and outsource vendor.

- Failure to invoice client's customers.

- No strong commitment to fixing programming problems.

- Lack of security.

- Placing management in the position of having to choose between doing what is best for the health of the organization and doing what is best for the careers of their employees. This risk not only adds stress to the decision maker's life, it also raises the question of ethics.

- Calls for different rules of management "play" (i.e., keeping the existence of an outsourcing study under wraps).

- Employees who are forced to go to work for the outsource vendor, as part of the outsource contract deal, may not want to, might be unable to go, and be un-

© Rich Tennant, Rockport, MA.

happy, both personally and professionally. Employee morale suffers, as does the productivity, which leads to higher costs.

- The organization may become overly dependent on — and hence dominated by — its partners (i.e., outsourcing vendor or trading partner).

- Outsourcers have to be carefully managed and contracts painfully hammered out.

- Outsourcing requires an intense level of managerial diligence: performance goals and guidelines must be painstakingly pieced together and vendor efforts must be continuously monitored. (It should be noted that this item can also be included as a benefit of outsourcing. By its actions, management is forced to take a hard look, to really examine each of its functions (goals). By doing so, the organization should benefit in the long run.)

- Allowing outsiders to handle the tactical implementation of your organization's information technology needs is one thing, but permitting them to decide and define what those needs are is quite another. Most, if not all, major organizations' interests would be best served by retaining this strategic role.

- Outsourcing customers share in the responsibility (and subsequent risk) for complying with licensing policies of software vendors for the software used by their outsource vendors.

> Nobody wants to lose control of their strategic IS functions but, on the other hand, the idea that you have to hold on to it all is passe.
>
> — *Howard Anderson,*
> *President, The Yankee Group*

- One of the most dramatic role changes for management after outsourcing is one of learning to become a manager of contracts instead of being a manager of people.

- Deciding on which organization to choose as an outsourcing partner.

- While outsourcing may allow a firm to reduce personnel costs, that reduction is often not as great as organizations expect. This is because the firm fails to take into account relocation and severance costs associated with departing personnel.

- Organizations are demanding outsourcing payback within two years, which places unrealistic financial demands on the outsourcing contract.

- Loss of control over strategic operations.

> You don't abdicate management responsibility by outsourcing data processing.
>
> — *Charlie Eppinger,*
> *Executive Vice President and CEO,*
> *First New Hampshire Bank*

- Loss of in-house expertise (outsourcing forgoes the developing of internal expertise in favor of "renting" the expertise of others).

- Once an organization decides to outsource, the transition back to managing those functions in-house can be costly.

- Other hidden costs such as conversion costs for installation, software transition fees, and training costs all add up to some of the risks inherent with outsourcing.
- Other "hidden" costs would include termination of equipment leases and maintenance agreements.
- Transferring software licenses over to the outsource vendor can be expensive in some cases.
- Contract management costs are often unanticipated.
- Communication expenses can also be prohibitive. In many instances, the communications costs can become quite high if the corporation's remaining data center facilities are clustered in an area where the outsourcing vendor does not have a site or a network node.
- Not planning for future technology upgrades as part of the long-term outsourcing contract.

The Downside of Outsourcing

The potential as well as the opportunity for management to place the organization's financial future at risk through outsourcing has never been greater. For all the benefits and risks discussed, none is as great as the loss of financial stability. None of the strategies to be discussed herein can provide management with complete security from financial loss. As auditors it is our responsibility to identify those situations and conditions which may expose our organizations to financial risk. Three recent cases (briefly discussed here) provide clear evidence that risks abound under these new management strategies, and that the role of the auditor has never been more urgently needed by corporate management.

Outsourcing Everything But the Risk

Case #1 — Unauthorized Use of Property Software by Outsourcer

Minolta Corporation (the client) entered into a five-year data center outsourcing agreement with PKS International Services, Inc. (the outsource service provider). Minolta was hit with a bill for approximately $100,000 in license transfer fees from its software vendor, American Software, Inc. A spokesperson for American said the company (American Software) simply wrote a new agreement to enable PKS to run the software originally licensed to Minolta.

Several important audit-related control issues surface here. Two of the more critical questions which should be posed by auditors at this point are: (a) What effect, if any, does this extra payment have on the financial model upon which the decision to outsource was originally based?, and (b) Did Minolta's management have an available, viable alternative plan or strategy ready to go, had management been unable to afford to pay the license transfer fee, not want to pay the transfer fee, or convince American's management to relinquish or reassign the license to PKS?

In a second, closely related outsourcing contract gone sour (as of this writing), an ongoing legal dispute between Computer Associated International, Inc. (CA) and Electronic Data Systems Corp. (EDS) has forced UK's Inland Revenue to delay a major outsourcing contract and undertake a costly software rewrite.

A 10-year, $1.5 billion outsourcing agreement is on hold because CA's UK subsidiary refused to let EDS take over the licenses for the CA-IDMS database that Inland Revenue uses.

A spokesperson for CA said Inland Revenue has "mismanaged" the contract because it "made no attempt to ensure the outsourcer selected, EDS, was acceptable to CA." Once again, as in the previous example, the auditor's role in examining potential internal control weaknesses and exposures (i.e., no clear title of ownership to the critical database software) may have saved Inland Revenue from massive financial expenditures and costly legal battles.

As auditors, we need to ask some very basic questions as part of our proactive role in auditing outsourcing: Does the firm (or client) have clearance from all software licensers, or has the firm (client) paid a fee to all appropriate licensers, which ensures that currently utilized, critical software can be made available to the outsourcer of record? Has the fee for this "right" been built into the cost justification model for this outsourcing venture? Has a contract for such reassignment of fees been approved by legal counsel? The question of software license ownership takes on heightened importance when viewed in terms of an outsourcing contract. Not only is assignment of license rights important, but also ownership of software source code should the software vendor cease to operate, be acquired by a competitor, or decide to abandon the outsourcing/software industry. The importance of securing all necessary components, which will ensure a successful outsourcing endeavor, should never be underestimated. The auditor's role in this process will only increase in importance as the number of outsourcing contracts written annually continues to increase.

Case #2 — Lost Business Opportunities Due to Outsourcer's Faulty Computer System

Once the outsourcing marriage has been consummated, the need to regularly examine internal controls and conduct ongoing operational audits of the outsource provider becomes critical. Simply because your organization (client) has outsourced a particular business function or functions, the stockholders of your organization have not outsourced the responsibility to ensure that these functions continue to perform and operate in a manner consistent with management's objectives!

Texas State Bank is attempting to collect more than $365 million from outsourcer Electronic Data Systems Corp. (EDS) largely for what bank officials claim are lost business opportunities as a result of faulty computer operations.

In its suit, Texas State Bank alleges EDS misrepresented itself in 1988 when the outsourcer claimed that it was knowledgeable of and familiar enough with the bank's existing computer systems (provided them by Fiserv Inc.) to be able to convert the bank's Information Technology (IT) operation to an EDS system within three months.

Deposition papers filed by Texas State Bank indicate that nothing could be further from the truth. EDS's conversion and post conversion data processing and automated teller service system were disastrous, causing service problems to the bank's daily operations and growth. It is believed that EDS used a banking software system it had acquired through its purchase of another banking client. This "software system" is not used widely by EDS at other accounts.

The bank is seeking $300 million in exemplary damages, plus an additional $63.5 million for what bank officials claim are lost business opportunities (two bank acquisitions at $17.5 million and $46 million in lost business from customers). Bank officials claim that the primary problem with EDS's system stems from unreasonable amounts of downtime, a system that calculated interest based on the wrong number of days, inaccurately applied loan payments to customer accounts, and prevented bank customers from using their ATM cards.

The opportunity for audit involvement in the pre-decision making process, prior to signing the outsource contract, could not be more justified than in this case. One outstanding question looms in this case, which may be answered during the trial: Did Texas State Bank auditors (or the bank's external auditors) conduct financial, operational, or IT audits of the outsourcer's proposed systems prior to entering into an outsourcing contract? Note that the alleged system's compatibility question *may have* been misrepresented by EDS; however, a thorough audit of EDS's proposed system by appropriate, knowledgeable, and qualified auditors *may have* detected incompatibility weaknesses in the beginning. These weaknesses could have been brought to the outsourcer's attention and their correction to State Bank's satisfaction could have been made a condition of signing the outsource contract. These findings could have at least alerted State Bank officials and provided them with enough lead time to seek out an alternative outsource vendor.

As a postscript to this particular case, a jury in Texas has ruled that EDS *did not* commit fraud or fail to comply with its data processing agreement with Texas State Bank as charged. The bank has been ordered to pay EDS $500,000 for interfering with the outsourcer's attempts to do business with two other banks that have merged with Texas State Bank. George Carruthers, Texas State Bank's chief financial officer, indicated that the bank's attorneys are deciding whether to appeal the decision (Halper 1994).

This ruling should clear the way for a similar suit filed by First National Bank of Edinburg (Edinburg, Texas) against EDS. The suit alleges EDS overburdened the bank's data processing system after EDS took over operations from Mtech Corporation in 1989. The bank is also claiming that EDS failed to provide daily account balance information in a timely manner. First National seeks unspecified damages in its actions against EDS.

As the stakes continue to rise and the dependency upon third-party service providers continues to grow, involvement of the auditing department in a variety of reviews (examinations) is becoming more critical. Closer scrutiny should be given to the reengineering of the auditing function in the months ahead.

One can only predict a closer working relationship between auditing and the firm's (client's) legal department in performing co-audits of outsourcing contracts, for example.

Case #3 — Employees Claim Loss of Severance Benefits Due to Outsourcing
In one of the higher profile outsourcing contracts (estimated at nearly $1 billion over 10 years), ex-employees of Blue Cross and Blue Shield of Massachusetts sued their former employer 11 weeks after the organization's management consummated an outsourcing deal with EDS.

The ex-employees allege that they had been wrongfully denied Blue Cross severance benefits, which they were legally entitled to. At the trial's conclusion, the judge found that Blue Cross had unfairly placed limitations on the employee's range of options (i.e., requiring them to work for EDS or resign, and not offering them the option of being laid off from the organization with severance benefits and access to potential unemployment benefits as well). The court found in favor of the 480 employees who brought the class action suit, and awarded them $9 million in severance benefits, interest, and attorney's fees.

Although this case is currently under appeal, the potential risks to organizations considering outsourcing (should the employees in this example win and overturn the appeal and set precedent) is dramatic. First, and most clearly, a message is sent to the organization's management — employees will not and should not be considered as parcel and subjected to wholesale "business decisions" without regard for their personal well being and financial security. Secondly, employees have voices, loud ones, and most are aware of their legal rights and availability of the legal system to work for them. Employers who do not consider the "human element" and the downstream ramifications of their outsource decisions on this human element (or their employees) should stand ready to pay the costly consequences of their employees' dissatisfaction.

Again, in a related case with a slightly different twist, employees of Kodak (Kodak Network employees) who along with their network operations function were outsourced to Digital, sued Digital (the outsource vendor). It appears that the employees were not excited about being forced to work for Digital and losing their benefits in the process. The slight difference in this case is that the employees sued the outsource vendor, not their former employer (at least not as of this writing).

As was the case in most issues, not until the bottom line was affected (and significantly) did the more humane and emotional issues associated with outsourcing contracts attract management attention. Since most outsourcing deals are struck for economic reasons, historically, the social issues and concerns have been pushed aside or flatly not dealt with at all. This attitude will change! Increasingly management will need to become aware of the impact of their outsourcing decisions on personnel and not solely on profits. As auditors, in our responsibility to identify the potential exposures, the financial risks will also require us to look more closely (more operationally) at the people issues and not just the financial issues. Our audits or pre-audits of outsourcing decisions should include an examination of the social elements of this decision and the associated costs and potential long- and short-term liabilities. Not only is the potential for risk and loss from employees who feel abandoned or wronged high, but the resulting negative media exposure and potential for confidential company data being disclosed in courts warrants the involvement by the audit function proactively in all outsourcing/third-party arrangements. No longer will (nor should) the audit function be restricted to providing an opinion on just the financial stability of the organization.

These cases demonstrate the growing need for auditors to become more proactively involved in the examination of contracts and contractual wording. Our profession may eventually see the skill set of an internal auditor include formal course work and/or training in the law of legal contracts. For now, however, it may be prudent for auditors to begin establishing closer relationships with their in-house (or external) legal counsel and to include the joint review of contracts (for each external third-party service) as part of the auditor's "standard" audit program.

© Teletoons, Joseph Louis Troise, Sausalito, CA.

What are the Impacts/Effects of Outsourcing on Organizational Behavior?

> Outsourcing means using experts to assume traditional, ongoing staff responsibilities in financial arrangements that are at least in part based on the bottom line of their work.
>
> — *Mark Hoewing,*
> *Executive Director, International Association of Corporate Real Estate Executives*

The implications of outsourcing on organizational behavior are many, and some of the more critical and far-reaching are detailed as follows:

- Both positive and negative changes are made to management behavioral styles.

    Negatively, many organizations may not communicate to employees that an outsource deal is under consideration for fear of losing key people if the outsource deal does not go through. This lack of communication (in attempting to prevent a disgruntled employee from harming company assets) may backfire when the announcement is actually made confirming the outsource decision.

    Positively, outsourcing is forcing management to take a harder look at personnel issues and begin a more open, up-front communications process with its employees.

- The strategy or decision to outsource provides the organization with a period of reorientation, i.e., an opportunity for the organization to view itself differently. Subscribing almost to a philosophy such that we (the client) should treat our customers in the same fashion as we would want to be treated by our outsource vendor.

- According to J.P. Richards, outsourcing analyst at the market research firm Input, the factors forcing management's hand toward outsourcing include increasing profits. Many firms are under extra pressure from the prolonged recession and brutal competition to scramble to top one another's service levels.

- Paul Cooke, Senior Vice President of Real Decisions Corp., states, "At the business level, outsourcing can often play an important role in dealing with acquisitions, decentralization, leveraged buyouts, divestiture of operations, or other forms of corporate restructuring."

> Even though many companies are downsizing, these same organizations need to expand operations in order to compete. As a result, they are turning to outside vendors whose expertise is needed more than ever in this new downsized, yet rightsized environment.
>
> — *William Stevens,*
> *Group Vice President,*
> *Decisions Unlimited, Ltd.*

- Outsourcing forces management to take a hard look at each and every operation. This focuses management's attention on the core business and being efficient at that business.

- Outsourcing places management in the position of viewing every action, every operation with an eye toward a cost/benefit relationship.

Types of Outsourcing Arrangements

According to Wagner (1994) the two major outsourcing arrangements are the partial transfer of computing activities and the outright sale of all computer assets. Each of these arrangements has advantages and disadvantages.

Partial transfer: From an accounting perspective, outsourcing is defined as "the transfer of an internal service function to an outside vendor" (Friedberg and Yarberry, 1991). This sort of arrangement is not necessarily new and need not be comprehensive. In the MIS area, this type of outsourcing may provide lower costs or greater access to advanced technology. This type of outsourcing could include externally processing payroll, while developing decision support systems in-house (organizations that processed clerical systems externally were known as "service bureaus" until relatively recently; now this is known as a specific type of outsourcing) (Wagner, 1994).

Reacting to the concerns of many MIS managers, Valovic et al. (1990) point out that outsourcing is "not giving away the strategic parts of your business — it's maintaining management visibility and control over it, it's being manager of the process and deciding who is going to do which parts." This might include hiring contract programmers, although such "one-shot" situations are not usually considered in discussions of outsourcing. "A good MIS manager will outsource only his or her weaknesses while keeping strengths in-house" (McCusker, 1991).

Purchase of assets: Several large outsourcing vendors (e.g., EDS, IBM, Andersen Consulting), states Wagner (1994), may purchase the entire set of MIS assets of the organization. The assets (i.e., computers and peripherals) will not physically move from the original organization's location. IBM purchased Eastman Kodak's mainframes and now runs Kodak's computer facility as a profit center rather than as a cost center. The MIS employees may be transferred from the original organization's payroll to the vendor's. Superficially, nothing changes. The employees will still report to work at the same location, will still have the same responsibilities, and will do the same jobs. This particular type of outsourcing provides a great infusion of cash into the organization at the time of the sale of the assets.

Potential Advantages of Outsourcing

Transfer of risk: One of the major advantages of outsourcing is the shifting of various risks from inside the organization to outside the organization. While a major advantage of outsourcing is the transfer of risk, it is from risk that an organization may acquire competitive advantage. In particular, technological advances developed by knowledgeable staff will not be possible; the staff will not have access to the technology. There will be no incentives for the vendor's staff to develop new and exciting uses of technology for the organization. The road to success for the vendor's staff will lie in carrying out daily tasks efficiently, not in developing new uses of technology or new technologies for the original organization (Wagner, 1994).

Reduced costs: In addition to reducing risk, outsourcing may also reduce actual costs for the organization. The vendor must be able to utilize economies of scale in order to achieve lower costs and make a profit. Reduced costs are not themselves a disadvantage, comments Wagner (1994). However, the emphasis on economies of scale for the vendor may result in the use of inappropriate technology for a particular organization. In addition, the vendor's economies of scale may lead to disaster recovery related questions. If the outsourcing vendor has all the clients' MIS work on one large computer, and if this one large computer crashes or experiences a disaster, which client organization will be brought back up first?

Improved service and access to new technology: Improved service may also be obtained through outsourcing. Because the vendor is not burdened with the other aspects of the organization's business and need only concentrate on the MIS area, the time between the request and the response may be dramatically decreased. However, because the vendor may be burdened with many other organizations, the business and needs of the original organization may not be the first priority. A new opportunity perceived as urgent by the organization may not be solved (or even worked on) in a timely fashion.

Management focus: The high-level managers of an organization may be better able to concentrate on the "real" business if they have outsourced the MIS activities. However, the potential loss of corporate continuity may be quite dangerous; viewing the organization as a set of very loosely related parts is often ineffective. A long-range vision, shared by the entire organization, is an important factor in successful organizations.

Increased ROE: The purchase-of-assets type of outsourcing (i.e., outsourcing the entire MIS department) provides a particular benefit to organizations wanting to increase their ROE ratio. The purchase-of-assets type of outsourcing mathematically leads to an increased ROE if profit remains constant or increases. However, in a slightly different scenario, the organization may decrease profit by paying an outsourcing vendor more for newer technology (i.e., sell the old computers in order to gain access to new ones). While this may still result in a larger ROE, the overall profit margin (the ratio of profit to sales) will decrease. Such a decrease may be distressing to analysts and vendors and should be carefully considered in advance (Wagner, 1994).

Nolan's Stage Model

A useful devise for planning in MIS is Nolan's Stage Model (King and Nolan, 1991). Nolan's Stage Theory helps the MIS planner decide where the organization is now, where it should be in the future, and what problems it is most likely to encounter as it journeys toward its goal of satisfying the organization's information needs. Nolan's Theory is based on understanding that the organization's personnel must first learn to perform old tasks using the new technology and then learn to use the new technology to solve new problems. Such knowledge is used by the planner to anticipate problems and their solutions, thus maintaining relatively smooth growth at an appropriate pace.

Dickson's Hierarchy

Dickson's Hierarchy (Dickson and Wetherbe, 1985) provides another way of looking at the systems in an organization, from lowest level (clerical) through information reporting systems and decision support systems, to the highest level (expert systems). The lowest two levels, clerical and information reporting, can be outsourced with relative ease. They are stable and easily described by rules. In fact, payroll systems (clerical) have been outsourced by many organizations for decades. The successful use of decision support systems and expert systems, on the other hand, requires so much extensive knowledge of the particular organization that outsourcing such high-level systems may be too difficult and inefficient. The MIS manager should analyze the particular characteristics of the systems under consideration for outsourcing and decide the appropriate action carefully.

Extent of End-User Computing

An organization that relied heavily on end-user computing may outsource those systems with which the end users do not interact. If the decision is made to outsource systems which do directly affect the end users, the MIS manager must be sure that the change will be transparent to these users. The goal of outsourcing is to improve the organization; unhappy users will render this goal completely unattainable (Wagner, 1994).

Summary

Outsourcing is not confined to the IT arena; in fact, outsourcing is relevant to every area subject to fulfillment by a service-based strategy. Perhaps the most important strategic outsourcing allows an organization to focus all its attention on the areas that add the most value per unit of input. This creates entry barriers for would-be competitors in a variety of ways. Because they are leaner, these organizations can respond faster to customers and move more easily to form the cross-functional teams that best provide innovative products for new market needs. Because they have fewer management levels, less bureaucracy, and more opportunities for employees' personal and entrepreneurial development, they can often attract the best people. Finally, they can leverage managerial talent — their most limited and most crucial resource — because their executives no longer need to waste time and attention on peripheral activities (Quinn, 1990).

Global sourcing, volatile currency fluctuations, fast-changing communications and information technologies, and the increased leverage of services are combining to restructure organizational philosophies, behavior and styles, as well as entire industries. The bottom line is simply, whenever an organization outsources, sets up a joint venture, or enters into a strategic partnership with a major service company — as most will — the organization is destined to encounter a totally new set of potential opportunities as well as risks.

The necessity for an independent, third-party review of the level of internal controls, as a result of the organization's move toward a pattern of non-traditional organizational behavior, has never been more justified. Control of potential exposures, due to the inherent risks of outsourcing, will be addressed in Part 3, Third-Party Service Organizations: The Impact On In-house Operations (Audit Questions).

Outsourcing is a business — not a technology — decision. It is a shift in the balance of power and a surrendering of control.

— *Paul Cooke,*
Senior Vice President,
Real Decisions Corp.

Tips for Picking a Client/Server Outsourcer

What should you look for in a client/server outsourcer? Here are some tips from the experts:

- Since client/server applications tend to be spread over several locations — and maybe several continents — look for an outsourcer that can go to where your facilities are — statewide, nationally, or globally. And if it doesn't have local officers, make sure it has agreements with reputable subcontractors.

- Make sure the outsourcer covers all of the basic services — help desk, training, application enhancement, and maintenance. Even if you don't need a particular service now, considering the rapid pace of change in client/server technologies, you may need it tomorrow.

- Closely evaluate the technical and managerial skillset of the outsourcer's people — "not only their technical knowledge, but also how well they understand your business," says Input Inc. analyst Steve Kerns.

- Set down performance metrics — ideally in business terms — to measure an outsourcer's performance. Are reports being generated on time? Are production requirements being met?

- Finally, make sure the outsourcer has appropriate network management skills. "If they don't have good network management skills, the network can bring you to your knees," states Kerns (Ricciuti, 1994).

Thanks to Outsourcing

What are Organizations Outsourcing?
% of Respondents

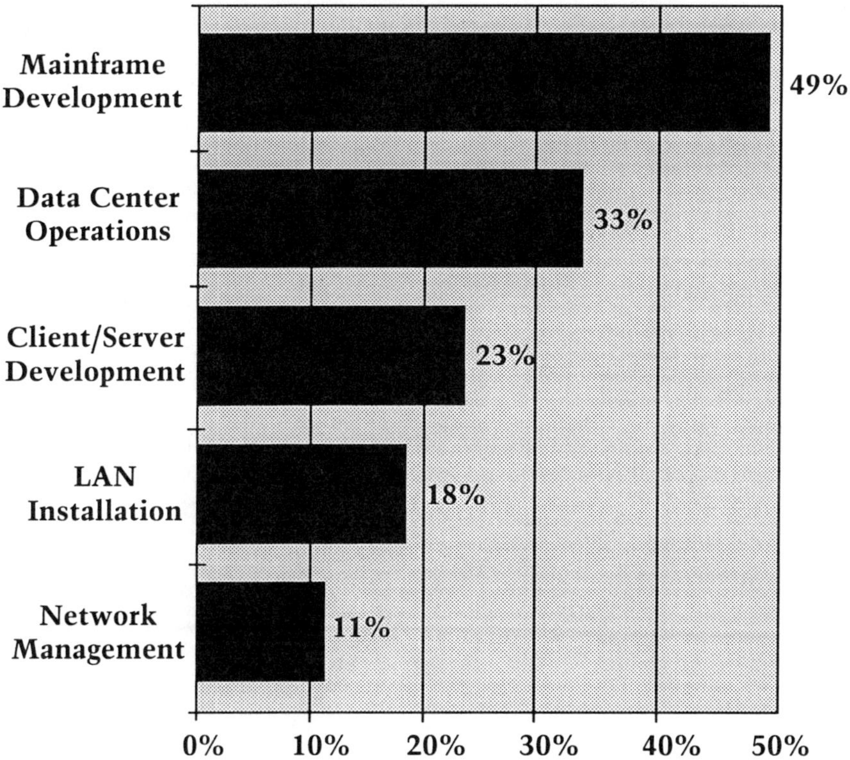

Reprinted with permission of *DATAMATION* magazine, March 15, 1993.

Outsourcing Market Leaders

The outsourcing market will jump from $10 billion in 1991 revenue to an estimated $26.5 billion in 1997, according to Input Inc. of Vienna, VA.

Outsourcing Trends

All companies are spending more on external training, but small companies spend the most

Company Size (No. of employees)	Percent of Budget Spent on External Training		Change (%)
	1993	1995	
Small (1 - 99)	27.5%	35%	7.5%
Medium (1,000 - 10,000)	15%	20%	5%
Large (10,000 - plus)	5.5%	13%	7.5%

Source: International Data Corporation, Framingham, MA (1994).

Outsourcing Outlook

U.S. Networking Outsourcing Revenue (in billions)

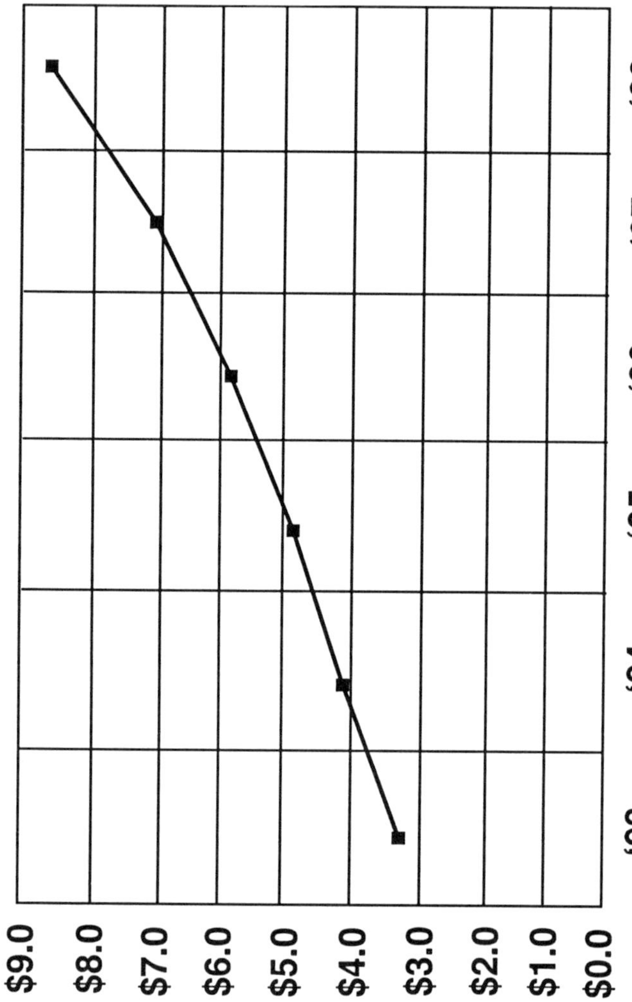

Source: Dataquest Worldwide Services Group, Framingham, MA. Copyright 1993/94 by Computerworld, Inc., Framingham, MA 01701. Reprinted from Computerworld.

Downsizing

> There is one guiding principle behind downsizing: Corporations will become more responsive (read more profitable) if key business resources are decentralized and distributed. What this means for managing the enterprise is cutting back or even dismantling an oversized bureaucracy and ushering in smaller, more dynamic groups. Client-server computing is central in the downsizing revolution. These distributed networks put data on the desktop and enable users to create simple programs in a fraction of the time it takes to develop a similar application for the mainframe. But while the client-server scheme addresses the needs of departments, it can have a negative effect on the flow of information between departments. Reintegrating the enterprise will be the toughest step on the road to distributed computing.
>
> — *Steven S. King,*
> *Contributing Editor,* Data Communications

Introduction

Although economists hesitate to use the term recession, the U.S. economy is in rough shape. Organizations both large and small are pinching pennies in efforts to buttress their bottom-line. Cuts are being made in almost every department, and times like these call for new management strategies. How do organizations remain competitive while reducing expenditures?

Information technologies (IT), recognized by most organizations as being their lifeblood, are rapidly changing and increasingly providing competitive advantages. To disregard the impact of IT would be nothing less than corporate suicide.

Corporate management is requiring the IT function to build and support more complicated, less costly systems. Through advances in technology such as open-system protocols, firms have tied ("linked") together many different types of computers. But managing these complex configurations and at the same time providing access to information for strategic decision making is more difficult than ever.

Most organizations will be required to spend more just to keep pace with the added responsibilities; however, spending increases are simply no longer possible. Outsourcing and downsizing are being viewed as possible solutions to this dilemma.

Is downsizing simply a fad? The terminology itself may be fleeting, but the idea behind it is here to stay. With the continuing advances in desktop technology in terms of price and performance, and with the increasing acceptance of standards-based operating systems and software environments, computer downsizing is almost an inevitable conclusion, especially for any business that wants to significantly cut costs, increase productivity, and improve its quality of service. And what business doesn't want to accomplish all three?

For all these reasons, a majority of computing industry analysts believe that downsizing represents a major paradigm shift in the way computing will be delivered in the future and the behavior of the resulting organization which is left in its wake. If such is the wave of the future, a clear definition of "downsizing" is the first order of business.

No longer is bigger always better. Along with streamlining operations and becoming more cost effective, organizations must now be prepared for a host of new challenges in managing ongoing operations in a restructured environment. In an environment in which personnel concerns may be in direct conflict with bottom line/expense reduction concerns, downsizing may not be a cure-all; however, one position is clear — the route an organization decides to follow will require a change in both management style and philosophy.

Downsizing Defined

Downsizing is a methodology — a management direction resulting in the moving or transferring of all or part of applications running on large systems, such as mainframes, to smaller, often lower-cost computer systems (i.e., microcomputers on local area networks).

Management must realize that downsizing is not primarily about technology. It is a holistic process that involves all aspects of an organization, from the physical plant, to personnel policy, to the most mundane aspects of day-to-day operations.

The remainder of this section will examine the benefits, as well as the risks, of downsizing and its impact on traditional organization theory.

What are the Benefits of Downsizing?

Downsizing provides management with the following benefits:

- More computing power.
  - Smaller systems are easier to program, and for the CPU power gained, cost less to buy, operate, and maintain.
  - The practical needs for downsizing arise because even the most powerful mainframes will slow down under heavy number-crunching jobs like statistical analyses or rate calculations. When this happens,

response time becomes too long for important tasks like on-line accounting. Then, transferring number-crunching applications to smaller computers can help.

- Improved network performance.
  - Downsizing can help solve network performance problems. When one computer interacts over a local network with many other computers or terminals, the resulting network traffic can seriously degrade communications speeds. Also, when some links in a wide-area network use low-speed data communications lines, performance over those links will be poor, especially when compared with local connections. Poor network performance will seriously limit users' productivity.
  - The key to increasing performance for both local and remote sites is to create subnetworks for storing and accessing copies of the data, eliminating the need to retrieve the data from a central system. The result is less traffic and better performance. Data stored on these subnetworks is periodically updated, often at night when the increase in network traffic is much less of a problem.

- Shorter application development cycles.
  - Packages are available for smaller platforms that often allow for very fast application development.
  - Often it is users rather than professional applications programmers who develop new applications with PC-based packages, thus, expediting application development.

- Improved data access.
  - Application developers for small computers expect users to manipulate and format data they need in their jobs.

  - Downsized applications supply a range of tools by which users of small computer systems can easily extract what they need from corporate data.
  - By entering mainframe or minicomputer-based data into downsized, PC-based applications, users can produce reports that mainframe operations are too busy to generate.

- Lower costs.
  - Whatever other advantages it offers, however, the underlying reason to downsize is to save money.
  - PC and workstation hardware and software cost less to maintain than comparable mainframe counterparts.
  - Increasing network performance increases productivity, which can save personnel costs.
  - Improving user access to data by making management more efficient can save costs in everything from personnel to raw materials.

- Empowered end users.

- A reduced number of computer vendors will force a cut in costs and reduce maintenance contract complexities.

- Newly redesigned downsized client/server systems will place report-writing tools directly in the hands of end users, allowing IS staff to concentrate their time and efforts in other areas.

- Establish a larger computing base by dispersing computing intelligence among more people.

- Maintenance contracts are typically based on the equipment's original purchase price. The cost of maintenance on a downsized $20,000 server is much less than the cost of maintaining a $1 million mainframe system.

- Perhaps one of the biggest benefits of downsizing is the opportunity it provides to incorporate new technologies on the organization's network. Multimedia applications, wireless technologies, pen-based systems, and other advanced products are very expensive to implement on a mainframe, if they can be supported at all.

What are the Risks of Downsizing?

For all of the benefits provided to organizations by downsizing, there are many inherent risks associated with this strategy:

- Running important business applications such as accounting and payroll systems on smaller platforms (i.e., PCs) requires adherence to similar standards for developing applications, operating the systems involved, maintenance, and security that are applicable to traditional mainframe and minicomputer environments.

- Low-end mini-and microcomputers, at least as they come out of the box, cannot offer the stability and security that good data processing practices require, especially when programmed and managed outside the traditional data processing structures.

- Building high-level stability and security that good data processing practice requires into lower-end systems is likely to add significantly to their cost and will, to some degree, reduce the appeal of downsizing entire applications.

- Once a key application makes its way to a downsized platform, it should receive the same attention as when it ran on a larger system (i.e., costly uninterruptible power supplies, backup and recovery procedures, etc.). All of these increase costs substantially and most of these tend to decrease the chance that enhancements to an application can be made quickly.

This is about as far as we can downsize our host applications without running into serious difficulties..
Phil Frank

- Applications for downsizing might not have enough room to grow. PCs, even those with high-end 486 processors, are likely to run out of steam (i.e., processing capacity and storage capability), and to some extent may push the limits of currently configured Pentium processors, before larger systems would.

- Downsized applications lead to easier access to data, leaving the door open for unauthorized persons to view, alter, delete, or copy it.

- When systems are downsized, it is especially important to consider the need to segregate responsibilities in order to meet internal control standards.

- Cost of migration/reorganization of the work environment may exceed any anticipated savings.

- Loss of mainframe-level profits.

- Increase in end-user support costs.

- Increase in education costs associated with learning to operate in a new processing environment.

- Policy changes to include the new computerized environment may be required in all areas and functions of the organization.

- End users, ironically, are also the primary obstacle in a smooth migration to a distributed platform. The learning curve required for users to solve their own computing problems is an impediment that management should be keenly aware of and address in a forthright, direct manner.

- Political infighting can destroy a downsizing project quicker than anything else.

- Local area networks and high performance servers (destined to be the backbone of a downsized system) are not yet as robust as a mainframe.

- Personnel within IS may lack familiarity with the applications development software and LAN technology used in downsizing projects.

- Cost savings from the move (from mainframe-based systems) to client/server systems are deceptive.

- Few CIOs are ready to ditch the trusty old mainframe in favor of machines that were, until a few years ago, mere toys.

- The full impact of application compatibility, operating system coherence, system-wide security, and data integrity has not yet been extensively tested. There is apprehensiveness in moving from legacy systems to PC-based LANs and client/server technology.

- Organizational downsizing creates personnel-related stress and security problems. Just the rumor of layoffs will have a negative impact on personnel.

- PC users (on a downsized client/server LAN) require more support than terminal users because they have more software at their disposal.

- End users may need additional training to make sure they perform regular backups, follow password procedures, adhere to software licenses, and manage disk space and software distribution tasks properly.

- New staff (to replace those who leave or are forced out) will need added skills to work in this client/server environment.

- It is sometimes tricky (and often darn near impossible) to align downsizing strategies with corporate-wide goals.

- Application development can be hampered because:
  - Few development packages are currently available for client/server platforms.
  - The lack of integrated tools forces the use of many different products.
  - Replacing mainframe screens and reports can be a long and laborious process.
  - Building GUIs is slower than on a mainframe application.

- Unlike proprietary shops, downsized IS must interact with multiple computer, network, and software suppliers which can be chaotic.

- In this changing environment, there is a potential for substantial personnel problems. These include employees' (including management) short-term and long-term motivation levels, their active involvement with or commitment to the organization, the actual and/or potential for career growth and development in the redefined company, the introduction or strengthening of an organized labor group or subgroup, and a person's actual or perceived loss of responsibility, authority, or status within his or her peer group, function, or organization.

- If computer security is lacking during a major staff downsizing effort, the consequences for organizations can be both embarrassing and damaging.

What are the Impacts/Effects of Downsizing on Organizational Behavior?

The implications of downsizing on organizational behavior are many. Some of the more critical are detailed here.

Downsizing:

- Forces organizations to examine their current operating practices to seek out newer, better, less expensive ways of accomplishing the same task.

- Is a change agent — it changes the traditional way an organization views itself and its operations.

- Will (or at least it should) require an organization to more thoroughly examine its internal control structures.

- Will require an extensive examination be made of the organization's ability to backup and recover data residing on the downsized systems. Disaster recovery planning will take on a renewed significance.

- Will require management to look at their customers and the requirements of the business in more detail. An examination at this level and of this detail may uncover weaknesses, or better yet, opportunities for improvement, as well as reductions in expenses and a trimming of the "excess" resulting in a leaner, more competitive, more successful organization.

MAINFRAMITUS MANAGEROUS
ENDANGERED SPECIES
REASON FOR ENDANGERMENT: LOSS OF HABITAT FROM WIDESPREAD SLASH AND DOWNSIZING BUSINESS METHODS.
PRIMATE HOUSE

- Sometimes has a negative connotation associated with it. Offloading mainframe computer applications onto LANs may mean the eventual layoff of personnel. Management may be advised to reassess current personnel policies, to address countering the potentially negative feelings created by downsizing, stop rumors, and confront personnel fears directly. Downsizing may indirectly and directly restructure personnel policies and procedures long held to be the foundation of the organization.

- Will initially result in a significant employee exodus. An industry average is approximately 50 percent.

- Is emerging as a broad trend that includes a variety of ways of distributing corporate data to the largest possible cross-section of workers (empowerment of the 1990s).

- May create unrealistic management expectations (i.e., "more for less," without a loss of competitive advantage or a reduction of IT performance and resources).

- Provides personnel with an opportunity to learn or develop new skills and adopt to new roles within the organization as a result of various operations/functions being downsized.

- Brings cultural change, especially when it is part of a conscious reengineering effort.

- Would most likely make mainframe programmers and systems analysts victims of change in a downsizing effort. Many of these people will have to learn a new career discipline in order to stay on with an organization that is abandoning or downsizing the mainframe. What will be the organization's "social" policy toward these displaced employees?

- Will keep downsizing at many sites to a one-application-at-a-time affair for much of the early 1990s because of the billions of dollars of investment in COBOL code.

- Will not result in mainframe being eliminated, at least not in this decade. Organizations will need to create strategies which will incorporate both large (mainframe) and downsized (PC-LANs) computers into their long-range IT plans.

- Will require IS to first adapt its traditional role as a central point for control and security to a client/server architecture. That means getting the traditional IS structure, with its separate departments, to work as a team and to provide a single point of responsibility for the system.

- Will require organizations undergoing downsizing to expect many staff changes. For one, the operations staff may virtually disappear as most centers will be managed and controlled from outside the computer room.

- Will begin with an inventory of an organization's people, not with an inventory of software or hardware. With such dramatic change, the human factor is the most crucial item in downsizing.

- Will require every migrating company to develop a strategy for dealing with the fear and ignorance associated with downsizing. Ignorance is most easily overcome by explaining the migration process.

- Will require corporations selecting downsizing to develop plans to accommodate rapid changes in technology, which render traditional training techniques inadequate.

- Often presents another important aspect that is sometimes overlooked; the acceptance (or rejection) of the downsized (reorganized) firm by former employees, as well as the local community's acceptance and support of the surviving employees, former employees, and the newly restructured organization.

- Is requiring IS managers to make tough decisions. They can either assign portions of their operating budgets to the reeducation of mainframe and COBOL programmers or hire new workers already trained in mission-critical, client/server technologies.

Summary

While downsizing has some obvious advantages, downsized systems, even when built and run properly, will probably deliver fewer benefits — especially fewer cost savings — than anticipated. At the very least, organizations considering downsizing as a management strategy for competitive advantage have a lot to consider.

Despite the many problems associated with a move toward downsizing, many users have found that downsizing is the route to go. Significant savings in hardware, software, maintenance, and personnel are the norm, but the real proof comes from those users who have successfully navigated their way through a corporate-wide downsizing effort.

Their success may be the greatest confirmation that the move away from mainframes is not just a passing phenomenon.

Shrinking Applications

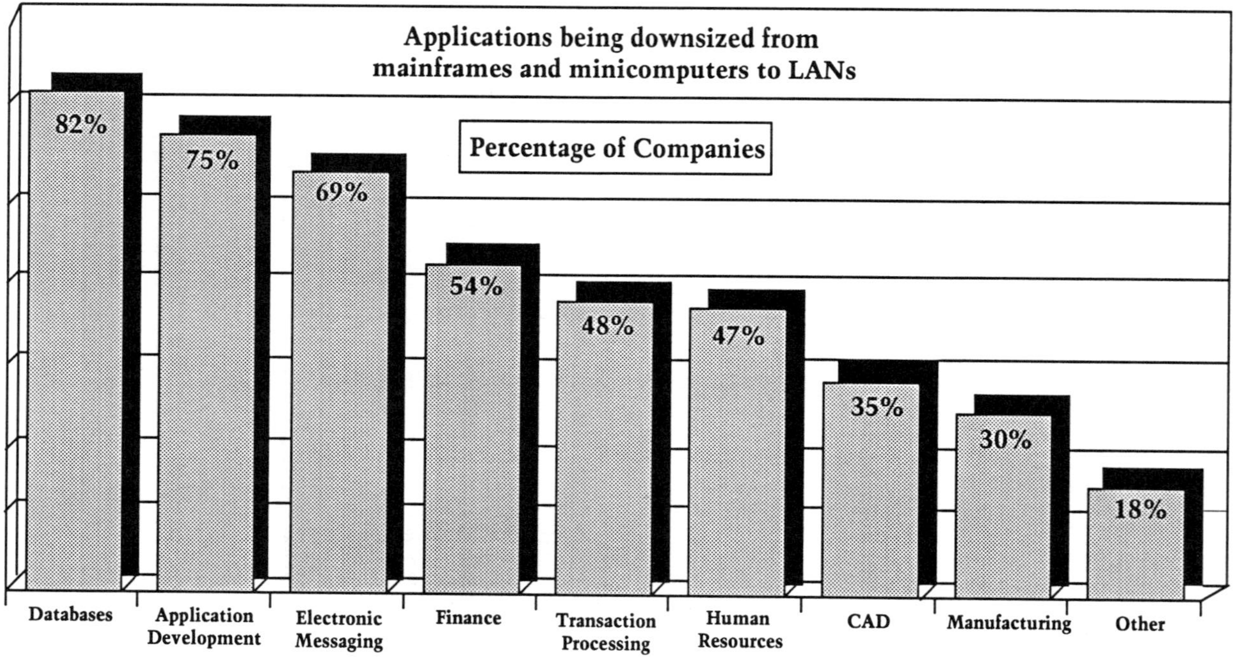

Figures are based on a survey of 71 companies currently engaged in a downsizing project. More than one response was accepted.

Downsizing has gone mainstream...

Percentage of companies that have downsized mainframe applications to LANs or plan to do so:

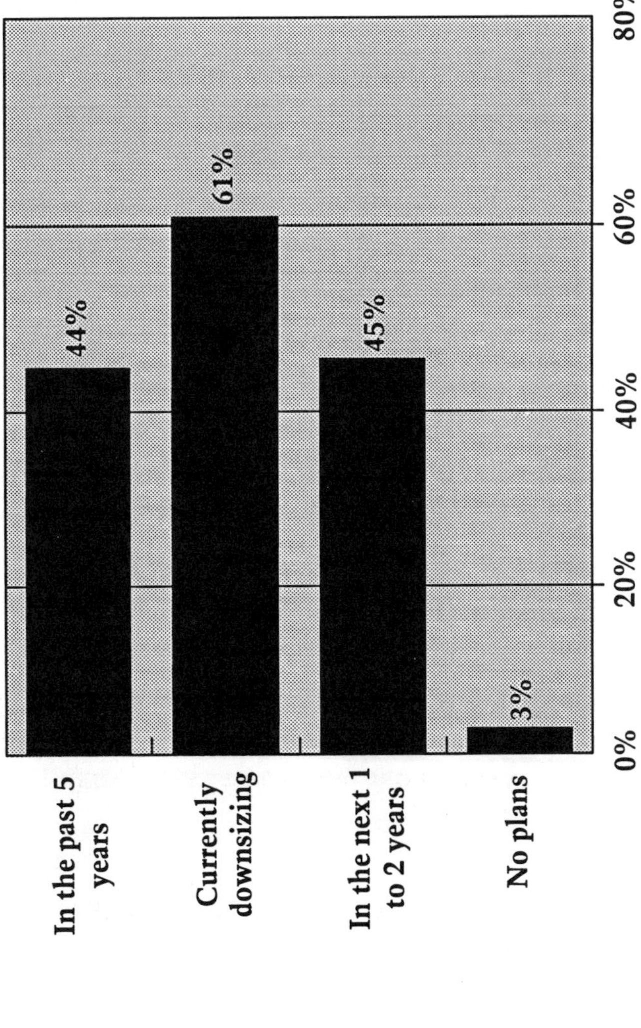

Rightsizing

Properly restructuring or "rightsizing" an organization will position it for future success and competitive advantage and enable it to engage in continuous self-renewal.

— *Kathryn Koening,*
"Rightsizing,"
Bank Management, June 1990

Introduction

The limitation of downsizing is that it merely describes a direction and defines an action. It does not address each component of the enterprise, or provide methodologies or principles to be followed.

End users complain that IS cannot respond quickly enough with new applications and/or modifications of existing applications. The price of slow responsiveness can be an organization's inability to take advantage of change including new legislation, mergers and acquisitions, internal organizational shifts, and new market opportunities.

The push to rightsize is a major part of the growing pressure to do more with less, to increase productivity and efficiency without tapping additional resources. The rightsizing movement is enabled by the ready availability of low-cost and easy-to-use computing resources, and is fueled by the expanding computer literacy of the end user.

Through it all, the motivation for rightsizing remains the same: getting the most out of a computer environment in order to address real business concerns.

The most commonly held view of rightsizing is actually that of downsizing — simply picking up an application and moving it to a new platform. This narrow view, however, can limit an organization's ability to meet its business needs.

A particular downsizing solution may reduce costs, but does it provide timely and accurate information to users? Does it meet customer demands? Exploit market opportunities? Increase an organization's ability to compete?

What is needed is a broader definition of rightsizing — one that embraces the benefits of centralized and personal computing, combining the power of the mainframe with the feel of the PC.

The broader view of rightsizing focuses on getting the right information to the right people at the right time. An organizational strategy aligned on the concept of rightsizing calls for a business function approach, aligning what users need to do, with what information is required to accomplish those tasks.

Rightsizing, therefore, is a process; one which can only identify the questions to ask. It is a strategy which, if adopted, can move an organization closer to where it wants to be. It has a beginning, perhaps a middle, but no end. With this as our focus, let us examine more closely the concept of rightsizing, the risks as well as the benefits of such a managerial approach, and the impact of the "process" on organizational behavior.

Rightsizing Defined

Rightsizing begins with a disciplined approach to information gathering from an organization-wide perspective. In order to implement the best process for rightsizing, management must first establish where the organization is today and determine where it is going. Management can then develop the IS requirements to get the organization where it needs to be.

Rightsizing must also take into consideration the organization's mission, goals, and objectives, as well as the specific goals and objectives for each department. The people, information, and technology currently in place must be evaluated from both the enterprise and the department perspective to determine how well they support the organization's goals.

To be successful, rightsizing must be viewed as an iterative process. It doesn't begin at the top, then move to lower levels, and finally reach an end point. At each step along the way, the findings must take the implementors back up the organization to make sure that the CEO and CIO are in sync, and that departmental goals, objectives, and skill sets are in line with the enterprise goals.

> For rightsizing to work, IS organizations — working cooperatively with user groups — need to take the lead in opening information up to their various users across organizational and geographical boundaries. Users need immediate access to answers and they need them to be faster and more accurate than ever before.

Given this "view of the world," the following discussion will sort out the issues involved in rightsizing business applications, starting with definitions of the terms involved. Just what is meant by "rightsizing" and "mission-critical"? Why would an organization consider selecting this strategic route? What are the benefits? The risks? These questions do not have clear-cut answers, of course, but asking the questions and seeing the possibilities are essential first steps in successful rightsizing efforts.

Sacks (1994) states that rightsizing is simply a logical redeployment of existing or new applications to the platform on which they run best. These systems could be PCs, RISC-based workstations, minicomputers, mainframes, or various combinations of these technologies. Rightsizing often leads to a client/server design — a form of computing that breaks applications into clients (requestors) and servers (providers).

Rightsizing, therefore, is the process of choosing among available hardware, software, and connectivity options so that the actual needs of a given application are served correctly and the underlying business considerations are given their due. Stated more directly, rightsizing means the right tools at the right price for the job at hand. "Mission-critical" means anything critical to the mission of running the business.

Rightsizing may be a relative newcomer to the corporate-computing vocabulary, but it has certainly captured the business world's imagination. Two-thirds of respondents to a recent Dun & Bradstreet software survey said that 1994 will be a year of rightsizing or realignment of computer resources in their organizations. The study polled 1,100 IS professionals on a range of issues shaping the computer industry. Among the results were the following:

- When asked their main reason for rightsizing, respondents moving down from a mainframe or away from a proprietary system cited decreasing costs (46 percent) and increasing flexibility (44 percent). Of those organizations moving down from a mainframe, only 16 percent gave empowering end users as their primary reason.

- Respondents said the most influential forces driving automation were increased worldwide competition (28 percent), growing productivity (26 percent), and the need to cut costs (24 percent). Business-process redesign and continuous quality improvement both ranked low.

- 37 percent of respondents said they believe Microsoft's Windows NT will offer benefits that are not yet available with Unix.

- Forty-one percent of the survey respondents said their organizations have moved to an open-systems environment. Asked the most compelling reason for switching to open systems, 64 percent mentioned increasing flexibility. But the benefits are likely to be felt principally within the organization: Only eight percent selected customer service as their primary motivation.

There are three basic approaches to rightsizing information systems: low-end applications such as those in a networked PC LAN configuration can be "upsized," meaning that components can be upgraded to more powerful systems and servers; high-end mainframe and supermini-computer applications can be "downsized" to run on cost-effective computers; or the data processing workload can be redistributed through an existing network of computing systems.

This latter example, known as client-server computing, does not imply or require the sacrifice of existing computers. It simply means realigning the workload to match the user's needs.

Let us now turn our attention to the benefits and the risks in selecting rightsizing as an organizational strategy and a means to develop a competitive advantage position for an organization. This next section will also investigate the potential impact this organizational "style" will have on an organization's management philosophies, behaviors, perceptions, and expectations.

> Today's manager must understand the new technology and apply it to the business environment in order to survive. In a new world of "rightsizing," mergers, acquisitions, and change, the old adage "But what have you done lately?" is a question many of us should continually ask ourselves.
>
> — *Jane W. Videtich,*
> *President of the International Communications Association*

What are the Benefits of Rightsizing?

Rightsizing provides management with the following benefits:

- Decentralizes decision-making authority and accountability.

- Empowers business unit work groups and individuals to continually improve their functions.

- Choosing a different platform — either larger or smaller — can offer new and better choices of application development tools, which means the application will be much more flexible in terms of future adaptability to changing business requirements.

- The overriding theme that characterizes the trend in rightsizing solutions is diversity — diversity in hardware, software, and connectivity; diversity in productivity and development solutions; diversity in robustness and methods of recovery; and diversity in price.

- Redistribution of an organization's electronic workload so that each computer handles only the work it does best. Applications are relocated to the most appropriate platform, maximizing computer system efficiency and saving costs.

- The potential of rightsizing is enormous for improving information sharing, expediting new service development and deployment, and reducing expenses.

- The net result of rightsizing is that it frees up computer resources and decreases the processing time of both mainframe and server-based jobs.

- Rightsizing fulfills business objectives. The rightsizing process aligns business functions with appropriate information, processes, and applications. Viewing information systems from the top of your organization ensures that automation will support overall business goals. Decisions about rightsizing should start with the need for business information and the purpose and requirements of the application.

- Rightsizing takes a comprehensive, objective approach. The biggest risk in rightsizing is taking too narrow a view. A top-down approach goes beyond considering applications and databases, and even their associated networks and systems. This broad approach extends to the related development tools, skills, department, user community, and organization goals.

- Rightsizing is a planned, proactive process. Driven by the IS department in partnership with others throughout the organization, rightsizing examines where the enterprise is going relative to where it is now, and puts a plan in place to get it there.

- Rightsizing calls for proven methods and a full range of options. No outside vendor can prescribe a predetermined rightsizing solution for your organization; every organization has a unique combination of goals, competencies, and needs. You need a rightsizing "partner" who can apply a methodology for collecting all relevant information, knowing the right people to interview and the right questions to ask. They must then analyze the answers and match your organization with the most appropriate mix of rightsizing opportunities.

- Rightsizing is evolutionary, not revolutionary. Rightsizing reduces risk by retaining previously gained experience and creating modular applications. By identifying and retaining your current organizational strengths, you also protect your existing investment in systems, data, and people. Scalability is important; make sure that any rightsizing solution can scale up to meet expanding business needs, or down for the sake of cost savings.

- Rightsizing demands a flexible environment for growth so most organizations maintain successful rightsizing by using products that generate flexible and portable applications and databases. Rightsizing is facilitated by the use of "middleware" products that provide openness and interoperability. However, it is important that user applications and databases are well documented, enhanceable, and not tied to any single rightsizing path.

- Rightsizing includes application optimization and upgrades. Organizations should gear rightsizing toward providing structural improvements to applications — such as streamlining, splitting, and integrating. The point of rightsizing is to optimize what you already have in place, while evaluating feature and function improvements.

- Rightsizing requires coordination. Any distribution of business functionality or data requires a well-developed plan that maintains integration and data integrity. Concentrate on getting the right information to all the right people and avoid isolated solutions. Focus on identifying standards and establishing procedures for recovery and security.

- Rightsizing requires ongoing support. Make sure to include supporting organizations and functions in your rightsizing plans. These groups — including the help desk, technical support, operations staff, and LAN administration — are easily taken for granted since they are an automatic part of a mainframe environment which does not automatically transfer to a distributed environment.

> Rightsizing can be the technological equivalent of decentralization. It allows an organization to move resources where they can perform most effectively, improving response time and customer service.
>
> *— Doug Ehrenreich,*
> *Market Segment Manager,*
> *Telecommunications, Sun Microsystems*
> *Computer Corp.*

- Rightsizing is a dynamic, ongoing process. The process of rightsizing becomes a way of operating; it is not an end in itself. Changes need to be made as business needs change. Rightsizing continually ensures that the most effective use of computing, data, communications, and human resources lead to meeting corporate needs.

- Through rightsizing, simulation applications can be migrated to a RISC/UNIX workstation and processed locally in front of the user. The total time needed to complete the processing of a simulation decreases. The user can perform many more scenarios in the same amount of time and achieve more accurate results.

- Client-server [rightsizing] computing allows some applications, particularly database — such as operations administration and maintenance (OA&M), operational support systems (OSS), and operator services — to migrate from the mainframe onto other computers. This frees up the mainframe to perform successfully the specialized tasks for which it was designed, and reduces the backlog of user requests related to those applications.

  That means database users get faster response to queries, and jobs for mainframe users are processed faster. Likewise, PC users gain access to high-performance servers and are able to tap into and run the applications they need more quickly and efficiently.

- Rightsizing will also allow users to share information in multivendor computing environments.

- By delegating the application code and user interface functions to PCs and workstations, rightsizing frees the mainframe to handle database requests. Two immediate benefits are achieved — the mainframe no longer has to waste cycles on user functions, and users can access multiple applications from a single desktop computer.

- As a prime component in a rightsizing migration, UNIX workstations give users the added advantage of multitasking capabilities.

- Rightsizing also gives PC users access to the more powerful servers they need to remain competitive. Through new industry standard networking tools, PC users can gain access to multiprocessing servers for use in the surveillance of internal OSS systems; on-line transaction processing (OLTP) applications; database applications for billing services; 800 number services and transaction record-keeping; and computer simulation applications.

- Migrating via rightsizing to client-server computing will ultimately reduce design-to-implementation time or time-to-market of new services, network operations, and maintenance systems because, in the long run, it can facilitate software development. Therefore, creating a competitive edge for these proactive organizations.

- Development of applications on the UNIX platform instead of mainframe environments will save developers time because UNIX applications are less difficult to write and hundreds of excellent development products are available.

- Applications that were once available only on mainframes can be made directly accessible to the end user in the field. Services can be deployed into the users' locations, giving them the ability to customize products. The result: decision-support tools and mission-critical applications are available to users in remote sites, and decision-making authority can therefore be placed in the hands of the people who are closest to the customer.

- Rightsizing can also allow organizations to centralize information systems that operated independently in the past. Field offices with previously incompatible computer equipment and networks can integrate with corporate information systems, and the unified network can allow users to take full advantage of the entire organization's computer resources.

- Rightsizing would have a secondary effect in its ability to free up MIS (IS) personnel to spend more time serving users and less time dealing with clogged backup procedures, unavailable files, slow response time, and other common ailments found in non-rightsized environments.

- A move to client-server computing via rightsizing can contribute to solidifying the department's reputation for facilitating the process of getting the right information to the right people at the right time.

What are the Risks of Rightsizing?

> Whatever the impetus for a cutback — forward-thinking strategic change or necessary belt tightening — rightsizing remains a very difficult step, one that can have serious adverse consequences for an organization in a variety of areas. The business rationale should be well thought out and articulated to all affected audiences.
>
> — *Jill Kanin-Lovers,*
> *"Pay After Rightsizing,"*
> Journal of Compensation & Benefits,
> *September/October 1991*

For all of the benefits to organizations provided by rightsizing, there are many inherent risks associated with this strategy:

- Deep cuts across the board (in response to pressure from market forces) without clear strategic direction can produce lasting undesirable effects.

- Morale and commitment among "surviving" (remaining) employees can drop, impairing the organization's ability to improve productivity and spark innovation.

- Management must reduce work first, before reducing workforce.

- Improper, incomplete preparation prior to the initial rightsizing announcement can result in the inability to effectively motivate the remaining employees.

- Internal political games can prompt one special interest group to try to wrest control of an application from another group.

- Management may encounter the not-invented-here syndrome in which one group rejects the platform choice of another group and insists on installing a different and competing platform.

- It may be unrealistic to expect cost savings to be the real justification for rightsizing.

- There are major one-time expenses involved in the migration from one platform to another. It will take time to recover these expenses in terms of lower operating costs, and the payback time may be longer than the useful life of the application.

- A newly rightsized application will need ongoing maintenance and support; it is typical to underestimate these costs, which can wipe out any savings associated with the migration.

- Rightsizing might seem to imply (to die-hard MIS types, and those resistant to change) a certain loss of control over users, because users gain access to more resources through their own hardware devices.

What are the Impacts/Effects of Rightsizing on Organizational Behavior?

The implications of rightsizing on organizational behavior are many. Some of the more critical are detailed on the following pages:

> As organization structures flatten, whole levels of middle management are being removed. Complex vertical structures are being replaced by small, focused work groups who need tools, processes, and access to specialized information.

- Considerations of strategy and operational effectiveness in a system-change setting can outweigh the quantifiable financial factors of traditional cost/benefit analysis, especially when the features of prospective new systems are difficult to predict.

- The initiative for rightsizing often comes from the end users themselves. They may be tired of paying their share of mainframe overhead charges and want to save some money. Or they may be dissatisfied with the quality of the old application(s) which may be too slow, or too cumbersome, or too out-of sync with their real needs. This could lead to ineffective management and poor use of strategic information.

- Two misconceptions overshadow the move toward rightsizing: (1) that moving to LANs means abandoning a disciplined approach to development and maintenance, including disaster recovery and backup; and (2) that rightsizing means distributed databases, making data integrity difficult to maintain.

Today's LANs have more backup solutions than mainframes or minis ever had. In addition, hardware redundancy can be built into LANs without spending a fortune, unlike the mainframe environment.

The security being built into today's LANs offers most of the features necessary to protect even the most sensitive data. Some systems are not only equal, but better mainframe counterparts.

There is no equal sign between rightsizing and decentralization. No one says a business must relinquish centralized control. Only a few business applications demand truly decentralized data management.

- Where staff members are truly redundant, there is an independent business mandate to reduce unnecessary expenses, and rightsizing highlights that mandate but does not by itself cause the layoffs.

- Business policy will be affected and will have to change to reward doing the right thing (i.e., rightsizing) versus maintaining large mainframe-based applications/systems. And there must be a change in how users relate to their applications and data.

- As a new computing paradigm, rightsizing requires MIS to take a fresh look at computing resources and how they can best be deployed within an organization. Databases, for example, must no longer be seen as departmental applications, but as global corporate resources.

> Rightsizing is a major opportunity to institute substantial improvements, not only in the application, but also in the underlying business process that provides the rationale for all information technology.

Summary

The rightsizing trend is just beginning, and as more and more pre-1980s applications become candidates for rightsizing and new platform choices become available, the process will become more complex and confusing. Finding the best rightsizing solution may well become impossible, if it hasn't gotten to that point already. A better strategy would be to find a good solution, one that clearly works and doesn't contain booby traps for the future.

As a direct benefit to the organization and to management, the migration process to a philosophy such as rightsizing is a perfect opportunity for an organization to rethink its business, its mission, obtain a clearer view of its core business activities, and determine what it does better than anyone else in its product market or field. This, surprisingly, is the hard part. Old planning assumptions have a way of getting engraved in stone, repeating the sins of the parent and passing along the commonality of thought to succeeding generations. This is a fast-paced environment, but things change, and a firm may discover that it requires more security than it once had or even needed. And believe it or not, the world may not even come to an end if an application is out of service for a few hours.

> Modern businesses live or die on the basis of how well their information technology works for them, and users are the direct agents of the business. They have to play an active role in planning and carrying out the whole rightsizing process.

Rightsizing provides the opportunity to rethink exactly what mission-critical means to the organization. Rightsizing should focus on what the organization really needs, not on what the organization already has. Businesses must be on the lookout for organizational dynamics that could get in the way of rightsizing and road blocks created by empire builders, the exalted, the "old guard." These are facts of organizational life, and enterprise policy must address them, not pretend they don't exist.

As a managerial/organizational philosophy, rightsizing may be so closely aligned (related) to its downsizing cousin that identification of differences or separation of the two may be difficult. It might be more accurately stated that rightsizing is an action, a function based on or as a result of a philosophy and a methodology called downsizing. If organizational management elects to implement a downsizing strategy designed to build competitive position, the way to implement the strategy is through rightsizing.

The next examination of emerging management styles and organizational behaviors is that of reengineering. IS organizations have been called reactionary when reengineering their own operations. This seems strange in light of the fact that the IS group is viewed as inflicting change, maybe even chaos, on the rest of the organization.

The discussion which is to follow will analyze reengineering as a management strategy and as a shift in organizational behavior. Again, the benefits and risks of this course of action will be detailed as will the impact to the organization, resulting from a directive to implement reengineering whenever and wherever possible.

Why Rightsize?

- Expense reduction.
- Improved capacity.
- Better application development tools are available.
- Better user interfaces and connectivity methods.
- Direct response to end-user demands.
- More easily managed applications.

Reengineering

Prosperity is not without many fears and disasters; and adversity is not without comforts and hope.

— *Francis Bacon*
(De Auguments Scientiarum, 1623)

Introduction

A survey completed by more than 400 Chief Information Officers of major North American companies in industries ranging from manufacturing to healthcare shows a five-fold increase in the number of information systems applications running on client/server architecture.

According to the *Sixth Annual Survey of North American CIOs* by Deloitte & Touche, CIOs are reporting a high degree of satisfaction with reengineering projects, greater use of software development tools and an expanding role for open systems. Eighty percent of the respondents indicated that they have at least one business process reengineering (BPR) project underway and 81 percent expect the number of new projects to grow within the next two years. For the second year in a row, manufacturing led other industries with an average of 4.8 BPR projects launched.

Today's business world bears scant resemblance to the boom economy that once prevailed in American industry. Organizations that loathe defeat are redesigning their business processes from the inside out. Management must position itself effectively to deal with what is to come by asking itself, "Are we prepared?" The three Cs of business in the 1990s provide some answers to the pressing question, "Why reengineer?"

- Competition is hot and getting hotter.
- Customers have the upper hand.
- Change is the only thing that is certain.

As an organizational philosophy — or even more radical, a new shift in organizational behavior — reengineering is setting out to overthrow the most basic tenets of how American organizations operate. Imagine scrapping every belief, every method, and every process and then rebuilding the organization in entirely new ways. This is an accurate picture of what reengineering is all about, and the strategy is taking American industry by storm.

Forget quality circles, worker empowerment, or management by walking around. Those are nice — but we're not talking nice. We're talking radical, as in:

- Eliminating the marketing department — and every other department, for that matter.
- Letting customers calculate their own bills.
- Trusting employees to hire and fire colleagues.

Reengineered organizations don't have departments, they have processes — the process of acquiring clients or the process of filling an order. Salvation comes from redesigning one process after another until the old corporate structure and culture withers away. There are, of course, parables — tales of reengineering miracles. How Bell Atlantic Corporation cut the time it takes to design and install a new circuit from two weeks to three hours. How Ford Motor Company trimmed its accounts receivable department by 80 percent. How International Business Machines Corporation's credit department absorbed a 100-fold increase in transactions without adding a single new employee.

"Reengineering is not free. It is purchased in coin, denominated in suffering," states Michael Hammer. Is reengineering merely the latest in management fads? Or is it, as Hammer claims, nothing less than the undoing of the Industrial Revolution? Probably a little of both.

"Reengineering has become a label for every corporate change process that anyone has thought of — or wants to get funded," laments James Champy, Hammer's coauthor and head of CSC Index, a consulting firm. "The term has become so broad as to become almost meaningless," complained David Nadler, a New York management consultant.

But Nadler and other management experts say that, despite misappropriation of the term, the genuine reengineers may be on to something important and real. "This is very serious stuff," said Thomas Gerrity, Dean of the Wharton School of Business, where reengineering is now part of a required course. "It integrates a number of ideas that have been around for a number of years. What's new is that it insists that you do them all simultaneously."

The central idea of reengineering is to turn the old industrial model on its head. In this model — laid out by Adam Smith and Henry Ford — complex work is broken down into simple, repetitive tasks that are performed in sequence by specialists until the goods or service are delivered to the customer. The primary job of supervisors is to control the quantity, quality, and cost of the work performed. Employees were organized by function — sales, manufacturing, customer service, and the like.

In recent years, organizations organized along those lines have found themselves handicapped in a world of intense global competition and rapid technological change. They were spending too much time and money coordinating and communicating and too little time doing work that benefits customers, analysis found. Overhead costs were soaring while boundaries between departments had become barriers to change.

In the 1980s, some U.S. manufacturers began to develop new models. Instead of one worker performing one job, teams of workers — each trained in several jobs and equipped with computer-driven machinery — were given responsibility for significant chunks of the manufacturing process. Layers of supervision were eliminated. Designers had to work with marketers and production engineers to come up with products people wanted that could be made easily, quickly, and cheaply.

Now reengineering is taking many of those techniques and extending them to all parts of an organization — and of the economy, including the burgeoning service sector, where industries such as retailing, telecommunications, and financial services are in the throes of painful restructurings. In its crudest form, reengineering has proven an effective way to cut costs and reduce payrolls. But consultants who do it report that reengineering gets just as much impact from increasing sales as it does from decreasing costs, either by grabbing market share from competitors or generating new products and services.

> Reengineering is the fundamental rethinking and radical redesign of an entire business system — the business processes, jobs, organizational structures, management systems, and values and beliefs — to achieve dramatic improvements in critical measures of performance.
>
> *—Michael Hammer,*
> *President, Hammer & Company,*
> *and James Champy,*
> *President, CSC Index*

To establish a common ground for furthering an examination of reengineering, the following is a brief but compelling example of the changes and impact to the business process brought about by reengineering. Mutual Benefit Life, one of America's larger life insurance companies, uncovered through analysis that in order to process a client's insurance claim, the process itself involved 19 people, across five different departments, over a three-day period. Acknowledging the importance of the increases in information technology, management realized that by utilizing shared databases and networks, all of the data necessary for decision making could be made available to one person, and an expert system could help the less experienced claims processor make valid decisions.

The use of IT allowed Mutual Benefit to redesign its claims processing activities so that a "case manager" can now process a client's claim in as little as four hours, compared to the previous *three days* it took before. The cost savings to the firm alone are staggering, let alone the increase in efficiency and client satisfaction.

> Business reengineering reaches into the heart of an organization and into its guts, rips them out, and reassembles them in the context of today's changing business world.

This is a classic example of a business process reengineered. Many large American organizations are going to collapse and fade away, or be swallowed up by the competition unless they make radical changes over the next few years. Most firms today are still at the point where they are just considering reengineering, evaluating it, and working to understand the concept.

Reengineering Defined

Once again, Dr. Michael Hammer, President of Hammer & Company and widely recognized pioneer and authority on the use of IT and reengineering, provides an excellent definition of reengineering. Mr. Hammer's definition is included here to set the stage for further development of this organizational philosophy. Hammer states, "Reengineering is the radical redesign of business processes to achieve dramatic performance improvements. It is not about looking for marginal improvements. Reengineering is about making quantum leaps in performance — factors of two and above, not factors of 10 percent. It's about fundamental, not superficial change" (Hammer 1992).

Baline Maring, Assistant Vice President of Information Systems Architecture at GTE, defines reengineering as technological redesigns that are drafted to facilitate new business blueprints. Rochester (1991) defines reengineering as the process of recapturing the essential design, structure, and content of a complex computer system that has the power useful in running the business. When the system is understood and defined, reengineering is used to rewrite the system to take advantage of new technology, such as relational databases or advanced telecommunications, while maintaining all the functions and features that were useful in the original system. James Champy, Chairman and CEO at CSC Index, Inc., provides yet another definition, "The real power of technology is not that is can make old processes work better but that it lets you destroy outdated assumptions and create new ways of working — that is reengineering."

Whether it is called reengineering, total quality management, business process reengineering or business process restructuring, firms across America are reevaluating how they do business, exactly what their business is (identifying core business activities), and how IT can help them better conduct their business as they respond to ever increasing competitive pressures.

> In an environment of rapidly changing technologies, treacherous competition, and escalating customer demands, only the strongest companies will survive.
>
> — *Raymond Manganelli,*
> *President and CEO,*
> *Gateway Management Consulting*

Business Reengineering: Where to From Here?

> **Who is Reengineering?**
>
> About 25 percent of large companies are doing it. These efforts often involve an early project or two, not widespread rollouts.
>
> **Ahead of the Pack:** Insurance, telecommunications, long-distance carriers, RBOCs (Regional Bell Operating Companies), electric power utilities, the auto industry, and the auto parts business.
> **Middle of the Pack:** Electronics, consumer goods, pharmaceuticals, and chemicals.
> **Just Getting with the Pack:** Retailing, the defense sector, aerospace, and airlines.
> **Back of the Pack:** Banking.
>
> — *Joseph Maglitta*

A brief review of business practices will show that American businesses have for decades been using technology to automate old ways of doing business, many of which date back to the Industrial Revolution. America has based its work process on specialization of labor and economies of scale. Jobs are task-oriented and designed to use "simple" people for "simple" work. Management is based on pay for time and is control-oriented, using the traditional hierarchical approach designed to enforce discipline in the ranks.

This approach, however justified, is dated and attuned to a period of intense growth necessary for gearing up supply to meet a large and increasing demand. This behavior addresses issues of execution, standardization, making and meeting plans — issues that are critical in a boom economy. The cold reality is that we are no longer functioning in a boom economy. Instead of limited supply, we now operate in an environment of limited demand. In this kind of market, a model of American business fashioned after the Industrial Revolution era is absurd; in fact, it is safe to say such a model is useless in today's economy.

Hammer (1992) states that by automating existing methods we are simply becoming more efficient at doing things the wrong way. We need a different model that lets us be flexible, innovative, customer-focused, and oriented toward quality and service. That is what reengineering aims for: the creation of an entirely new model of how businesses work.

The recent history of General Motors (GM) offers a case study in how reengineering differs from earlier attempts at corporate renewal. To save on its labor costs, the giant automaker embarked on an estimated $40 billion modernization drive 15 years ago, much of it centered on using robots to replace the work of humans on its assembly lines. But the effort did little to reduce the cost of production, while GM's market share continued to decline.

At the same time, GM launched its Saturn project, intended not simply to produce cheaper cars, but to reinvent the car business. Instead of automating the old single-product assembly line, Saturn designed its assembly process around self-managed work teams and flexible production lines. Perhaps more significant, every other aspect of the business was reengineered as well — from the way that cars were designed to the no-haggle pricing on Saturn showroom floors. Saturn now is so successful that it recently increased its production rate by 25 percent, while inventories of unsold cars are running at one-third of the industry average. GM's operating profit margin on Saturns is among the best in the business, according to analysts.

"Reengineering is not restructuring or downsizing," states Hammer. "Downsizing is about doing less with less. It's not automating — automating is paving the cow paths. . . . Reengineering isn't about fixing anything. It's about obliterating what you have now and starting from scratch. It's about transforming practically every aspect of your organization, often beyond recognition. And if you're not prepared to do that, don't start."

Unlike most management theories which have their origins in corporate consulting and business schools, reengineering's roots are in technology. Many of its practitioners, like Hammer and Champy, have degrees in computer science. And nearly every reengineering project involves using technology to allow people to work quicker and smarter.

Purchasing managers at Procter & Gamble Co., for example, don't wait to receive an order before sending diapers to Wal-Mart. P&G's computer talks directly to Wal-Mart's and does the reordering automatically. When the drive-up line starts to back up at Taco Bell, an employee with a hand-held computer walks the line to take orders and sends them electronically to the kitchen. The restaurants can double their lunchtime capacity without having to add expensive seating areas or drive-up windows that sit unused most of the day.

Ironically, what drew many of these tekkies into reengineering was the realization that expensive new equipment had failed to yield the kind of bottom-line results that had been expected in many organizations, particularly in service firms. The technology was used to automate old processes rather than devising wholly new processes. For service companies in particular, reengineering is born of technological frustration. That was the case at Showtime Networks Inc., the premium cable television programming service. About 18 months ago, Jerry Cooper, Showtime's chief financial officer, found that the company had spent $1 million trying unsuccessfully to upgrade his department's computer system. The bulk of the work in Cooper's department involves collecting monthly fees from cable systems. Because the fees were based on complex formulas negotiated in 10,000 separate contracts, however, Showtime and its customers rarely agreed on what was owed.

To adjust a bill, the accounts receivable clerk needed permission from a supervisor, a manager, and a director, who would often check with the salesperson handling the account — who in turn would check with the vice president for sales. In addition, Showtime's audits of its customers often uncovered major underpayments. The process of collecting the money often embroiled the customer and the finance and sales departments in a three-way dispute. In the end, Showtime wrote off about $10 million a year, an amount equal to 10 percent of its profit.

Wondering whether he could even automate this process successfully, Cooper decided to scrap it altogether and design a system in which customers, in effect, bill themselves. Today, the finance department bears little resemblance to its former self. Most employees have been trained in all the accounting department's functions and are organized into self-managing teams. Team members are given wide latitude in settling accounts with customers, eliminating two of three levels of middle management. But more important, the number of adjustments is rapidly declining as Showtime works with its customers to establish computer systems that allow customers to generate their own bills. And for the first time, finance staff members are involved in contract negotiations in an effort to simplify contract terms and avoid discrepancies before they arise.

The department's newfound efficiency will allow it to handle billing for new channels without adding personnel. Cooper intends to use the sales data gleaned from customers' computers to help the cable systems better market premium channels. "This was not intended to be a cost-cutting or head count-reducing exercise, but to provide us with a strategic competitive advantage," said Thomas Hayden, the Showtime salesman who oversees the effort (The Washington Post, 25 July, 1993, pp. H1 and H4).

Simply stated, IT's role is essential to the successful implementation of reengineering. It is the single most powerful tool for breaking traditional assumptions and rules, and the factor that makes new ways of operating possible. Technology makes it possible for information to be available in multiple locations concurrently. Geographically dispersed resources can be linked to headquarters to create a new organizational structure — a hybrid or a centralized/decentralized organization — two approaches which do not conflict.

New technologies will continue to support reengineering efforts. The availability of high-performance networks and hardware, for example, facilitates widespread real-time decision making for complex issues. An organization that cannot change the way it thinks about IT cannot reengineer. An organization that equates technology with automation cannot reengineer. An organization that looks for problems first and then seeks technological solutions cannot reengineer.

> Technology has the potential to challenge a business to rethink the way it operates, to break rules, to reengineer.

Hammer and Champy (1993) claim that to recognize the power inherent in modern information technology and to visualize its application requires organizations to use a form of thinking that business people usually are not taught and with which they may feel uncomfortable. Most executives and managers know how to think deductively; i.e., they are good at defining a problem or problems, then seeking and evaluating different solutions. Deductive thinking skills are critical to organizations looking for competitive advantages. Staying on top of new technology and learning how to recognize and incorporate it into an organization must be an ongoing effort — no different from research and development or marketing. Regression, heavy foreign competition, and a desperate ongoing search for making technology investments pay off have helped to both fuel and sustain reengineering technologies.

> The really hard part of technology is not that it can make old processes work better but that it lets you destroy outdated assumptions and create new ways of working — that is reengineering.

Benefits of Reengineering

Reengineering provides management with the following benefits:

- New technologies will continue to support reengineering efforts.

- Reengineered applications generally have shorter development times.

- Empowerment of workers through reengineered applications, which includes ownership of the assets employed in the applications.

- The decentralization of assets, network controls, and system controls in reengineered applications will require fewer central-site professionals who will be performing different tasks.

- Improved customer service.

> Where theoretical discussions of reengineering fall down is by misleading the gullible into thinking that organizational structure and workflow are all that must change. Considerable attention also needs to be paid to remapping people's attitudes and orienting their intellectual, philosophical, and even emotional relationships toward work and toward their customers.

What are the Risks of Reengineering?

For all of the benefits to organizations provided by reengineering, there are many inherent risks associated with this strategy:

- End users' resistance to change.

- Programmer unfamiliarity with new development tools or application platforms.

- Hidebound technology infrastructures.

- Top management misconception of actual, realizable benefits.
- Vendor mistakes in application software design and hardware configuration.
- Up-front capital requirements.
- External economic events within the industry, national, and international marketplaces affect an organization's strategic plan and operating goals.
- Reengineering attempts to change the way people behave.
- Empowerment of workers, including ownership of assets through reengineered applications, makes centralized control of networks and computer systems difficult.
- Shorter development times for applications makes forecasting network requirements and traffic loads difficult.
- The mission-critical aspect of the applications will magnify the uptime requirements for networks.
- Many existing hardware, software, and communication systems service contracts will require renegotiating.
- It is clear that one of the key networking imperatives of reengineering will be LAN management.
- Turf battles may erupt when functional boundaries are crossed to redefine jobs.

- Failure to obtain the sometime outrageous goals inherent in most reengineering programs may derail future projects and make management apprehensive.

- Eliminating positions and dealing with widespread anxiety over losing jobs can raise serious questions about the security and safety of personnel and data.

- Support costs for client-server systems — desks, extra technicians, etc., — may outstrip projected cost savings.

- Tremendously large telecommunications bills await unsuspecting organizations who enter reengineering unprepared, ill-prepared, or without adequate technology planning.

> Reengineering is difficult. It is a philosophical change leading to a dramatic breakthrough — it questions almost everything done in a particular function and asks, "Why do we even have this function?"
>
> — *Kathryn Hayley,*
> *Information Technology Consulting Principal,*
> *Deloitte & Touche*

What are the Impacts/Effects of Reengineering on Organizational Behavior?

The implications of reengineering on organizational behavior are numerous, and what the author believes to be the more critical are detailed here:

- When you change a process, the entire business system needs to undergo transformation as well. The belief of the organization, jobs and organizational structures, and management systems may all be altered.

- Reengineering will require organizations to change how performance is measured, how compensation for that performance is determined, and even how to go about hiring and developing new employees.

- One prerequisite for successful reengineering attempts to overcome the status quo is executive leadership with real vision, commitment, consistency, and maybe even a bit of fanaticism.

- The close contact created by reengineering can turn historical vendor/supplier adversarial relationships into partnerships. This win/win attitude is one of the more powerful impacts of reengineering on organizational behavior. It has created a change of mindset, and how organizations view the world around them and their role in the new order of things.

- In short, reengineering means radical, dramatic change. Why are organizations suddenly willing to endure the cultural upheaval of reengineering? The long answer references the deregulation of basic industries, the growing computer literacy of the workforce, the globalization of supply and markets, increased mass communications, and the prevailing management theories of worker empowerment.

- Three systems that must be addressed in any successful reengineering effort include:
  - The physical system, including workflow, hardware, software, and group and team assignments.
  - The support system, which includes the metrics for measuring project performance, the reward struc-

ture for implementors and users, and the management structure.
- The value system or organizational culture and employee attitude.

> The change agent is not someone who is going to win a lot of popularity contests. Nobody likes disruption, and few like the person who instigates it.
>
> — *John Kohler,*
> *Chief Information Officer,*
> *Kimberly-Clark Corporation*

- Reengineering has prompted organizations to reexamine their priorities and contract out those tasks they believe other organizations are better equipped to handle or upon which they do not wish to focus.

- Career paths for networking professionals will succumb to technical expertise, operational management skill-set requirements will change, and the physical locale of network management will change.

- The telecommunications network will become more complex and tougher to manage. It will, however, become more important to an organization; the network will be decentralized and will demand more performance and reliability.

- Jobs will change radically after most reengineering efforts, and only senior management is in a position to make such changes. When one is designing an application that cuts across functional boundaries, he or she wants and needs all of the players (senior management) to be involved.

- After years of splitting jobs into smaller and smaller pieces and creating inward-focused, highly matrixed organizations, executives at many large corporations are realizing that something is very wrong. The functional divisions are intently focused on their own small piece of the pie rather than on the big picture — creating great products and satisfying customers.

- Employees are encouraged to take more risks with the understanding that some failure would be part of the process.

- The technological implications of reengineering may seem self evident, but the organizational ones are not. Often what is required is a dramatic reallocation of power within the organization. Many organizations find it difficult to give the decision making power to those doing the work because it is in direct opposition to the traditional functional hierarchy, which assumes that only those at the top of the pyramid are capable of making intelligent decisions.

- It is critical to involve the end user not only throughout the design and implementation stage, but also once the system is up and running. Typically, workers using the reengineered application will find additional opportunities for reengineering.

Summary

> Reengineering is not for the timid.

Reengineering requires redefining fundamental business decisions, ranging from basic mission statements to how service and support will de delivered. As such, top management must be the initiator of the driving force behind reengineering projects. Because the role of IT is central in reengineering, the challenge facing MIS is how to assist in making often difficult reengineering projects succeed, and in doing so, earn the respect of the business side of the "house."

> To qualify as reengineering — and produce dramatic results — an improvement program must enhance quality, increase revenue, *and* optimize costs.
>
> — *Raymond Manganelli,*
> *President and CEO,*
> *Gateway Management Consulting*

Only time will show whether those MIS managers who have made a difference in their organizations are the ones who could adapt the fastest and most effectively in an atmosphere of constant change. If one thing is certain about reengineering, the process is anything but predictable.

The technologies emerging today are designed to deliver dramatically more value for the dollar, more productivity, more performance, and more applications. Managers must get aggressive about proving the value of their services and they must express that value in hard numbers (Eskow 1992).

Overcoming the Obstacles

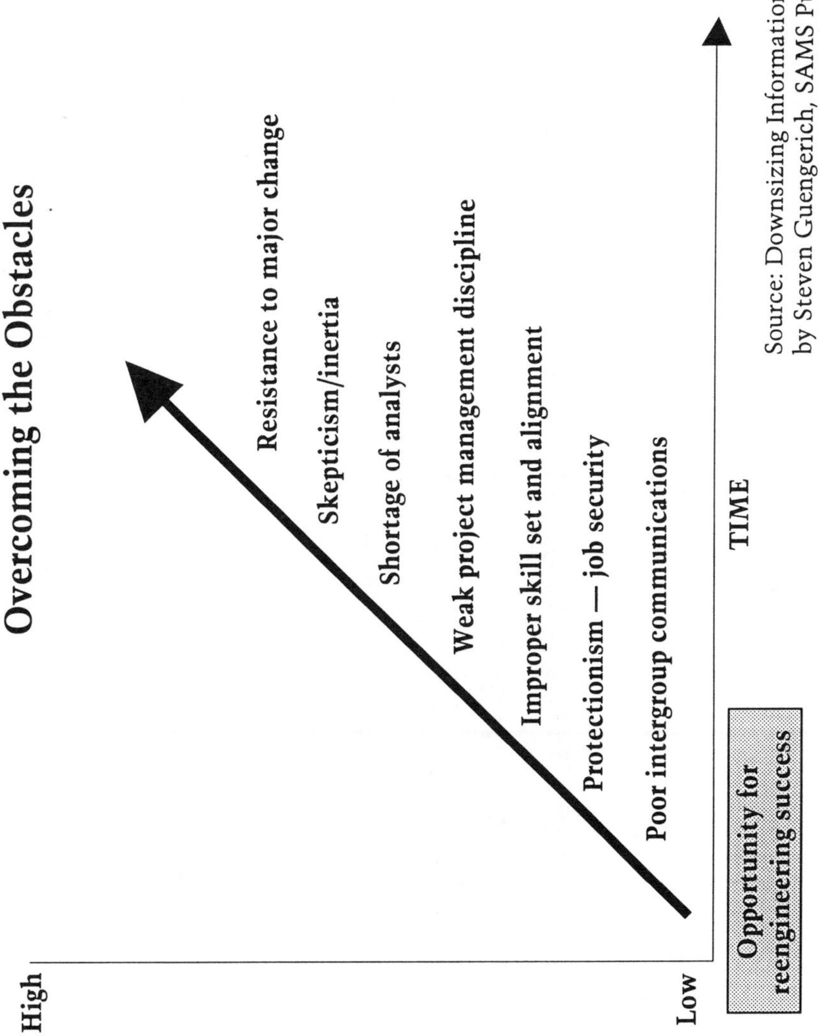

Source: Downsizing Information Systems, by Steven Guengerich, SAMS Publishing, 1992

Overreaching Expectations

In spite of the increased popularity of business reengineering, CIOs report that the actual benefits of reengineering projects have fallen short of expectations.

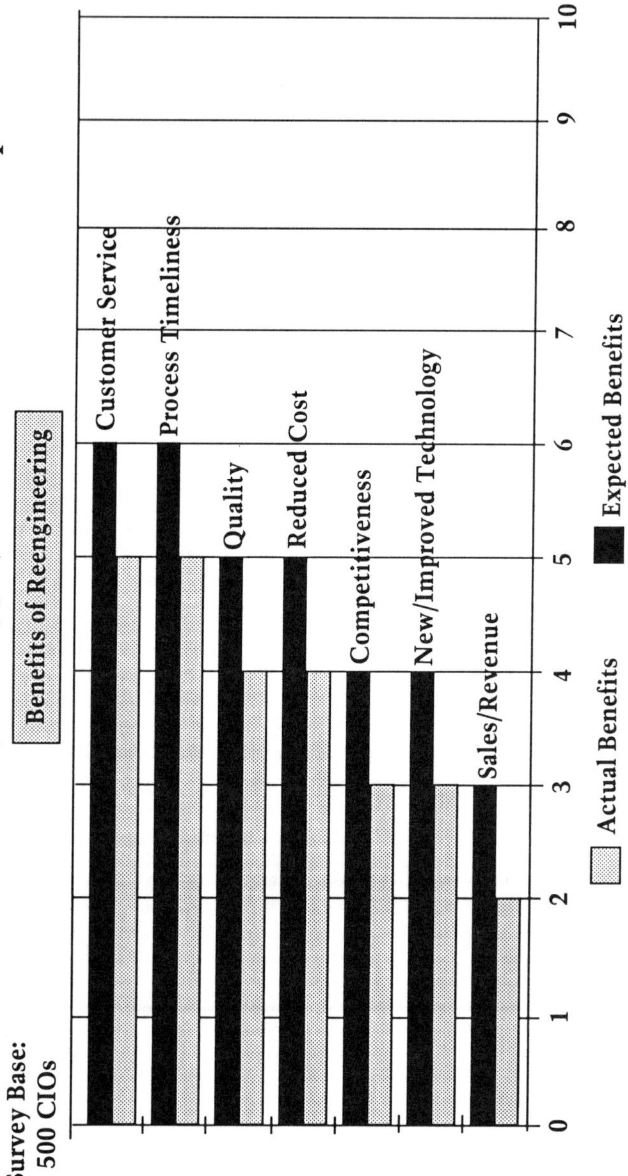

Scale: 1 = Limited Benefits, 10 = Significant Benefits

Responding to Technology with Reengineering

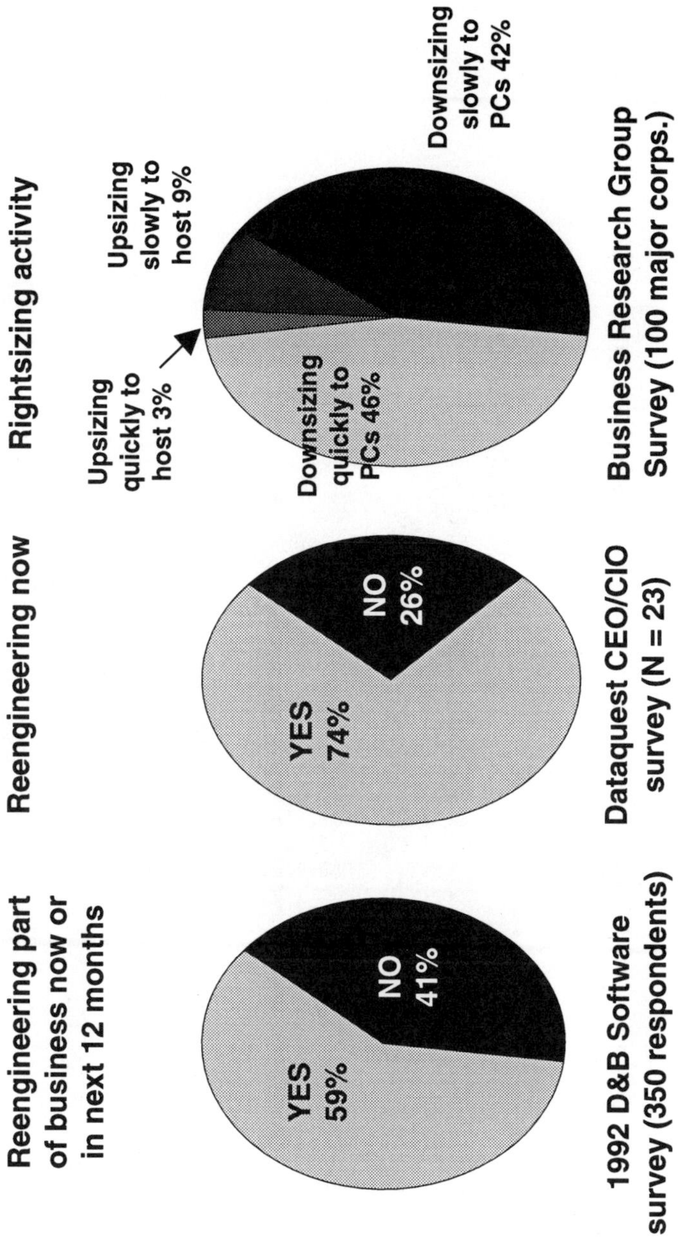

Source: *Networking Management*. January 1993.

Reengineering Slammed

Did Your Company Experience Unanticipated Problems From Reengineering?

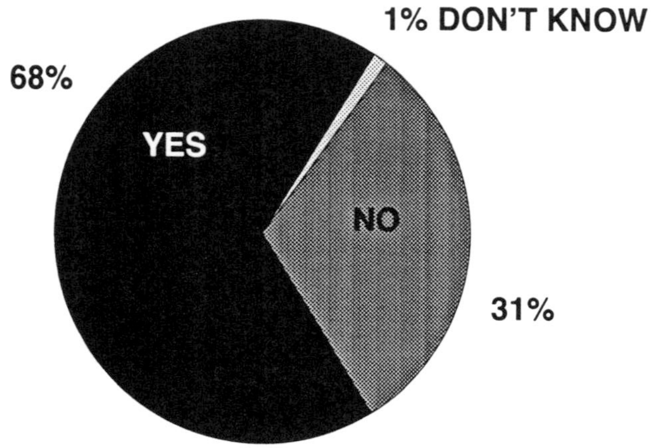

Base: 350 executives in 14 industries

"But Is It Really Reengineering?"

Organizations often believe they are reengineering. But many are actually only designing single processes, the least complex type of change. Reengineering and invention involve much larger degrees of change.

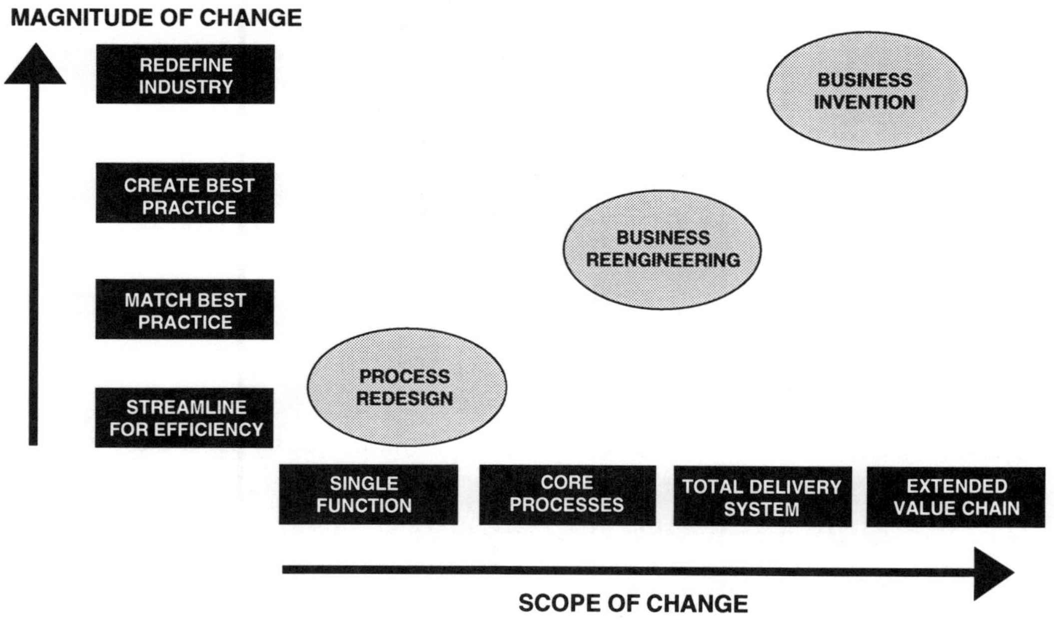

Japan Reengineers

Will business reengineering catch on in Japan?
Despite formidable obstacles, reengineering will be adopted by corporate Japan, according to three quarters of the respondents.

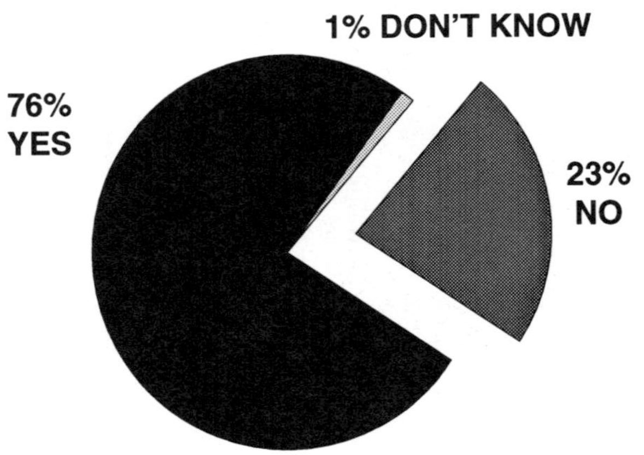

Number of Respondents: 53

Workers Cool to Reengineering

Emloyees' Reactions to Reengineering Initiatives

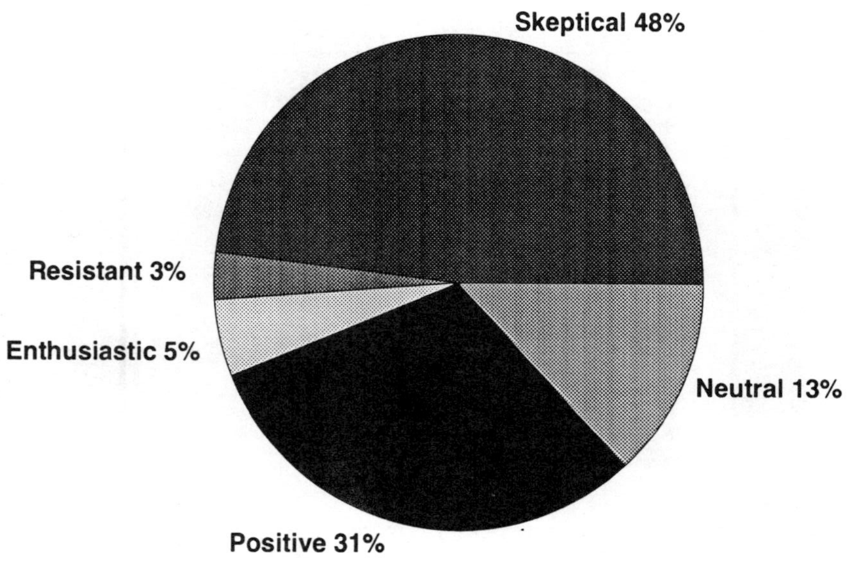

Source: Survey of 182 North American senior executives. Kepner-Tregoe, Inc., Princeton, NJ (1994).

...and nobody's happy after reengineering (Top 5 reasons projects fell short)

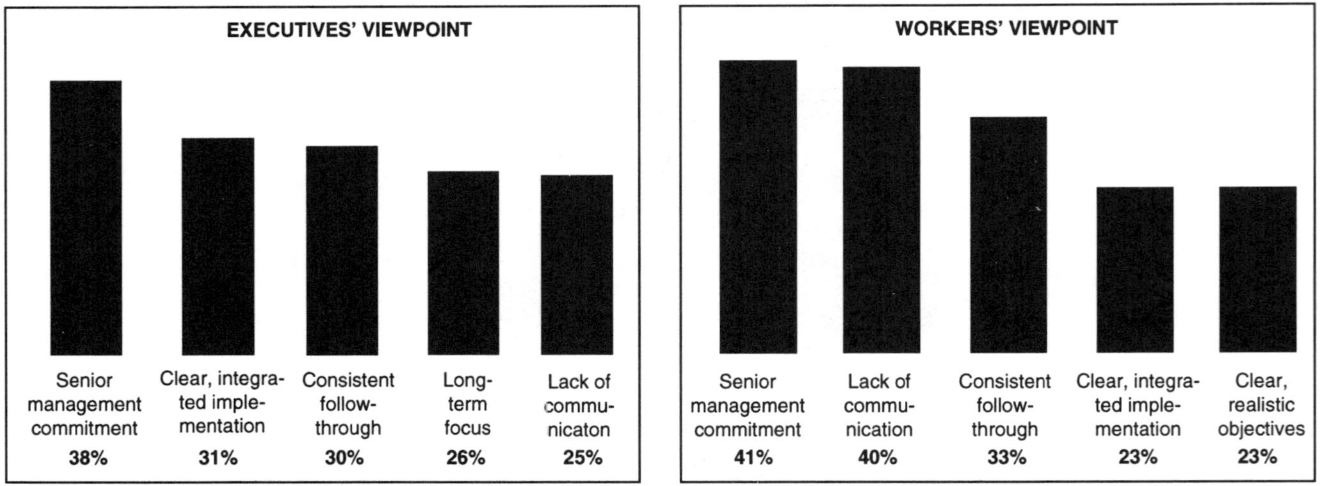

Source: Survey of 182 North American senior executives by Kepner-Tregoe, Inc., Princeton, NJ. Copyright 1993/94 by Computerworld, Inc., Framingham, MA 01701. Reprinted from Computerworld.

The dirtiest half-dozen...

Jitters and foot-dragging are the biggest threats to reengineering efforts, according to CSC Index (Percentage finding it very or extremely difficult)

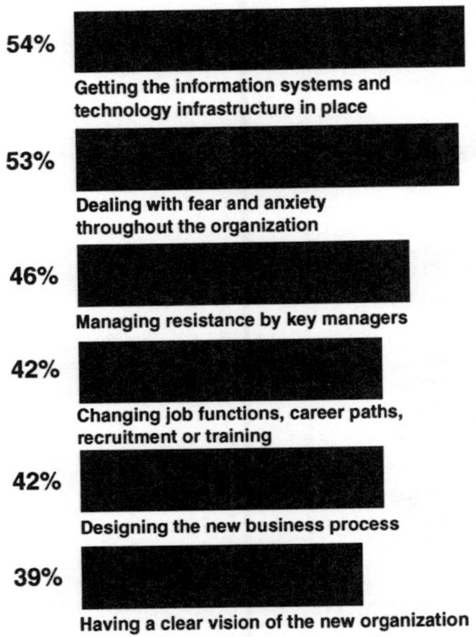

Source: CSC Index, Inc., Cambridge, Mass.
Survey of 497 senior North American executives.

...and a half-dozen more

A Deloitte & Touche study found almost identical problems (Percentage of respondents naming the factor as a significant obstacle to success)

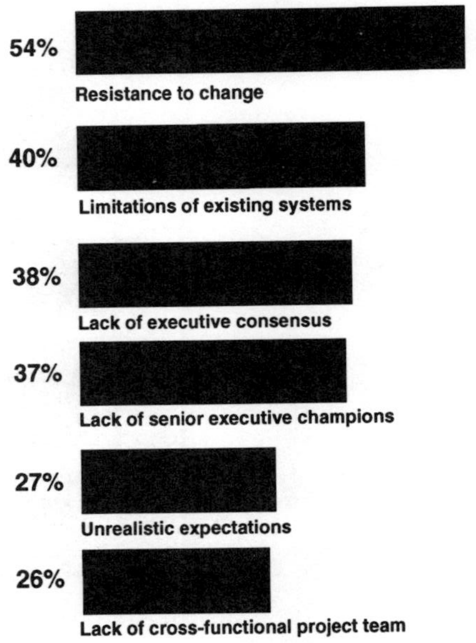

Source: Deloitte & Touche, Wilton, Conn.
Survey of 400 North American CIOs.

I Can't Hear You

Top managers say the biggest communications challenges in reengineering are keeping employees informed and calm

(Percentage finding it very or extremely difficult)

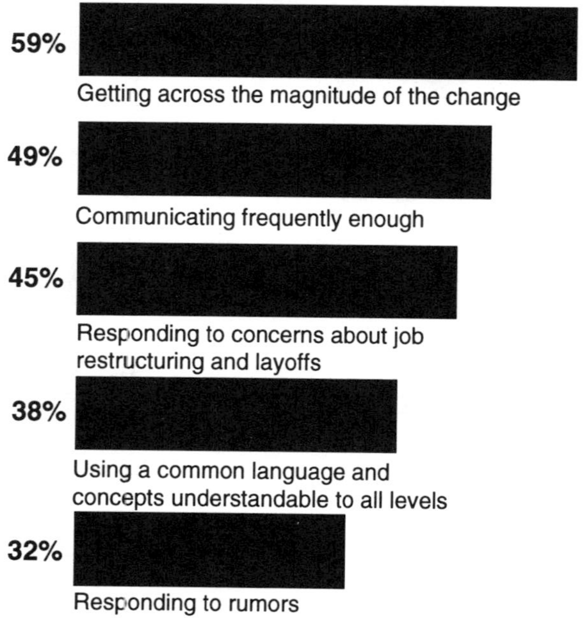

Source: CSC Index, Inc., Cambridge, Mass. Survey of 497 senior North American executives.

Reasons Reengineering Projects Fall Short
Executives' Viewpoint

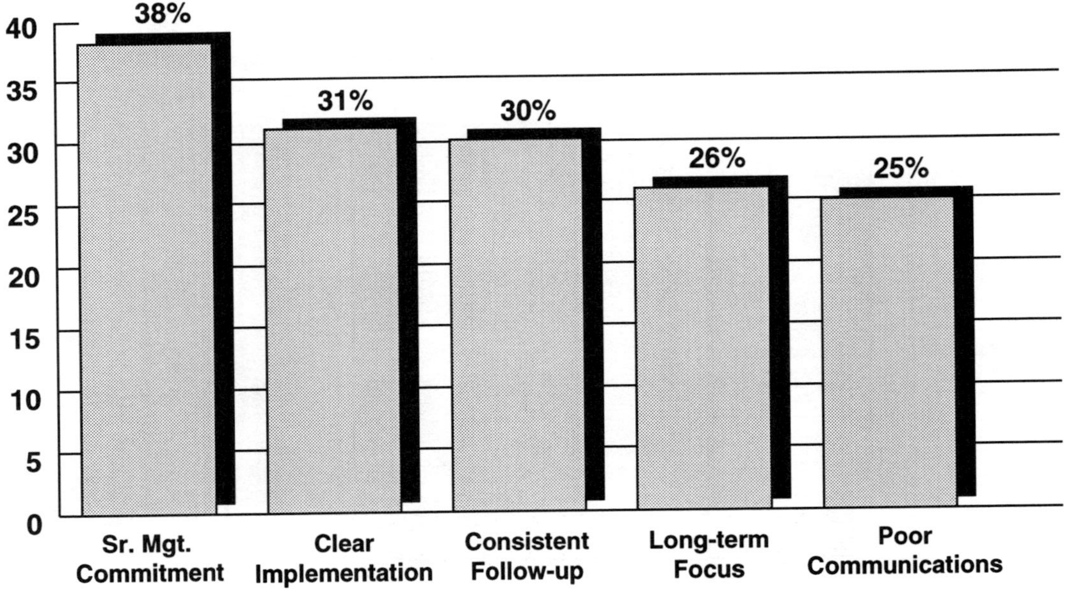

Source: Survey of 182 North American senior executives. Kepner-Tregoe, Inc., Princeton, NJ (1994). Copyright 1993/94 by Computerworld, Inc., Framingham, MA 01701. Reprinted from Computerworld.

Reasons Reengineering Projects Fall Short
Workers' Viewpoint

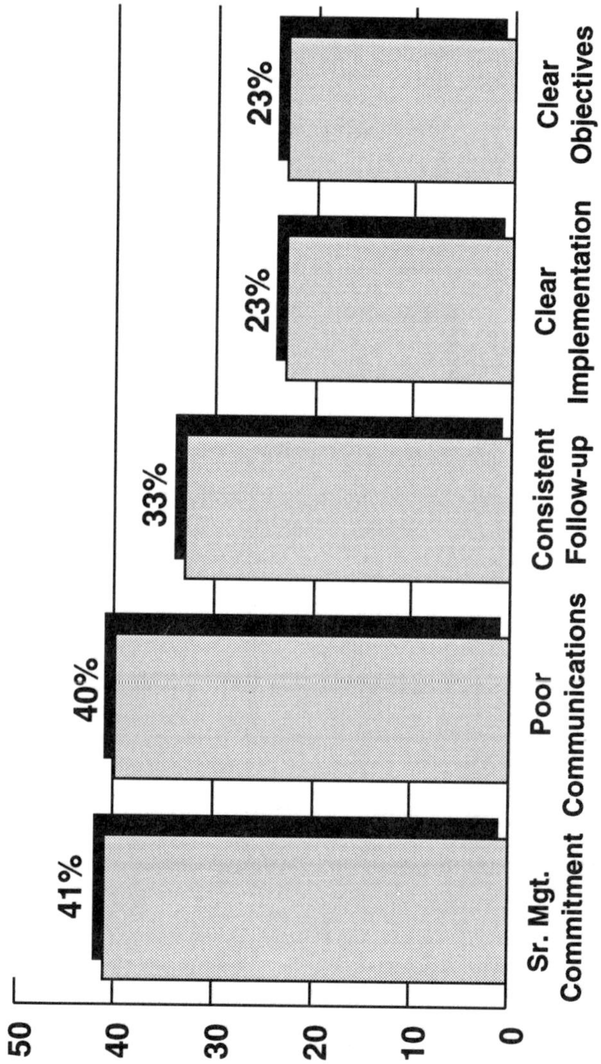

Source: Survey of 182 North American senior executives. Kepner-Tregoe, Inc., Princeton, NJ (1994). Copyright 1993/94 by Computerworld, Inc., Framingham, MA 01701. Reprinted from Computerworld.

Percentage of Respondents Naming the Factor as a Significant Obstacle to Reengineering Success

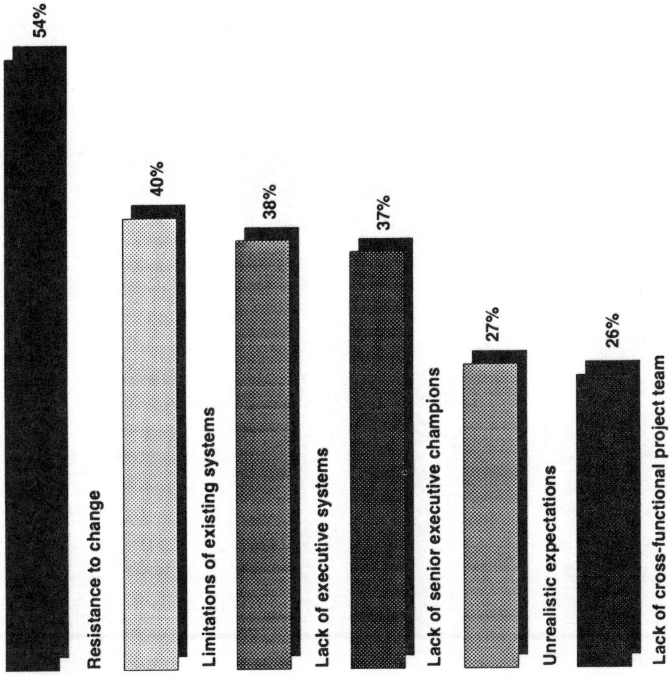

Source: Deloitte & Touche, Wilton, CT. Survey of 400 North American CIOs.

The Biggest Threats to Reengineering Efforts (Percentage Finding It Extremely Difficult)

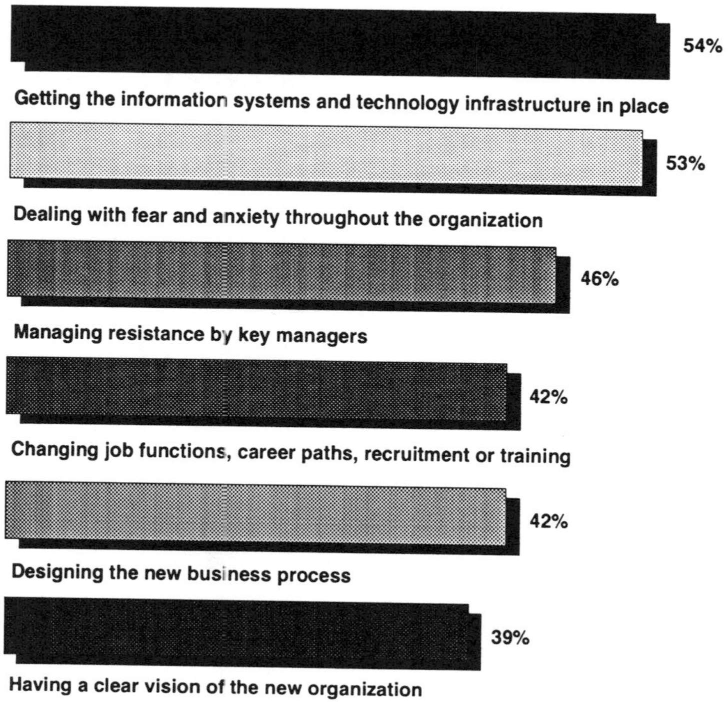

Source: CSC Index, Inc., Cambridge, MA. Survey of 497 senior North American executives. Copyright 1993/94 by Computerworld, Inc., Framingham, MA 01701. Reprinted from Computerworld.

Biggest Communications Challenges in Reengineering Are Keeping Employees Informed and Calm

Percentage of respondents finding it very or extremely difficult

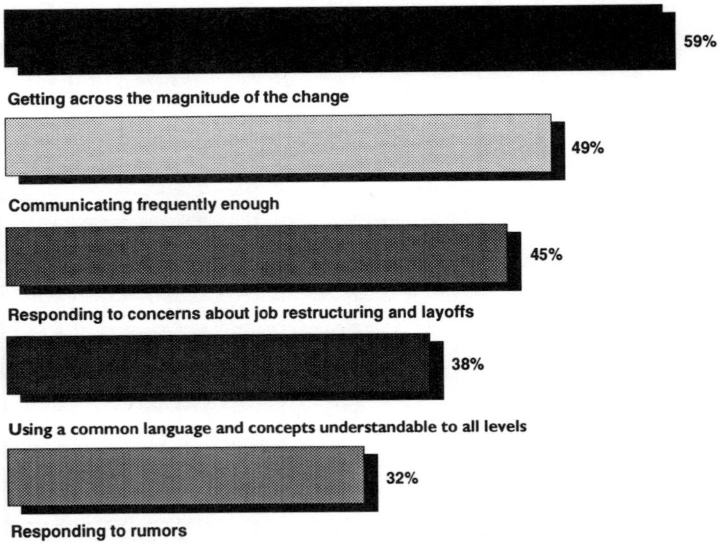

Source: CSC Index, Inc., Cambridge, MA. Survey of 497 senior North American executives. Copyright 1993/94 by Computerworld, Inc., Framingham, MA 01701. Reprinted from Computerworld.

Who's Doing Whom

Company	Function/Dept. Reengineered
ABB Europe	Product development and customer order process
ABB Vetco/Gray	Order fulfillment
ACCO USA	Order management process
ALCOA (Industrial Chemicals)	Customer service
American Express	Worldwide accounting and finance operations, vendor management process
Bank of America	Finance processes
Bell Atlantic	Service delivery
California State Automobile Association	Underwriting services operation
Cargill	Finance
Cigna Dental	Customer service
Cigna Property & Casualty	Support organization processes
Cigna Group Insurance	Customer service
Commerce Clearing House	Customer management, product management, information systems
Delta Airlines	Performance measurement process
Department of Housing and Urban Development	Grant application process
Dun & Bradstreet	Global shared services
E.I. DuPont de Nemours	Supply chain
Federal Mogul	Operations strategy
GTE Cellular Communications	Fraud cost control

Who's Doing Whom

Company	Function/Dept. Reengineered
GTE	Billing, credit, and collections; product development and finance
GTE	Customer service
Hallmark	Financial reporting processes
Harley-Davidson	Product development and manufacturing
Honeywell	Product sales
International Paper	Mill-based processes, including marketing and customer service
Kraft General Foods	Human resources, accounting, facilities management, payroll, benefits
Lever Bros.	Supply chain and business management processes
Levi Strauss	Supply chain
London Fog	Operations
Marion Merrell Dow	Business and customer service
Mass Mutual	Pensions systems
Mazda	Parts-supply system
MBNA America Bank	Finance
Mellon Bank	Integration of new acquisition
Mercedes-Benz	Business processes and information technology
Mobil	Finance and TQM implementation
Newsday	Finance
Nynex	Waste and cost control

Who's Doing Whom

Company	Function/Dept. Reengineered
Ontario Ministry of Revenue	Tax collection
Premier Bank	Lending, new accounts, and transaction processes
Procter & Gamble	Global planning and management
Quaker Oats	Supply chain
RCI Europe	Customer service
Reebok	Worldwide supply chain
Ryder System	Finance
SaskTel	Telemarketing
Sears	Merchandise-return process
Texas Department of Human Services	Payroll and personnel
Union Carbide	Finance
United Technologies	Order fulfillment
Vanguard	Institutional investor services
Washington Mutual	Business processes
Zeneca Agricultural	Business processes

What's Being Reengineered?
Some 45% of financial executives report departmental reengineering efforts. Those underway include:

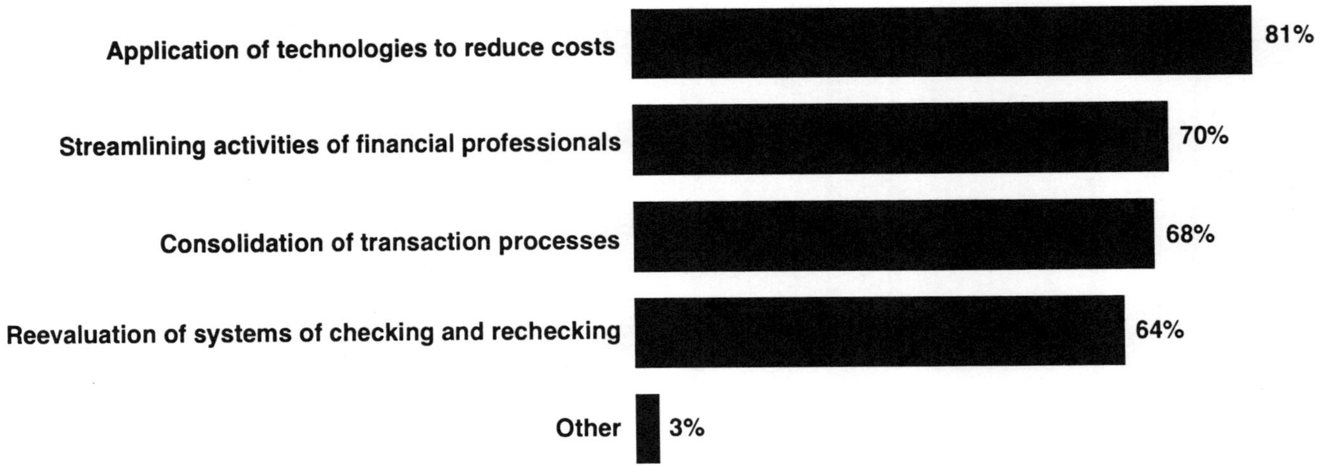

Reprinted with permission from the October 1994 issue of *CFO, The Magazine for Senior Financial Executives.* © 1994 CFO Publishing Corp.

Partnering

Introduction

> A company decides to partner because it wants one or more of four things from an ally: marketing, manufacturing, technology, or finance.

Partnering is defined as a long-term commitment between two or more organizations with the goal of achieving specific business objectives by maximizing the effectiveness of each participant's resource.

Many industries are interested in partnering. However, it requires a cultural and a behavioral change on a corporate-wide basis as well as a commitment from top management.

Too often, however, the history of partnerships in the high-tech industry reads like a poorly written three-act play; great promise, uncertain commitment, and bitter divorce. Organizations going into a partnership often plaster their announcements with terms such as "strategic partnerships" and "new paradigms," with little idea of what they are getting together to produce.

For example, the plummeting of the ACE (Apple Computer, Commodore Computers, and Epson), the failure of U.S. Memories, and the cantankerous feuding between IBM and Microsoft are but three cases of once-trumpeted partnerships that have fallen into disrepair.

For American organizations to continue to strengthen their competitive positions in the world economy, they must shatter existing contract paradigms ("us" versus "them" attitudes) and find new methods to improve quality (win-win attitudes). Corporate executives, in general, are learning to ask two questions when confronted by the latest, greatest breakthrough promises from the latest, greatest partnership deals just struck: What will be produced and when will it be available to the market? If these basic questions cannot be answered, the success of the partnership is severely at risk.

The results of a Construction Industry Institute task force suggests a number of reasons for establishing a partnering relationship, including: (1) lack of personnel, (2) emergency response capability, and (3) cost reduction. Any move toward this new organizational philosophy will entail a reorganization of management thought and a reshaping of corporate cultures.

When an organization's partnering strategy is put in action, it can have ramifications for every aspect of the organization's business-to-business marketing operations. This can include the way an organization manages its sales force, the way it uses trade shows and advertising, the kind of market research it does and even the decisions that it makes about its product mix. Since a partnering strategy reaches into all corners of an organization, fundamental changes in organizational behavior must be undertaken to allow this strategy to succeed.

What is the Partnering Process?

Partnering, as previously defined, is an alternative management process that seeks to produce organizational change to resolve the traditional organizational/contractual problems such as: (1) organizational "posturing" instead of problem solving; (2) retaining critical project information; and (3) "us" versus "them" attitude which continues an adversarial position.

The objective of the partnering process is to design for each project an effective problem-finding/problem-solving management team composed of personnel from both parties, focused on creating a single culture with one set of goals and objectives for the project. The primary advantage of partnering is that it recognizes and honors the objectives of all parties, thereby creating synergy for true project success.

> No one is doing it well yet. It is so difficult because it is so totally different from doing business the old-fashioned way, where you have confrontational "beat-em-over-the-head" relationships as opposed to partnerships. The only way to learn how to do it is to go out and experiment. It is like reading a book on how to play golf, and then giving someone a club and telling them to go out and shoot par. Partnering takes a lot of practice.
>
> — *Bob Kearns,*
> *Operations Manager,*
> *Sonoco Fibre Drum Division*

Traditionally, each party to a contract makes decisions based on the goals and objectives of their organization without consideration of the impact on the other party. The decision process is treated as privileged information and the other party is not involved. Members of management from both organizations engage in diversionary tactics rather than attempting to solve the problem(s) at hand. Many times, the confrontational process is conducted in order to reach decisions that can be defended through the legal system if challenged by the other party. This type of adversarial relationship, for example, is reflected in construction delays, difficulty in resolving claims, cost overruns, litigation, and a win-lose climate. Partnering is designed to eliminate this traditional management practice/attitude/philosophy/behavior.

Partnering is generally established through a structured, facilitated process, normally consisting of organized workshops to bring the participants together. The process is designed to provide an environment for developing the cooperative attitude and commitment needed to drive the partnerships.

Strategic Partnering Pitfalls to Avoid

- Partner having little strategic alliance experience.
- Selecting cash-rich silent partners.
- Integrating different management styles.
- Not building consensus and alliances right from the start.
- Moving too fast on too many fronts.

— *Earl Landesman,*
Principal, A.T. Kearney, Inc.

Moore, Mosley, and Slagle (1992) present eight steps in establishing a partnering process. These eight steps, in various renditions of the same theme and principal concepts, appear many times in the current literature addressing partnering. The Moore et al. version is presented here, both for its clarity in its presentation of the important partnering concepts and to assist the reader in gaining a better understanding of the partnering process in general.

According to Moore and his colleagues, the eight steps in establishing the partnering process are:

1. **Begin early**. If partnering is to be used effectively, the decision by both parties is needed as early as possible, and the process initiated before the contract is awarded. In the solicitation for bids, a general statement of intent is helpful. Typical wording is shown at the top of page 127:

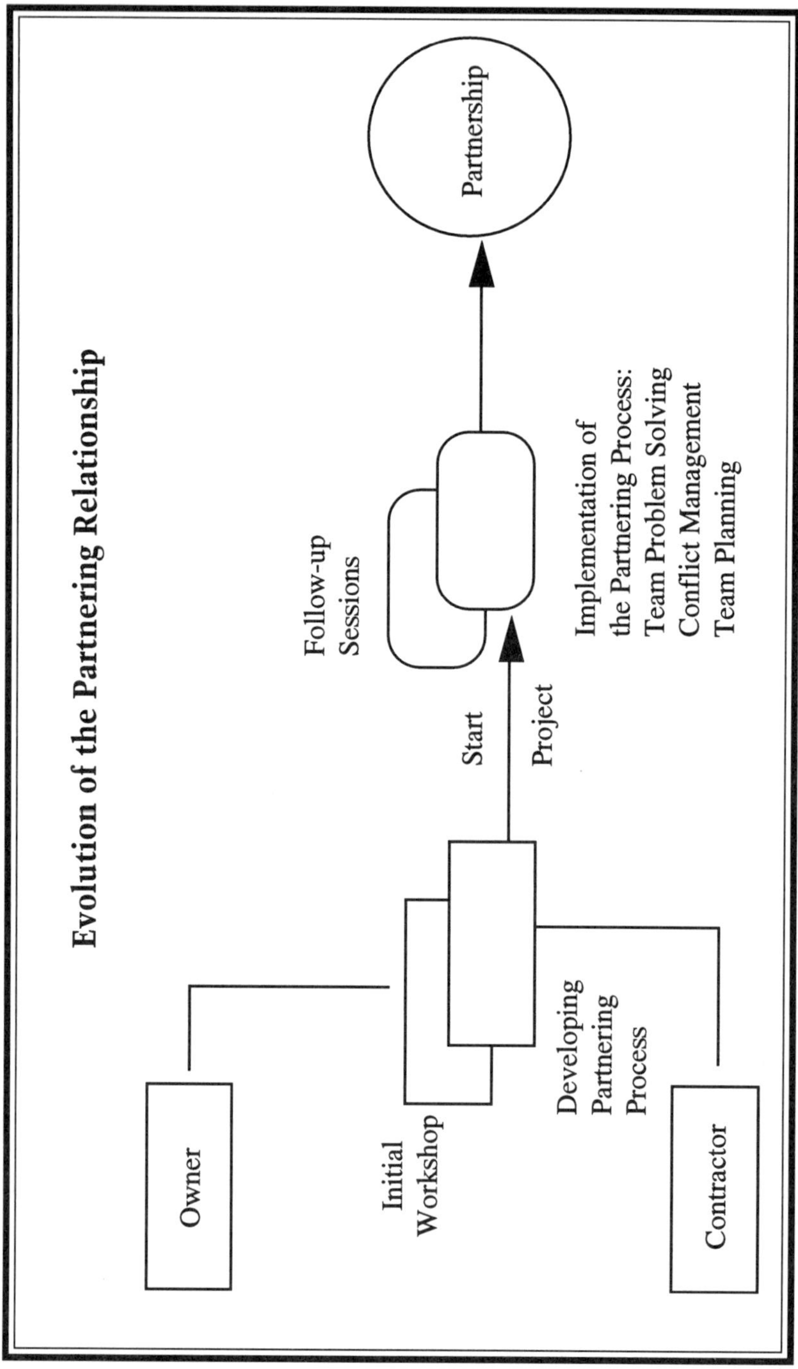

Reprinted from the *Project Management Journal* with permission of the Project Management Institute, 130 South State Road, Upper Darby, PA 19082, a worldwide organization of advancing the state-of-the-art in project management.

> In order to most effectively accomplish this contract the owner proposes to form a cohesive partnership with the contractor and its subcontractors. This partnership would strive to draw on the strengths of each organization in an effort to achieve a quality product done right the first time, within budget and on schedule. This partnership would be bilateral in makeup and participation will be totally voluntary. Any cost associated with effectuating this partnership will be agreed to by both parties and will be shared equally with no change in the contract price.

The essential concepts in the statement are "voluntary" and "cost-sharing." To work, partnering must be a process that both parties want and for which both are willing to pay.

2. **Obtain commitment from top management**. Because of the additional efforts, new behaviors, and up-front costs required for partnering, top level management in both organizations must be fully committed to the concept and process. Without the continuing commitment and active support of management, the process will have little chance of success. The commitment must clearly run from the top down. Chief executive officers from both organizations will have to provide visible support and involve other key middle managers from the home office.

3. **Select members of the partnering team**. The number of participants will vary from project to project, but there are some general guidelines. The core of the partnering effort will be the on-site managers. Included in this group are the resident engineers and their associates. The site team is the primary contact point in the partnering process. Most of the interorganizational communication, problem-solving, and decision-making will take place within this group.

In addition, there will be a Home Office Support Team, composed of staff from both organizations, including those involved with design, scheduling, and purchasing. Care needs to be exercised in providing a balanced team. If the team is "loaded" with owner personnel, the contractor might feel outnumbered and perceive the role as being unequal. The total number will be kept as small as possible to facilitate teamwork. The larger the group, the less efficient it becomes.

Plans are made early in the process to bring "new players" into the team as needed. Some team members will be transferred to other projects during the construction phase and at times specialists will be brought in to cope with specific issues.

4. **Identify a "champion."** No matter how committed management and team participants are, the partnership will not run itself. In order to track, care for, and build the process, individuals from each organization must be assigned responsibility for maintaining the momentum of partnering throughout the life of the project. These individuals will provide the administrative and logistical support that is required to make it work. These activities include scheduling and arranging for follow-up meetings, distributing information to all parties, and follow-up on procedures and plans developed in partnering meetings. Partnering promotes the same goals that are of paramount interest to the project managers of both organizations — quality, safety, cost management, and profit. Thus, project managers are the logical choice for champions.

5. **Select facilitators**. Independent facilitators are recommended to build and maintain teamwork; trust and open communications are needed to sustain the process. The facilitators are not members of the technical or managerial groups, but rather are independent, objective partici-

pants skilled in team-building and group dynamics. They have no vested interest in the decisions reached by the group but serve to manage the process of the meetings, not what is decided. They focus their attention on how decisions are made. At times they may serve to gather information for all team members to support the decision making process. The facilitators must remain neutral on the subject under discussion and their goal is to assist the team in reaching consensus. The primary skills needed to facilitate a partnering effort are in the areas of management training, organizational development, and communication.

6. **Conduct the initial workshop**. To develop the foundation for a successful partnering effort, an initial facilitated workshop should be scheduled as soon as possible after the contract award. Generally the workshop will be held over a three-day period and conducted at a neutral location away from the site or the offices of the participants where a "retreat" atmosphere can prevail. A "retreat" atmosphere fosters the group dynamics that are necessary if partnering is to succeed.

   The goals of the workshop are to open communications, develop a team spirit, establish partnering goals, develop a plan to achieve them, and gain commitment to the plan.

7. **Follow-up**. Detailed maintenance has to be incorporated into the implementation plan. Follow-up sessions should be scheduled at regular intervals to reinforce team-building skills and to assess the progress of the partnership. These follow-up activities are essential for maintaining the momentum of the partnership. The initial workshop focuses on changing the attitudes of the participants from the traditional "us" versus "them" to the team-spirited "we." This change in attitude requires periodic reinforcement. The follow-up sessions also offer an opportunity to engage in team problem solving of current project issues and to revise plans in view of the present project status.

8. **Perks**. Consider developing a team logo for the project and providing keepsake items such as coffee mugs, caps, etc. These are effective and inexpensive extras that add to team spirit.

These eight elements contribute to the development of a climate within which a healthy partnership can grow and evolve. When successful, the implementation of partnering merges two or more previously independent entities into one team, at least for the duration of the project. (Moore, et al. 1992)

When picking a partner, the first question management must ask of itself is, "Why?" not "Who?" Why ask Why? Finding a compatible partner requires figuring out what your firm has to offer that another firm desires and, conversely, what your firm needs that somebody else might have.

According to John Grillor, a partner in the San Francisco investment bank, Robertson Stephens & Co., "The best strategic partner is one whose interests are the same as yours. They need you as badly as you need them. Finding one like that, where they can live up to their half of the partnership, is the critical issue." All customers and supplier firms that do business together have established some sort of working relationship.

> A lot of midrange companies are entering into these relationships (partnerships), and I'm not sure they're giving them the full thought they warrant. It's like a marriage. You should choose wisely, because if you don't, it's going to cost you.
>
> — *Jim Franch,*
> *Director of Technology,*
> *System Software Associates (SSA)*

At one end of the spectrum is a purely *transactional relationship,* where the customer and the supplier focus on the timely exchange of basic products for highly competitive prices. Purely *collaborative relationships* anchor the other end of the spectrum. The latter kind of relationship comes about through partnering.

It is important for the reader to note that partnering, as it has been defined, is a complete reversal of traditional organizational philosophy and behavior. Its acceptance as a management strategy for the 1990s and beyond will depend on management's ability to break long-held traditions and the mold of traditional management behavior — pitting customers (the firm) against the supplier. Success and acceptance will depend on management's ability to see beyond tomorrow, to view the bigger picture, and to position the firm as a competitive player within the industry for years to come. Success will also depend on management's ability to select the most appropriate partner to help achieve both short- and long-term corporate goals.

Henricks (1991) provides five ways that management can increase its chances of finding and living with a fitting partner. These include:

1. **Don't rush into a deal.**
   Begin the process by selecting 20 to 25 potential partners for screening. The targeted firms should appear to have the desired marketing, operational, or technological characteristics deemed critical for continued success. Examine each potential partner's markets, products, key customers, image, finances, facilities, management backgrounds and, naturally, other partnering arrangements.

   There is one essential question management should ask: Is the organization really interested in partnering? With that, two additional questions arise: Will an alliance with the organization enhance the firm's competitive advantage? And, what will convince management to enter into such a deal?

Strategies for Sizing Up a Partner:

- Approach several potential partners.
- Seek high-quality, experienced forms.
- Seek supplementary strengths.
- Concentrate on horizontally related partners.
- Employ step-by-step relationship building.

— Earl Landesman,
Principal, A.T. Kearney, Inc.

2. **Check the corporate culture.**
How does your potential partner's organization function? Do you know exactly how decisions are made? Will the decision making style conflict with your firm's style? How compatible are the separate management teams? Will decision making be an independent process or will it require a committee decision?

   Before inking a partnership contract, ensure that you understand what is going on inside that potential partnership's organization.

3. **Establish clearly defined goals and performance milestones.**
For a partnership to work, experts say each partner has to know *exactly* what to expect of the other, what is expected of itself, and how to measure whether expectations have been achieved.

4. **Find a corporate champion and develop a personal relationship.**
   No matter how formal the management's arrangement with a partner has been defined, it takes commitment from the heart for the partnership to work. The key people involved must truly believe in the necessity of the alliance and never fail in championing it.

5. **Plan an exit strategy.**
   Getting out of an alliance can be as tricky and unpleasant as breaking up a marriage.

   Pegging an alliance's continued existence on objective measurements, such as sales levels or market share, can provide a timing mark for when an alliance will be over.

   A way out can also be provided by a clause in a contract calling for the firm's partner to live up to certain requirements at certain times — regular cash payments, timed equity purchases, specific customers "landed," sales levels achieved, and so forth. If the conditions are not met, the alliance can be automatically dissolved.

Imperfect Alliances

> Software companies are abandoning the old attitude that they must develop everything themselves. Our customers want increased functionality such as EDI and demand forecasting capabilities, and there are companies out there that already do these things very well. It makes more sense for us to form strategic partnerships with them than to commit resources to develop those features in-house.
>
> — *Patrick Engesser,*
> *Distribution Products*
> *Marketing Manager,*
> *Lawson Associates*

Most American retailers acknowledge the benefits of forming quick response (QR) partnerships with their suppliers. But only a few are aggressively making the changes to their corporate cultures and operating environments necessary to implement QR. So concludes a survey conducted for Coopers & Lybrand (C&L) by Louis Harris and Associates.

Quick response is to the retail supply chain what just-in-time is to manufacturing. It can improve customer service and lower inventory and operating costs. C&L identifies six initiatives that are essential to successful QR efforts:

- Sharing inventory data among trading partners.
- Sharing sales and marketing data among trading partners.
- Using bar coding to track sales and inventory.
- Enabling customers to order through EDI.
- Managing stock replenishment for key customers.
- Using automated stock replenishment systems.

Only 28 percent of the manufacturers and 38 percent of the retailers surveyed had undertaken at least four of these initiatives. While the majority had some of the individual elements in place (and many even said they were implementing a QR system), "A surprising number view the alliance as merely a means of speeding up orders and deliveries..., not as a partnering approach to accelerate operational processes," said C&L Partner Len Olin.

The report is based on interviews with 210 general managers of strategic business units within consumable-products manufacturing companies and 79 general merchandising managers of retailers, all with revenues exceeding $500 million. A significant number of respondents, particularly among the manufacturers, said they will never share sales and marketing information with suppliers or implement automated stock replenishment systems (seven out of 10 retailers said they currently share sales, marketing, and inventory information with their suppliers; only four out of 10 manufacturers do so).

"Most consumer-products companies are currently focused on their short-term concerns, product quality being chief among them," Olin said, "And while they're right to be concerned with quality, they are missing the mark by ignoring longer-term partnering opportunities that can do more than any other activity to increase productivity across the entire supply chain."

> Partnering will continue to be a core strategy for our company as it seeks to penetrate medical, remote sensing, and other promising industries. We hope to build strategic relationships with companies in many different application areas.
>
> — *James Anderson, CEO, Applied Intelligent Systems, Inc.*

What are the Benefits of Partnering?

Partnering can provide management with the following benefits:

- Partnering can improve efficiency in the area of interaction between customer and supplier, providing better customer service and cutting operating costs.

- Partnering creates a formidable competitive barrier. Partner relationships bind the customer to the supplier and make it difficult for anyone to take the business away.

- The increased focus on partnering with customers also is prompting organizations to help their sales force develop new sets of skills, especially those necessary for gathering research information.
- The primary advantage of partnering is that it recognizes and honors the objectives of all parties, thereby creating synergy for true project success.
- Forging strategic partnerships whether it be with large or small organizations — be they suppliers, customers, or even competitors — enables partners to save time and money when designing, building, and marketing new products and services.

> The fragility of interorganizational alliances stems from a set of common "deal busters" — vulnerabilities that threaten the relationship. Partnerships are dynamic entities, even more so than single corporations, because of the complexity of the interests in forming them. As a partnership evolves, its parameters are never completely clear at first, nor do partners want to commit fully until trust has been established. And trust takes time to develop. It is only as events unfold that partners become aware of all the ramifications and implications of their involvement.
>
> — *Rosabeth Moss Kanter,*
> Becoming Pals: Pooling, Allying, and Linking Across Companies

What are the Risks of Partnering?

For all of the benefits to organizations provided by partnering, there are many inherent risks associated with this strategy:

1. **Shifts in Business Conditions.**
A partnership begins with a mutual agreement to a predefined set of goals and objectives intended to last for the life of the project. If conditions change, resulting in unexpected delays, cost overruns, etc., the feeling in the partnering organization could regress to an "us" versus "them" attitude and undermine the agreed upon win-win objective.

2. **Uneven Levels of Commitment.**
The efforts and energies which should be committed to a project will be affected by prior partnering endeavors or lack thereof and size of firms. All parties involved in the partnering must take all steps possible to balance the commitment among all participants so that each participant can feel like an equal partner.

3. **Failure to Share Information.**
Open, frank, and timely communication between all parties of a partnering team is essential. Failure to communicate important issues when they arise to the site team instead of reporting them back to the "Home Office" will cripple any partnering efforts. Such failure to share information is an indication of a regression to the old adversarial relationships and "us" versus "them" attitudes.

4. **Lack of Momentum.**
The champions from both sides of the partnership must take all actions necessary to keep the partnership active, alive, and focused. Once the initial fanfare and meetings fade from memory, it is often difficult to keep motivation levels charged and excitement at record peaks.

Consummating and managing a partnership is often compared to marriage in its complexity. And because of the variety of its forms and the demands of its management, a partnership is unlike anything else in business.

In any form of partnership, picking the right ally and attending to the details can lower your risk dramatically.

What are the Impacts/Effects of Partnering on Organizational Behavior?

The implications of partnering on organizational behavior are many. Some of the more critical are detailed below:

- Partnering is an attitude and strategy that imbeds shared values as a path to excellence and elevates problem resolution to a joint venture based on a "win-win" philosophy.

- Risk is an ever present element in partnering. All risks must be shared by both parties, and everyone in the partnership is responsible for maintaining a healthy partnership.

- Successful partnering will change the corporate culture of the organizations involved. It will produce a new positive strategy for doing business and change the management style of the members of the partnering team.

- Partnerships are being driven by several worldwide business pressures, including:

    - **Shorter product design cycles**. With the fast, ever-changing pace of technological innovation, many organizations in a variety of industries realize that it is cheaper to buy than to build — and, therefore, are looking outside their own R&D efforts for new products.

- **Increased global competition**. Foreign competitors are targeting American markets, making the lure of partnering for quicker responsiveness to market opportunities even more attractive.

> In the same way that companies need a market strategy, a company needs a partnering strategy that is figured in as a key part of that overall market strategy.
>
> — *James Anderson, Professor of Marketing and Wholesale Distribution at Northwestern University*

Summary

As demonstrated in the C&L survey previously cited, partnering has not established a firm foothold in management's arsenal as a strategic policy or practice. As previously noted, to embrace this philosophy, this management style will require a significant change in organizational behavior. This degree of change will not come easily or overnight.

However, the potential for success and improved corporate productivity is great, and over time, partnering will come into its own and experience varying degrees of success. Like outsourcing, downsizing, rightsizing, and reengineering which preceded it, the concept of partnering will need to undergo a trial by fire, establish a proven track record, gain a wider acceptance from organizations at all levels, and erode long-held management beliefs in an "us" versus "them" view of the world, before it is fully embraced by industry. The future, however, is close at hand.

> We are doing things to try to better prepare our salespeople to meet the challenges of today's industry. We are trying to help them learn to focus on the concept of value rather than on the concept of cost or price.
>
> — *Ron Kegarise,*
> *Director of Metallurgical*
> *Engineering and Quality Systems,*
> *Alcoa Aluminum Co.*

As demonstrated, working relationships with customers are a significant asset of any supplier's business. Through partnerships, a supplier can leverage its limited resources through joint efforts with customers, gain benefits of customer ideas and experience, and garner higher profit margins from value-added services. On the other hand, transactional relationships offer the supplier the opportunity to prune elements of the product offering that customers deem superfluous, yielding a more competitively priced offering while at the same time easing pressure on the supplier's profit margin (Anderson 1991).

When developed and implemented properly, a strategic partnership provides small organizations with the flexibility needed to compete in an increasingly global and competitive market (Henrichs 1991).

While the previously discussed strategies of outsourcing, downsizing, rightsizing, and reengineering dealt mainly with the corporate IT function, partnering (as we have seen) deals with yet another important element within organizations — the sales and marketing functions. Partnering can be tied to technology, but not exclusively. Partnering as an organizational behavior and a management philosophy of the 1990s will prove to be a powerful force as it is teamed with outsourcing, downsizing, rightsizing, or reengineering strategies.

Organizations that seize this opportunity and strategically implement this one-two (i.e., partnering/outsourcing, partnering/downsizing, etc.) combination, will be positioning themselves as industry leaders and global competitors well into the 21st century.

> One of the most attractive sources of capital for a small company is a strategic corporate investor.
>
> — *Thomas S. Shattan,*
> *managing director and head of the*
> *private equity financing group at*
> *Kulder, Peabody & Co. Inc.*

Part 3
Third-Party Service Organizations: The Impact on In-House Operations

Introduction

> Between 20 percent and 30 percent of the financial institutions surveyed by the General Accounting Office, the investigative arm of Congress, were found to have some form of hanky panky in their outsourcing contracts.
>
> — Information Week,
> *January 6, 1992, p. 13*

In recent years, increased foreign competition has resulted in downsizing and outsourcing in many organizations as they attempt to cut costs. In addition, the downturn in the American economy has led most major corporations to reduce staff positions at all levels and within all departments. This reduction in staff and the outsourcing of financial and IT functions raises concern with respect to the internal controls over these functions which either (a) are no longer processed in accordance with the concept of segregated duties, or (b) are no longer under the control of user management.

The migration to new technology requires a migration in responsibility within the organization. Many of the control issues associated with the mainframe environment must now be assumed by the end user, and likewise, data processing must now assume some new responsibilities.

Users will become responsible for the applications and data processed locally on LANs even though they may not be ready for the job. Effective management of this new responsibility includes policy changes and education of the user department managers in the area of data processing controls and security.

Additional responsibilities are placed on the internal auditing department. Since there are fewer organizational controls built into PC networks, internal auditing will have to perform more reviews to verify a given level of control (Sirkin 1991). Although there is much to be gained through outsourcing and downsizing, there is also the risk of a resulting loss of control and internal control weaknesses.

The Trade-offs: Are They Worth It?

A good starting point is to analyze why outsourcing is being considered in the first place. Questions that are being asked include: "Are costs getting out of hand?" "Are existing staffers overwhelmed by their workload?" "Is it time to shift in-house talent away from fire fighting chores so that they can tackle strategic projects?" "Do staff members even have the ability to handle special projects?" As previously discussed, part of this corporate self-analysis also must include how well outsourcing fits into the way an organization conducts business — its corporate culture, as it were.

Most businesses today have plans for downsizing and decentralization. When those plans become fact, it is likely the IS control groups — including internal and EDP audit, data security, and quality assurance — will suffer more than their fair share of reductions. Why? They are labeled as "overhead." Worse yet, they are often regarded as inhibiting cost centers — blocking productivity, innovations, and quick response.

Although control specialists do not deserve sacred-cow status, they should not be sacrificial lambs either. If anything, they are more necessary than ever in this world of rapid downsizing, outsourcing, redeployment, and reengineering.

When an enterprise embarks on structural and operational overhauls, those business changes are often accompanied by a restructuring of its information processing operations. As that occurs, information responsibilities and mechanisms should also move, grow, and adapt. Far from achieving state-of-the-art controls for their state-of-the-art hardware and software, many organizations still rely almost entirely on control and protection procedures from the early 1980s. This might not be a major problem if they are using their information systems in the same way and for the same purposes. But in most instances, they are not.

> Most outsourcing contracts identify financial implications of failures to meet agreed-upon terms. Thus, it is important to accurately assess the value of your data and to determine potential damage if things go wrong.
>
> — *Ladd Willis,*
> *Managing Vice President,*
> *First Manhattan Consulting Group*

Through most of the 1980s, the single vendor, mainframe-based data center dominated the scene. Technology-based controls were reasonably easy to understand and attain. Essentially, if you provided the right tools and instilled a sense of control responsibility in the people who ran the data center, that was enough. The end user was dependent on the mainframe for direction and for access to transactions and information and could do only what the mainframe allowed. Now, in place of one system or application platform, there are rapidly changing options with varying degrees of compatibility. Using micro- or minicomputers, today's end users have become fully privileged processing partners.

To achieve even comparable levels of control for your critical information systems, you may have to contend with hundreds of independent, powerful, and sometimes dissimilar systems. These systems, under the command of these independent processing partners, are often linked in complex, dynamically reconfigurable, overlapping networks. There are far more complex processes and relationships. Most importantly, there are more people involved. Decentralizing information systems relocates information resource ownership and processing responsibility, placing it directly at the user level where control does not always get the needed priority. A small and sparsely equipped staff of control specialists using older, data center oriented control techniques is ill equipped to contend with this new world without additional resources, training, and facilities.

Information protection and control requires explicit direction, measurement, and reinforcement. To apply appropriate controls to the resources, applications, and environments that really need them, you need to have experience, professional advice, and good judgment.

Information protection also requires well-planned action programs. While line management is a key component in such programs, specialists are needed to help design, support, and measure these activities. Most organizations have too few specialists and many of those are trained only in mainframe protection techniques. To make their presence felt in telecommunications, network management, distributed systems, shared data and application design, they need to expand their skills.

They must participate in the application design and development cycle, ensuring that controls are developed along with the process. Retrofitting controls is the most expensive, least effective way of establishing necessary controls. It is also the reason that many poorly controlled applications and systems are put into production.

It is dangerous to assume that, when faced with major changes, staff reductions, and general upheaval, you can maintain the same or better level of control on a shoestring budget. Generally, the opposite is true. When it comes to control, smaller may not be better.

> Outsourcing information systems operations means entrusting someone else with your company's data. But if you think you're also transferring the liability for that data, think again.
>
> — *Robert E. Zahler,*
> *leading authority on outsourcing law*
> *and Partner at Shaw, Pittman, Potts and Trowbridge*

Xenakis (1992) makes several inaccurate generalizations based on a few bad outsourcing contracts rather than focusing on the many successful arrangements. He says, for example, that organizations should "deal with service and pricing issues separately." But service and price are interrelated. On-line availability of 99.9 percent is more expensive to obtain than 95 percent. A 24-hour, seven-days-a-week help desk is more expensive than a first-shift-only help desk, and dedicated resources are more expensive than as-needed resources. It is more important for the CFO to have the bidding outsourcers price the contract using the performance standards he or she wants — usually, the same standards currently demanded of the in-house MIS department.

In addition, Xenakis's article states that "almost every long-term outsourcing contract negotiated prior to 1992 will be substantially altered before its completion." Renegotiating contracts, however, is quite common in the business world. As a matter of fact, renegotiation provisions are provided for in large outsourcing contracts, recognizing that the parties will have to reset certain terms every two or three years, especially if there is a sale/merger/bankruptcy of the customer or a fundamental change in data processing direction or requirements. If a contract is properly structured, future events should not have a negative impact on a customer. For example, a clients' contract could be materially unchanged for four years even though the client may go through bankruptcy, substantial reorganization, and a pending sale/shutdown of a significant portion of its operations during this period. The contract pricing mechanism using the "compute utility" concept (that is, pay for the technology actually used) should address this issue.

It is also clearly unfair to offset the cost of *new* services against the savings expected on *existing* services by stating, "When extra services are needed, the outsourcer charges time and materials, and that eats into any hoped for savings." It is precisely these new services that can create out-of-control MIS costs in an in-house environment. In a typical request for proposals, the CFO should compare in-house MIS annual projections, excluding *new services*, with those of the outsourcer. Based on discussions with industry analysts, an in-house MIS department is simply not able to compete against a reputable outsourcer regardless of whether the services are new or existing. The economies of scale are simply too great.

Finally, recommending that "short-term contracts will be the safest and best bet" is a gross generalization and is only true for organizations that choose flexibility as their number-one priority.

Short-term contracts are the most flexible and the *most expensive.* If a customer is willing to sign up for a longer term, then the outsourcer will be able to lower the monthly fee. A properly structured contract will provide customers with the pricing benefits of a long-term contract while at the same time retain the flexibility to modify certain terms of the contract based on changes in technology and/or changes in their business environment (Rich 1994).

> Outsourcing the network to a single vendor may not provide optimal operating efficiencies, and it eliminates the competitive environment that keeps vendors responsive to user needs.

Audit and Control Observation

The 10-year outsourcing contract between General Dynamics (GD) and Computer Sciences Corp. (CSC) will provide GD with immediate balance sheet benefits by converting its data center assets to cash.

John Hammitt, the former Information Systems Chief at United Technologies Corp., states, "It is hard to imagine an industry more dependent on IS than aerospace and defense." A question to ask then is can an outsourced IS function cut time to market, improve customer satisfaction, and improve product quality?

A broader question is raised from the point of view of audit and control standards. As a result of the outsource contract, 2,600 IS employees left General Dynamics to join CSC. With this exodus, and considering the very nature of the line of business at General Dynamics, how does CSC propose to maintain the same level of internal controls, information security, access control, and government programming standards as were required by GD, a government contractor?

Outsource vendors have contracts with a number of varied clients to maintain systems and provide services. Before entering into an outsource agreement, the auditors should assist the company in determining whether the outsource vendor can provide the same levels of control and meet the same regulations (or adhere to the same requirements) posed by external regulatory agencies. If the outsource vendor cannot provide the same level of control, the auditor should raise serious questions concerning the vendor's capabilities and caution the user to exercise extreme apprehensiveness when entering into a contract with that particular vendor.

Additionally, if the outsource vendor does not meet governmental requirements for classified IS processing, entering into a long-term outsourcing contract may subject the outsourcing client to fines, penalties, legal action, and/or the loss of the government contract. The internal auditor should assist management in examining these requirements before entering into any outsourcing contract.

In order to manage multiple outsourcing vendors, companies need to do several things:

First, they need to recruit people with program management experience who know how to monitor and manage outsourcing vendors.

Second, companies need to make it easier to outsource parts of their operation. They can do this by establishing both realistic network performance measurements that outsourcing firms will have to meet or exceed, and setting well-defined job descriptions and functional areas within the network department.

(Continued next page)

> Finally, companies should undertake a comprehensive audit of all networking-related expenditures so they can evaluate the validity of cost-saving estimates offered by potential outsourcing firms.
>
> — *Howard Frank,*
> *Professor,*
> *University of Pennsylvania's Wharton School*

A Question of Independence: Outsourcing Internal Auditing

Chicago's Continental Bank has outsourced the bulk of its internal auditing function by expanding its relationship with Price Waterhouse, its external auditor since 1985. Under this unusual arrangement, internal and external auditing work will be integrated.

Continental has been in the forefront of the trend to outsource service functions not considered vital to an organization's major role. Last year it entered into a 10-year contract to outsource its information systems functions to an IBM subsidiary supported by Ernst & Young which is said to involve annual savings of $10 million. "We hope to derive some significant cost savings" from the internal auditing arrangement, says Dick Anderson, Continental's general auditor.

Two-thirds of the bank's 72 internal auditors are expected to join Price Waterhouse. The remainder, including the General Auditor and audit management, will stay with the bank to oversee the new strategy. According to Anderson, "This approach keeps Continental's Board of Directors and management in total control of the auditing function."

The examples just highlighted — General Dynamics and Continental Bank — demonstrate not only the extremes, but the realistic direction and impact outsourcing and downsizing are having on organizations.

Independence

> The audit staff should have read-only access to the organization's data on a demand basis. If special forms or other administrative procedures are needed to obtain access, the efficiency of the audit may be severely hampered. With unrestricted access, the auditor will not have to seek either user approval or service center approval to evaluate data.

What has not been addressed, especially in Continental's case, is the question of auditor independence.

The status of auditing as a useful service to the public is based on the fact that the financial community perceives auditors to be independent of both (1) the financial information audited and (2) the preparers and users of that financial information. Were it not for independence, an auditor's attestation function would be meaningless.

The concept of independence relates to both the real independence of individual auditing practitioners (practitioner-independence) and the apparent independence of all auditing professionals collectively (profession-independence). Practitioner-independence is a state of mind, an attitude of impartiality and self-reliance that pervades an auditor's approach to audit examinations. To successfully maintain an impartial attitude toward financial information, preparers, and users, an auditor must be aware of conditions or factors that might impair his or her independence. Mautz and Sharaf (1961) identify three fundamental dimensions of practitioner-independence that can minimize or eliminate potential threats to the auditor's impartiality:

- **Programming independence** — freedom from control or undue influence in the selection of auditing techniques or procedures and in the extent of their application. The auditor must have the freedom to develop his or her own program, both as to steps to be included and the amount of work to be performed, within the overall bounds of the engagement.

- **Investigative independence** — freedom from control or undue influence in the selection of areas, activities, personnel relationships, and managerial policies to be examined. This requires that all legitimate sources of information be open and available to the auditor.

- **Reporting independence** — freedom from control or undue influence in the statement of facts revealed by the examination or in the expression of recommendations or opinions as a result of the examination.

Thus, practitioner-independence requires freedom from restrictions regarding audit techniques, areas audited, and the auditor's reporting obligation. To be independent, an auditor's professional judgment should be neither subordinated to nor influenced by any other interested parties.

Profession-independence, in contrast, is a perception held by members of the financial community and the general public about practitioners as a group. Perceptions, however, are sometimes inaccurate and occasionally damaging. To the extent that the profession is perceived as lacking independence, the impartiality of individual practitioners is suspect. Thus, profession-independence has a direct impact on the effectiveness and indeed the livelihood of an auditor. As a result, maintaining an image of independence has been a major preoccupation of the profession.

At the AICPA's Nineteenth Annual Conference on Banking (November 4, 1994), Walter D. Schuetz, Chief Accountant for the U.S. Securities and Exchange Commission (SEC), in his prepared speech, made several statements which questioned the independence of external auditors who executed audit procedures that traditionally were performed by internal auditors. In addition, Mr. Schuetz also raised serious questions concerning the logic behind management's decision to outsource the internal audit function (Schuetz, 1994).

Mr. Schuetz referred to the issuance in 1993 of the AICPA's Ethics Ruling 97, "Performance of Certain Extended Audit Services," which addresses independence issues relating to internal audit outsourcing. Specifically, the AICPA Ruling states that external auditors cannot: (1) perform management functions or make management decisions, (2) be a part of the client's approval process, or (3) be a part of the client's internal control system, without impairing their [the external auditors'] independence.

Mr. Schuetz further examined the intent of the AICPA's ruling and its implications to external auditors by stating:

> "The guidance in Ruling 97, read carefully, is very restrictive. The auditor cannot perform management functions or make management decisions. That means, for example, that the auditor cannot determine the projects to be performed under the scope of the "internal audit" work. Also, the auditor cannot become part of the approval process for specific transactions, such as the loan approval process, because that is a management function. In addition, to the extent that federal or state banking regulations require an internal auditor to be under the control of management, the agreement

> by an outsourcer to function in that employee role is fundamentally inconsistent with the notion that for external audit purposes this same auditor would be considered independent from management" (Schuetz, 1994).

In his closing remarks, Mr. Schuetz revealed the position which the SEC has taken on the question (practice) of outsourcing internal audit, and by doing so, sent a clear message to management:

> "The SEC staff informally has advised external auditors that it [the SEC] would question independence, consistent with Ruling 97, when external auditors perform procedures that are management functions or internal control functions. Practitioners are advised to give careful consideration to the implications that attend such outsourcing arrangements and the resulting effect on the accountant's independence" (Schuetz, 1994).

The reader is advised to obtain and analyze a complete and detailed copy of Ruling 97. Is your company's senior management fully aware of the potential ramifications of their decision to outsource the internal audit function? In retrospect, is outsourcing the internal function still a wise idea? Are long-term controls being sacrificed for short-term savings?

Ethical Conduct

Ethical conduct within a profession deals with the study of ideal conduct which is a special application of general ethics. However, general ethics is but one of five fields of study in philosophy — the others being esthetics, the study of ideal form or beauty; logic, the study of ideal method in thought and research; metaphysics, the study of ultimate reality; and politics, the study of ideal social organization. Thus, ethics in auditing refers to the *ideal conduct* of a professional independent auditor and is a philosophical issue rooted in the study of general ethics.

Even though it is an abstract issue, ethical conduct in auditing requires reasoned and logical solutions to practical auditing questions.

Although discussed separately, the above concepts — independence and ethics along with evidence, due audit care, and fair presentation — are very much related. They provide a way of thinking about auditing, a conceptual overview for understanding auditing practice (Ricchiute 1989).

The question then is how does a firm retain its audit independence if it has outsourced its auditing function? What degree of independent verification and reporting exists if the same external auditing firm is now directing the internal auditing function and preparing the audited year-end financial reports? An unbiased, independent point-of-view is questionable and probably even unlikely.

The objective of this final section is not to debate the pros and cons of outsourcing the internal auditing function, but rather to present an audit program/guide for performing audits of services which have been outsourced and are maintained by third parties.

When commenting on the outsourcing of the internal auditing function, the following question should be raised: Should the work of the external auditor be examined by an independent third party (i.e., not being paid by the firm under review)? Does an opportunity for a less-than-objective examination exist if the external auditing firm performing the audit is being paid by the organization the external firm has originally been hired to audit?

This scenario would be a perfect opportunity for Company A (the firm requiring an audit) to undergo a peer review and not taint the perception of independence by hiring their external auditing firm of record.

Several questions have been raised in this introduction and the answers are not immediately available. The concept of auditing third-party service providers, although not new, has taken on a broader perspective and a greater sense of urgency as more and more organizations opt to include outsourcing of non-critical operations as a management strategy for the 1990s.

> An organization's most important asset, its information, is especially vulnerable when career-wrenching changes such as outsourcing, downsizing, and mergers hit.
>
> — *Dr. Sanford Sherizen,*
> *President,*
> *Data Security Systems*

Industrial sabotage is not new; only the motivations change. With many financially strapped organizations in the throes of staff reductions, information systems managers and security professionals have a new beast on their hands.

"When jobs are eliminated, computer systems are frequently seen as a great place to take out your revenge," says Charles Cresson Wood, an independent security consultant in Sausalito, California.

Security experts recommend that IS managers develop preventive measures to keep disgruntled employees from seeking revenge on the organization's source code.

> When a financial institution turns over its data processing chores to a third party, it also hands off some control over the most precious resource the institution owns — its relationships with its customers.

"Prevention and preparation will save you every time," says Sid Diamond, an independent security consultant in Stevenson, Maryland, who served as Vice President of Worldwide Information Services at Black & Decker Corp. during several staff reductions.

Experts say people are an organization's greatest resource, but they can also be its greatest risk. If computer security is weak during a major staff downsizing effort, the consequences for IS security personnel can be both embarrassing and damaging (Daly 1993).

Inside Job

Out of more than 1,000 respondents to a recent Datapro survey, fully a quarter were "extremely concerned" about the risk of systems damage by angry employees.

Percentage "Extremely Concerned"

Disgruntled Employees	25%
Information Leaks	18%
Network Hackers	18%
Unauthorized System Access	34%

The remainder of this material provides the reader/auditor with a litany of questions that should be asked before entering into a third-party contract or once a third-party relationship has been established. The questions are presented under several general headings:

- General/Overview.
- Management.
- Security.
- Third-Party Contract.

The questions in these categories are presented in such a manner as to allow the reader and/or the practicing internal/external auditor to select specific questions and design his or her own customized third-party audit program. While the nature of the work may remain the same, the type of service performed by a firm's third-party service provider may differ widely (e.g., payroll, payables, personnel, IT, disaster recovery, warehousing, or even internal mail room and photocopy services). It is with this knowledge in mind, that these audit questions have been developed.

Summary

The auditor and end-user management in general should remember that the client-outsourcer relationship is a "hard-nosed" business deal and the auditor should be aggressive in seeking audit rights. While the vast majority of outsource vendors seek to provide quality service, audit rights are not a high priority for them.

> The absence of audit rights can virtually nullify the effectiveness of the internal auditing function.
>
> — *Dr. Alan Friedberg,*
> *Associate Professor, School of Accounting,*
> *Florida Atlantic University,*
> *and William Yarberry,*
> *Director Operations Analysis,*
> *Enron Corporation*

Auditors who simply ignore the control exposure and allow the default or standard third-party service agreement to be accepted as is are placing themselves and their clients at risk. Accepting the vendor's standard contract without alterations could lead to financial liability. Without a right-to-audit clause, the auditor may find that access to the data necessary to perform the required auditing procedures is unavailable. This would then prohibit the auditor from reaching an independent conclusion about the accuracy of the data, and he or she would therefore be unable to express an opinion as to the financial soundness of the third-party service provider or the organization's data maintained by that service provider. (The reader may wish to refer to Appendix XXIX for a list of items that should be addressed in a right-to-audit clause.)

The audit questions that follow, when properly used in the context of an auditing program, will assist the auditor in determining the degree and level of internal controls that exist within an organization as a direct result of the organization's outsourcing, downsizing, rightsizing, and partnering strategies.

The current research suggests that outsourcing may lead an organization into a downsizing strategy while, conversely, downsizing strategies could lead an organization to consider outsourcing its remaining non-critical functions.

Rights to audit general controls should include, but should not be limited to, the following:

- Systems information (for example, operating system parameters).
- Systems change controls.
- System development life cycle controls.
- Disaster-recovery controls.
- Data security and other general control areas.

(Note: The use of the terms end user, you, user, client, and auditee in the following section — Audit Questions — is intentional. These terms are used interchangeably to demonstrate the flexibility of the questions. These questions can be used by internal and external auditors as well as other professionals who work with clients to evaluate the state of internal controls within third-party service organizations.)

The questions do not represent an all-inclusive listing, but rather are offered as a starting point with the expectation that the reader will expand and modify the questions as appropriate for his or her audit requirements.

© Rich Tennant, Rockport, MA.

Audit Objectives and Audit Rights

> In some situations, outsourcing certain elements of information systems functions may offer substantial benefits. However, internal auditors cannot afford to underestimate the importance of audit rights.
>
> — *Dr. Alan Friedberg,*
> *Associate Professor,*
> *School of Accounting, Florida Atlantic University,*
> *and William Yarberry,*
> *Director Operations Analysis,*
> *Enron Corporation*

Depending on the extent and sophistication of the data processing service outsourced, the user's internal auditing department will require different audit rights to satisfy its audit objectives. Therefore, audit rights should be negotiated based on audit objectives. To illustrate this point, Friedberg and Yarberry (1991) state that audit objectives and the associated audit rights, can be organized by three increasingly sophisticated classes of service: (1) batch processing only; (2) batch processing, on-line processing, and related telecommunications; and (3) systems development, maintenance, database administration, and full processing services. Exhibit 1 identifies audit objectives and the desired audit rights for each of the three classes of services defined. Each class of service is considered to include the prior class, so audit objectives and rights for class 2 should include those for class 1.

Exhibit 1
Audit Objectives and Rights Organized by Class of Service Provided

Typical Audit Objectives	Rights for Class 1: Batch Processing	Rights for Class 2: On-Line Processing with Telecommunications	Rights for Class 3: Systems Analysis and Design, Database Management and Processing
Review data integrity and validity (provide substantive tests and tests of controls).	Unrestricted access to: (1) entity's data and (2) access control information about entity's data including security tables for proprietary programs. Right to third-party review of (1) general controls; (2) access control information covering entity's applications; and (3) center's systems and utilities. Unrestricted ability to test entity's application controls. The ability to independently execute audit software.	Right to third-party test and evaluation of general on-line processing and communication controls. Unrestricted access to systems files and tables concerning access to entity's on-line and communications-based applications.	Right to third-party test and evaluation of systems development and management controls (e.g., controls to prevent over-allocation of database DASD and segregation of functions.) Unrestricted access or right to monitor: (1) entity's physical data; (2) entity's global and user schemas and dictionaries; (3) security tables; (4) actions of the database administrator; (5) systems development process.
Safeguard existence of assets (e.g., the entity's data, programs, documentation, and other proprietary information).	Right to third-party review of: (1) continuity plans; (2) backup and recovery capabilities; (3) physical security measures; and (4) off-site provisions for storage of backup data. Review should include right to observe and participate in regularly scheduled tests of the system. Unrestricted access to on-site and off-site storage of entity's files. Ability to operate audit software.	Right to third-party review of both primary and alternative telecommunication equipment and links and tests of the system.	Unrestricted access to documentation of: (1) ongoing systems development efforts, and (2) database documentation. Third-party ability to test backup and recovery of database management system including entity's files.

Exhibit 1 (Cont.)
Audit Objectives and Rights Organized by Class of Service Provided

Typical Audit Objectives	Rights for Class 1: Batch Processing	Rights for Class 2: On-Line Processing with Telecommunications	Rights for Class 3: Systems Analysis and Design, Database Management and Processing
Establish validity of billings from outsource vendor/ evaluation of system efficiency.	The service center must maintain resource consumption data organized by clients who share the same hardware and software to form a basis for billing. Unrestricted access to raw resource consumption data. For example, IBM SMF type 30 records may be needed to determine if CPU time billed is correct. Access to tables or other criteria used to distinguish between billable and non-billable activities.	Unrestricted access to raw technical data and information that serves as the basis for line and other telecommunications charges. Right to access data from various on-line monitors (e.g., PERFORM for IDMS, TMON for CICS, and RMF for overall system performance). Must be able to determine if certain on-line activities are "overhead" and thus non-billable.	When different processing costs apply for development rather than production activities, must have access to tables or other criteria (e.g., job class) which segregate production from development activities. Ability to monitor systems development productivity measures and personnel records to compare with contract standards.
Evaluate system effectiveness.	Right to access system performance data. For example, SMF data will indicate the "percent CPU busy" in an IBM environment. At high levels of CPU utilization, the same workload will be more costly because the system is thrashing (examine paging) more. Right to examine system parameters such as SYS.1.PARMLIB whose files indicate how well performance groups are set up as well as other key processing information. Service level information of all types should be available. For example, monthly frequency of abends and late reports.	Unrestricted access to telecommunications records and hardware including the ability to attach hardware monitoring devices. Third-party review of all telecommunications records and hardware with ability to attach hardware and software monitors.	Access to database auditor functions applied to entity's operations and third-party unrestricted access to these functions.

Source: Friedberg, Alan and Yarberry, William. "Audit Rights in an Outsource Environment," *Internal Auditor* (August 1991), p. 54.

General and Overview Questions

1. Have contract obligations with labor been examined and accounted for in the outsourcing decision? Items to be examined include transfer, pension and insurance contributions for severance payments, retraining costs and payments, employment taxes, contractual refunding of previous contract concessions, or workforce changes.

2. If the work is being transferred to another facility, have expenses for the remodeling or construction costs, training expenses, down-time costs, productivity costs, potential new labor agreements, and employee relocation expenses been factored into the overall cost savings projections?

3. Have expenses incurred for removing, shipping, storing, or disposing of material from the closed facility been considered? If so, are these expenses reasonably stated? Does the outsourcing option still appear to be feasible?

4. Have contractual obligations with outside vendors (telephone, office equipment, computers) and utilities (electrical, water and sewers, natural gas) been extended or canceled? What will be the related cost(s) respectively?

5. Has management considered internal costs related to productivity losses, reorganization of the information systems, or training costs as a result of restructuring elsewhere in the organization?

6. Has the outsourcing company worked with firms in businesses similar to yours? Do they have staff who know the details of information processing in your industry? Are they capable of bringing more than processing cycles to the planning of your information technology?

7. If your needs change in nature and volume throughout the year and over time, will the outsourcer negotiate an agreement that reflects those changes?

8. If you are relying on an outsourcer to help you make the transition from traditional host-centered computing to more modern technology, do they have proven skills in client/server, distributed computing?

9. If your organization is geographically dispersed, even worldwide, can the vendor handle that? And if you are running your own Museum of Computing History masquerading as a production IS department, does the outsourcer have the technical breadth needed?

10. When developing a RFP (request for proposal) has management determined what criteria will be used to select the winning vendor? How will the success of the project be measured?

11. Has management developed a response plan if the new system (operating arrangement, etc.) does not work as expected?

12. What steps are to be taken if the resulting hardware and software (from a downsize movement) are not *really* compatible with what your firm was using before?

13. Employees are expensive. Every day new government rules and regulations increase the cost of full-time staff to the point where expenses for each employee — including worker's compensation insurance and medical insurance — amount to more than that person's take-home pay. Has management determined a strategic plan to identify how the organization can make do with the absolute minimum number of employees?

14. Which applications should be downsized? Can mission-critical CICS on-line transaction processing (OLTP) applications be downsized? Are the tools available? What about batch applications? What about downsizing third-party packages?

15. When should applications be downsized? Is UNIX technology able to handle your organization's mission-critical applications today? Do UNIX systems really have the facilities for running your downsized applications?

16. How can existing SNA networks be used? Is it possible to access downsized applications from 3270 terminals? Will 3270 terminals still be able to access other mainframe applications and data? Will a separate TCP/IP network have to be installed?

17. What happens to the IS staff? Will they need to be retrained or will new people with new skills be required?

18. How can downsized applications be modernized? What actions may be required to upgrade to relational database management systems (DBMSs)?

19. Does the contract between the user and the service bureau describe exactly the services to be provided (e.g., conversion services, developmental services, ongoing services, input processing, report production, production of other items such as payroll checks, testing, correcting errors)?

20. Does the contract clearly define what hardware, software, and personnel will be used to provide the services? Is a level of service agreement included in the contract; i.e., will the system be available all day, everyday, or when? Is the capacity of the system able to handle user's workload? How will malfunctions be treated?

21. Are there timetables for all services to be provided? Are there penalties defined for delays?

22. Will the service bureau duplicate the user's data? Will the bureau keep duplicates in machine-readable form in a fireproof vault at an off-site location? Will users be given duplicates?

23. Are there provisions for recovery in case of a disaster? In case of flood, fire, etc., is there an alternative bureau available to handle work? Is there a disaster insurance policy in force?

24. Will the service bureau and their employees maintain confidentiality of the user's data? Is the user's ownership of data and the medium of storage clearly defined in the contract?

25. What are user responsibilities regarding: Providing accurate data? Using equipment compatible with that of the service bureau?

26. Is it clear how costs are to be calculated? Will charges be per transaction, per monthly flat fee, etc? Are there reduced fees provisions for late services? Is there a "most favored user" clause? Are deadlines for payment set forth? Is there agreement as to who pays taxes?

27. Are there warranties provided by the service bureau? Does the bureau represent that its system is able to perform as promised? Will bureau indemnify user against third-party claims?

28. Does the contract state how the contract may be terminated?

29. Does the contract set out remedies, indemnification, penalty clauses, and damages for early termination of the contract?

30. Does the contract provide for return of data, current source code, and documentation to the user in a timely manner?

> Someone should review the contingency plan after "downsizing" and redesignate key personnel and tasks. Keep in mind there will be fewer qualified employees from which to select.
>
> — *Roy Alzua,*
> *Vice President,*
> *Information Systems Security Association,*
> *Los Angeles Chapter*

Management Questions

1. To ensure success in any downsizing activity, an expressed commitment of both corporate and line management must be obtained. Has this commitment been obtained?

2. Has budget approval been obtained to pursue the downsize/outsource strategy?

3. Does corporate management support the idea of an information technology community within the organization?

4. Has corporate management been actively involved in establishing the business policies on which the community (organization) IT policies are to be developed?

5. In planning for a downsizing effort, does management understand the organization's overall position on IT and the constraints imposed by the organization's current technical, political, or personnel environment?

6. What are the key strategies and tactics in place for the organization to achieve its overall goals? How have these strategies and tactics been deployed within each operating division? What are the critical success factors to accomplishing those goals?

7. Is the organization growing or shrinking? Are acquisitions underway? Is the firm in a cost-control mode? What is the firm's relationship to the competition? Is a partnering decision at this point the most prudent course of action possible?

8. Has a broad technology principles guide been developed to identify the organization's use of information technology?

9. Has management determined:
   - specifically how the organization uses IT?
   - to automate?
   - to improve effectiveness?
   - to radically alter day-to-day operations?

   How does it work to use information technology in the long-term?

10. How many functional departments now use IT on their own? In what capacity? What exactly are they doing? What technologies or applications have they developed? What, specifically, is their cross-functional involvement?

11. What specifically is in your organization's applications portfolio? To what extent can you categorize those ap-

plications as enterprise, departmental, or individual systems?

12. What, specifically, is the experience of your user community? Can you rank the users in your various corporate departments according to their IT knowledge, capabilities, responsibilities, and interests?

13. Before beginning a downsizing effort, management must ensure that an appropriate organizational structure exists and that appropriate technical personnel are available to develop, implement, and maintain the organization's downsized systems. Have these issues been addressed prior to signing any contract?

14. Downsizing uses new hardware technologies, new operating systems, and new software products. It may also involve outsourcing non-strategic systems, as well as innovative development methodologies such as rapid application development and incremental design. Integrating these novel concepts is a key criterion for successful downsizing. Is management capable of coordinating such an integration of goals and technologies to ensure the prospect's success?

15. During a period of organizational change, senior and operating mangers must review a number of actions and decisions.

    a. Make sure the reorganization process is a planned proactive response to the situation.

    b. Make sure the downsizing is accomplished in as orderly a manner as possible.

    c. Make sure all legal agreements, contracts, and commitments are reviewed and honored.

d. Make sure the activities in each of the organization's functions or operations (including those that will be maintained, downsized, spun-off, or closed) are accomplished within the previously defined quality standards.

e. Make sure each operating policy or practice is reviewed for possible revision in view of the reorganization.

f. Make sure that the personnel performance review and reward policies are modified to reflect the new operational requirements.

g. Develop, expand, and maintain the lines of formal and informal communication to employees, customers, suppliers, the business and general media, and other interested parties that explains what is occurring within the organization and attempting to minimize the potential of rumors and/or additional surprise announcements.

h. Maintain the level of customer service and assistance.

i. Make sure internal operating and reporting requirements and standards are followed.

j. Continue operations within the organization in as normal a manner as possible.

Is there evidence that these issues and concerns have been addressed by management?

16. It can be much harder for network outsources to keep abreast of changing communication technologies than it is for data-center outsources to upgrade their computing resources. Has management ensured that options exist

to move quickly if the firm's outsource vendor falls behind its competitors? And if that *does* happen, will the firm be able to get special services at reasonable cost?

17. Once management has looked into an outsource vendor, how does management ensure that the firm gets the best price if the firm must relocate or shut down outdated, unprofitable locations? What if the vendor does not serve the new location (or serves it poorly)? How does management plan to obtain service of acceptable quality at a reasonable price?

18. Costs per unit of many types of long-distance communication services will fall drastically over the next 10 years, which is the typical length of an outsource contract. But if your firm is locked into communication charges based on today's economies, you may be at a competitive disadvantage in two ways: (a) your firm will be paying more for basic communications than your competitors, and (b) your firm may not be able to offer some applications offered by the competition. Is there evidence to support that management has adequately addressed these issues?

19. What is the real motivation for outsourcing? Is it purely financial or are there other reasons to be considered?

20. If cost is the driving factor, what alternatives to outsourcing (such as downsizing) the data center exist?

21. Are high costs in the data center a result of trying to meet unusually stringent Service Level Agreements (SLAs)? Should the SLAs be renegotiated?

22. If the data center is outsourced, will the vendor be held to the same service levels currently required of the data center?

23. Can the organization gain a competitive edge through outsourcing by allowing it to concentrate management attention on the core business?

24. Will outsourcing realistically reduce expenses over the long term?

25. How great is the risk involved?

26. Could the organization recover if, for any reason, the outsourcing vendor failed to perform?

27. Will outsourcing cause a significant loss of control over IS strategy?

28. Can outsourcing help the organization better manage seasonal fluctuations in its business?

29. Can outsourcing significantly improve the overall quality and service levels of the IS operation?

30. Can outsourcing provide better IS capabilities through access to more skilled employees or better hardware/software technologies than are currently available to the organization?

31. Should the outsourcing arrangement not work out as planned, does the organization have a backup plan ready?

32. What role will the vendor play in developing and implementing disaster recovery plans?

33. What types of backup arrangements are offered by the vendor in case of a disaster to the data center? Are these costs part of the standard processing fee or are additional charges involved?

34. What are the vendor's plans for implementing new technologies? Will additional costs be involved?

35. What is the vendor's track record in managing outsourced data centers?

36. Will the vendor use the existing systems software, such as automated production control systems, library management systems, change control and problem tracking systems, or will new systems be installed?

37. If new systems are installed, how will these impact the rest of the IS organization?

38. Will there be additional costs, either directly or training related, for the new systems?

39. Who will be responsible for the turnover of new applications into production?

40. How will technical support and application development interact with the data center?

> Outsourcing the information systems function results in shifting some of the risks associated with capital investment, technological change, staffing, and other areas to the service vendor. It is also seen as a technique for reducing costs, improving service, and permitting management to concentrate on the core business. These accomplishments are possible because the service vendor has converted a traditionally internal service function into a business.

Security Questions

1. When an employee, consultant, or third-party contractor is terminating his or her relationship with your firm, management should identify steps needed to ensure that:

   a. All property in the worker's custody is returned before the worker leaves the firm.

   b. As soon as the termination is known, notification is provided to all administrators handling the worker's computer and communications accounts.

   c. All other privileges of the worker are terminated at the time of departure.

   Is there evidence that these policies exist, are current, and are followed?

2. The data security and integrity of LAN-based systems also has drawbacks. Most network-based systems use the file server as a shared hard drive, with all processing occurring on the user PC. The lack of intelligent processing on the file server makes it difficult to centralize the enforcement of data integrity or to incorporate the transaction processing and disaster recovery mechanisms common to mainframes and minicomputers. Since a hardware or power failure can wipe out a database file, or corrupt a catalog or index, the only recourse is to go back to the most recent backup. However, the lack of centralized integrity controls means that even if backups are done on a regular basis, there is no guarantee that the data contained in the backup is not corrupt. Many users of LAN-based systems are living on borrowed time.

   Is there evidence of centralized integrity controls? Are policies and procedures in place which direct a timely and complete backup of the LAN databases and LAN servers? Is there evidence that these policies and procedures have been communicated to the end users? Is there evidence that these backups are performed on a regular basis?

3. Downsizing applications also leads to easier on-line access of data, leaving the door open for unauthorized persons to view, alter, delete, or copy the information. Have users been warned that data in downsized applications is just as sensitive as when it was available on a larger system?

4. Have policies been established that address the segregation of responsibilities between personnel as a result of the organization's downsizing strategy?

5. Will the firm's downsizing philosophy place an undue burden on IT personnel responsible for authorizing program changes, testing modified applications, and rewording said changes?

Corporate layoffs bring the fear of ex-staffers using computers for revenge or taking their revenge out on the organization's computer(s). Ensure that the following questions have been asked by management prior to publicly announcing the firm's intention to pursue an outsourcing or downsizing strategy:

6. Have problem employees been identified?

7. Are access control lists current?

8. Have obsolete user-IDs been deleted from the system?

9. Is there an up-to-date inventory of PC hardware and software?

10. Are security personnel prepared to change passwords and combinations?

11. Have PCs been checked with virus-detection software?

12. Are all keys and access cards accounted for?

13. Are there procedures and personnel assigned to review all application and system source codes that have been used by an affected employee?

14. Have PCs equipped with modems been checked to ensure that remote-control software (such as Microcom's Carbon Copy) is not in use?

15. Have employees been reminded of the organization's code of ethics? Is there a corporate code of ethics?

16. Has the need for a backup and recovery methodology and a guarantee of a successful recreation of the firm's source code been evaluated? Have existing disaster recovery plans been modified to reflect the downsizing of application platform?

17. Has the full disaster recovery plan been tested? If so, when?

18. Is it clearly defined via contract or other means which party has responsibility for the liability resulting from a security breach? How will the dollar amount of the liability be determined?

In accordance with The Performance Contract of November 1, Paragraph 6, Sub-Heading G - "Penalties for Poor Vendor Service"...
Phil Frank

Third-Party Contract Questions

> The ability to execute audit software should be guaranteed. This means that the audit software can be run on demand without prior permission of the service center. In addition, the service center should be required to provide assistance in installing audit software or providing technical information to access the data.

1. Has a review of the contract been performed to determine that the costs related to new systems design, application reprogramming, computer usage, existing management reports, special request reports, and other materials have been defined?

2. Are the user's responsibilities for activities such as the batching of input, data entry, and balancing specifically defined in the contract terms?

3. Has the service bureau's responsibility for activities such as reviewing the processing output for accuracy, the fixing of identified problems, and reruns been examined? Is the service bureau response rate within contract specifications?

4. Verify that the length of the contract and the terms for its termination are stipulated.

5. Is the service bureau required by the contract to annually provide a third-party review of its control procedures? If not, how are these procedures validated?

6. Does the contract permit the user's internal and/or external auditors to perform an audit of the service bureau operations?

7. Verify that the contract provides protection from the disclosure or loss of the user's data while it is under the control of the service bureau.

8. Does the contract require the service bureau to provide annual audited financial statements?

9. Does the third-party review report describe the control strengths and weaknesses of the service bureau's relevant operations? If not, how are these strengths and weaknesses determined?

10. Does the contract specifically state which controls are the responsibility of the user? Determine that the user has implemented these controls in an adequate fashion.

11. Has the service bureau been audited within the past two years? If yes, review the extent of the audit work performed, the findings of the audit, and the professional qualifications of the auditors involved. If it has not been audited, determine why not.

12. Have the annual financial statements for the service bureau been provided and examined prior to signing of the service contract?

13. Has the service bureau's financial stability been determined?

14. Examine the service bureau's user manuals to develop a general understanding of the application system inputs, processing, and outputs. Are the manuals complete and up-to-date? Can normal processing and full recovery from a disaster be accomplished using these manuals?

15. Does the contract require the service bureau to perform custom programming functions? If so, did the service

bureau complete the programming on time and to user specifications?

16. Obtain copies of the user manuals that describe this customized software. Are the manuals complete and up-to-date? Do they contain all necessary information required to process data through the newly designed applications?

17. Determine the accuracy and completeness of the user manuals through inquiry and observation of key application systems managed by the service bureau.

18. Analyze the user's current data processing disaster recovery plan. Ensure that critical applications processed by the user can be restored off-site by the service bureau before the user's activities are negatively impacted.

19. Verify that the service bureau's data processing disaster recovery plan is tested and updated periodically. What are the results of this periodic testing?

20. Ensure that management has considered the use of alternate service bureaus or other processing alternatives in the event that a data processing disaster at the primary service bureau's site renders that site unsafe or unusable.

21. Obtain the auditee's file on third-party relationships.

22. Request a list of vendor activity by cost center from the accounts payable department.

23. Determine whether there is a payable file for all third-party vendors utilized by the auditee and match the vendor activity list with files maintained by the auditee.

24. Review risk analysis questionnaires for completeness and accuracy.

25. If the vendor is a service provider, determine that an independent review of controls was performed. Determine that the review included an evaluation of the service provider's disaster recovery plan.

26. Determine that performance or reference checks were carried out.

27. Examine evidence that the vendor's place of business was visited by the auditee to look for indications of financial and/or operational weakness.

28. Determine that competitive bidding was performed.

29. Determine that a D&B or specialized industry report was obtained and reviewed prior to entering into an agreement. Examples of specialized industry reports are *Best's* for an insurance company, *Bureau of Credits* for a real estate related contractor, and *Sheshunoff* or *Thomas Bankwatch* for a bank.

30. Determine that audited financial statements were obtained and reviewed.

31. If the vendor is to serve as an intermediary by handling payments or cash or has access to the organization's computer programs/stored data, determine that the vendor is bonded.

32. Determine that a tracking system is in effect to monitor the vendor's performance on an ongoing basis.

33. Determine that the auditee has a copy of the contract/agreement and that it has been reviewed by the auditee's legal department.

34. Test the auditee's computation of the risk exposure factor for accuracy. See policy and procedures for calculation details.

35. For those third-party relationships that exceed the size threshold as established by the risk policies and procedures, determine that the credit worthiness of the third-party vendor was reviewed.

36. Determine that appropriate approvals were obtained for the third-party relationship and that the approvals are documented in writing.

37. For those third-party relationships that do not exceed the cutoff point, determine that approvals were appropriate and in accordance with the risk policy.

38. If any third-party relationships are excluded from the policy, determine that the reasons are appropriate and have been properly and completely documented.

39. Upon review of available documentation and discussions with the auditee, verify that the auditee has a clear understanding of exactly what services the outsourcing vendor will provide and what operations the auditee will continue to have responsibility for. How is this understanding evidenced?

40. Prior to signing the contract, has the auditee determined the market price for owned assets, the assignability of leases, and whether to give the third-party vendor any purchase options associated with equipment formerly used to run the auditee's IT operations?

41. Does the contract require the auditee to identify any liens or outstanding debt on equipment owned by the audi-

tee? If yes, is there information available and has it been provided to the third-party vendor?

42. Will the auditee be required to certify the equipment's maintenance record prior to acquisition by the service provider? If yes, is this information up-to-date and available?

43. Based on your review, is there evidence that before turning any software over to the third-party service provider, the auditee reviewed *and* understood the terms of existing software licenses?

44. Determine that the software licenses currently held by the auditee do not prevent the auditee from transferring that software to the outsource vendor. If the licenses are non-transferable, has the auditee contacted the licenser and obtained authorization to reassign the license? Has the cost (fee) for securing this "right of transfer" been figured into the potential cost-savings calculations which initially justified the outsourcing decision? Has the auditee established a contingency plan in the event the license does not grant authorization to transfer the license to the outsource vendor? If yes, what is this plan?

45. Since all outsourcing contracts should include a set of appropriate performance standards, verify that the contract contains appropriate performance standards for quantitative measures of such things as network availability, response times, and delivery of batch reports.

46. Determine that the contract also addresses performance standards that are not easily measured in quantitative terms, such as the quality of technical consulting, budgeting, and administrative support, as well as whether the vendor is making a satisfactory effort to implement the latest hardware and software technologies.

47. Determine that the contract, at a minimum, calls for the vendor to provide a level of service equal to the auditee's existing performance level.

48. Does the contract contain a catchall clause that calls for the vendor to provide service in a "workman-like" manner that meets generally accepted industry performance standards?

49. Performance standards serve little purpose unless users are able to effectively monitor and track vendor performance. Does the contract require vendors to produce a monthly performance report comparing actual performance against standards established in the contract? If not, how is the vendor's performance verified?

50. Is there evidence that the auditee closely monitors the vendor's progress in meeting contractually agreed upon performance objectives? How is this evidence documented?

51. Does the contract contain prenegotiated terms specifying the amount of damages the vendor will pay if the vendor's performance falls below a minimum standard stated in the contract or established by generally accepted industry performance standards? If yes, how will the amount of damages be calculated? (Typically, damages are specified as a percentage of the client's monthly payment under the contract.)

52. Verify that the contract addresses (in specifics) a methodology for resolving any disagreements, including disagreement over performance levels. Often, contracts specify that a senior executive from each organization who was not involved in the original contract negotiation should be called on to resolve the dispute. Is such language included in the contract?

53. If the executives fail to reach an agreement, determine whether the contract specifies that both parties will seek either arbitration or traditional litigation as the exclusive means for resolving the dispute. (Note: while auditees prefer arbitration to lengthy, often expensive litigation, the former usually favors the vendor over the auditee because arbitration occurs behind closed doors and limits the amount of information the client can request from the vendor regarding the dispute.)

54. Determine that the contract contains a clause that allows either party to terminate the contract if the other fails to resolve a serious problem in a timely manner.

55. Verify that the contract contains a termination clause which stipulates that the auditee can terminate the deal if the auditee's organization is sold or merges with another organization or if the auditee desires to end the relationship early.

56. Ensure that the contract specifies that upon termination of the contract, the current vendor is required to assist the auditee in transferring management responsibility for the network and information systems to another vendor or the auditee's own staff. (Note: unless the contract obligates the vendor to assist with the conversion, the auditee's right to terminate a contract may be meaningless.)

57. Verify that the contract contains a technology refreshment clause. This protects the auditee from being locked into obsolete technology by obligating the vendor to keep the auditee technologically competitive in its niche.

58. Determine that the contract spells out the terms and conditions for the final acceptance of a system, software, or other end item deliverable produced by the vendor for the auditee.

59. Does the contract specifically and clearly state each party's responsibility and liability for the use and protection of proprietary information? If not, how is the confidentiality of the auditee's proprietary information determined, established, and maintained?

60. If the service provider (vendor) is involved in new development work for the auditee, determine that the contract specifically addresses ownership rights, copyrights, and patent rights to be associated with the finished product.

61. Does the contract contain an indemnification clause? If not, how is the auditee protected against (from) potentially illegal acts carried out by the third-party vendor. Examples of such illegal acts include software copyright infringement, improper use of another vendor's software or hardware products, etc.

62. Does the contract include an extraordinary events clause (an escape clause) which allows the auditee to terminate the outsource agreement if costs exceed a predetermined amount? If not, how is the auditee protected (through the life of the contract) from uncontrolled, soaring costs incurred by the vendor and passed onto the auditee?

63. Does the contract state the number of backup copies of proprietary software that the auditee is allowed to make? If it does, are the number of copies restricted to making copies for the installation site and archival purpose only? Has management determined how it will recover proprietary software at a third-party owned recovery facility?

64. Just as there is an escape clause, ensure that the contract contains a "termination of operations" clause. This clause would require the vendor to provide the auditee with a timely notification (normally one year) of the

vendor's intent to either (a) not renew the contract upon completion of the original contract terms or (b) cease operations altogether and no longer provide services as an outsource vendor.

65. Does the contract provide a cap or limitation on the amount that maintenance fees can be increased by the vendor? If not, how is the auditee protected from vendor pass-along expenses?

> Several key factors to consider when reviewing prospective outsourcers are their:
>
> - R&D expenditures.
> - Ability to listen and not dictate.
> - Flexibility during negotiations.
> - International support capabilities.
> - Presence in your firm's specific industry.
> - Presence in your firm's operating regions.
> - Multi-protocol data/voice expertise.
> - Product/technology flexibility.
> - Ability to rush in emergency staff.
> - Internal network performance.
>
> — *Cathleen Hinderhoffer,*
> *Senior Vice President/Director,*
> *Boston Five Bank*

Part 4
End Note

"Outsourcing" Will Change Significantly the Nature of Internal Auditing

The growing interest in what is being described as outsourcing internal auditing will change significantly the nature of auditing. The outsourcing of internal auditing already has spread beyond the U.S. to the UK, Australia, Brazil, and Germany. The Institute of Internal Auditors has issued *The IIA's Perspective On Outsourcing Internal Auditing: A Professional Briefing for Chief Audit Executives* which sets out its position on this situation.

Not every internal auditor should expect to work under an outsource contract agreement. However, the manner in which these arrangements are structured most likely will become the standard by which the work of those auditing in other types of environments will be measured — especially by organizational senior executives and audit committees. This modification in the relationship between the auditing profession and organization executives gives every indication that its impact on both will be as profound as was the passage of the Securities Exchange Act of 1934 (15 U.S. Code). (That Statute, in effect, created the modern auditing environment in the U.S. Essentially, the Act required the routine annual review by an external auditing organization of the financial records of those entities whose securities have been registered with the U.S. Securities and Exchange Commission.)

Information systems auditors cannot avoid being affected by the switch to this different auditing arrangement. They can expect to have the environment in which they work altered dramatically by this process — even where they are functioning as a part of an external audit organization. For example, they will be expected to place greater reliance on automated auditing tools in order for them to realize greater audit coverage.

In preparing to work effectively in this new climate the information systems auditor should understand, at least, the uncertain nature of change, the concepts implicit in outsourcing, the auditing roles and relationships that are being modified, the organizational issues involved in this switch, and the basis for developing a fresh career strategy.

Understanding "Change"

In many ways, internal auditing has been an essentially stable environment. Introducing outsourcing into this environment creates a significant ongoing change.

Change is an inherently linear process. Once it has begun it is extremely difficult to reverse. Change cannot be backed up; it almost never is possible to return to square one. The original conditions, once modified, rarely can be restored exactly as they were. And, the very nature of change precludes predicting or controlling exactly the outcome of the process of change. That is true despite the most careful planning on the part of those trying to carry it out.

All that can be guaranteed when a modification as significant as the introduction of outsourcing to internal auditing will be is that both external and internal auditing — and the way in which they interact with organization executives, legislators, regulators, and the general public — will be altered profoundly by the change that is being made.

The Concept of "Outsourcing"

The goal of outsourcing, ideally, is to reduce the cost — and, at the same time, to maintain or to improve the quality — of a particular service function. (Such a function is some element of an entity's activities that is useful in its continuing operation, but that is not essential to enhancing its profitability. Any internal audit organization which has not demonstrated a significant contribution to profit improvement or loss avoidance will be highly susceptible to outsourcing.) In a typical outsourcing relationship the contracting organization eliminates the direct and overhead costs associated with the recruitment, training, and payment of the individuals involved in providing the service. Such an arrangement also eliminates a large part of the facilities management expenses and the equipment maintenance and replacement costs associated with the service.

Known originally as facilities management, the outsourcing process more properly should be described as contracting out. Since the end of World War II, this concept has been applied in the U.S. by many different types of organizations to a wide variety of service functions — including printing, warehousing, cash and treasury management, motor vehicle and aircraft operation, engineering and industrial design, advertising and public relations, food preparation, building and grounds maintenance, and site security. (U.S. government agencies continue to make extensive use of various types of outsourcing arrangements. These arrangements are viewed by some as privatizing these functions. Such outsourcing includes benefit payment and claims processing performed under contract.)

Under an outsourcing arrangement the contracting organization also gains stable and controllable costs for securing well-defined types of work over an extended period. At the same time this organization may lose some degree of control over the way in which these elements of its operations are conducted. And, the outsourcing organization that seeks to end such a relation before the end of the contract period may be assessed significant termination fees and, in some instances, may be forced to buy back its own data files or comparable assets.

It is possible, however, that some areas of dispute may arise between the outsourcing organization and the vendor. (Usually, these stem from poorly drawn contracts.) Among the possible points of contention may be payment for performing special services and the apportionment of liability for various types of risk exposures.

Many organizations that would be indifferent, otherwise, to the general outsourcing concept have entered into agreements that encompass data processing. These arrangements are typical of the contracts that cover other types of organizational services. The service provider owns the equipment and its supporting facilities and employs the individuals engaged in performing the work. Usually these people are located on the premises of the contracting organization and may be indistinguishable to the casual observer from its regular employees. (There have been disputes in some data processing outsourcing arrangements over such things as the ownership of data files and custom developed software products.)

Auditing Roles And Relationships

The work of external and internal auditors has been seen for most of the last 50 years essentially as being complementary to each other. Each type of auditor had a particular responsibility that did not overlap with that of the other. The external auditor evaluated financial reporting practices; the internal auditor evaluated management practices within the organization. (Information systems auditors have been unique in that routinely they have dealt with both financial reporting and management practices.)

For many years there was little interaction in most organizations between its external and internal auditors. (This practice began to change slowly in the U.S. after the 1975 issuance by the American Institute of Certified Public Accountants of its Statement on Auditing Standards 9, The Effect of an Internal Audit Function On the Scope of the Independent Auditor's Examination.) Representatives of the external auditor appeared once a year to examine and test the organization's financial records. These people often worked in space that had been reserved for their use (often known as the auditors' room that is kept locked between these visits), relied heavily on the representations of the organization's executives, and had little direct contact with the actual activities and processes reflected in the records with which they worked.

This practice began to change slowly in the U.S. after the 1939 disclosure of the massive McKesson and Robbins fraud in which, among other things, the external auditors accepted without question information provided by senior executives about purported status of inventories housed in what turned out eventually to be nonexistent warehouses. U.S. external auditors began to pay increasing attention to the processes that supported the creation and maintenance of computerized records after the 1973 disclosure of the extensive Equity Funding Insurance fraud. (It is documented in detail in *The Equity Funding Papers: The Anatomy of a Fraud* by Lee Seidler, Frederick Andrews, and Marc Epstein.)

The early internal auditors worked much more directly with the processes that supported the organization's records than did the external auditors of that period. The internal auditors and their predecessors were of two types. One was the accounts auditor who remained, typically, in an organization's accounting department. This person examined and tested the way in which various bookkeeping and accounting processes were carried out. (Often this person previously had maintained these same records.) The other type — known as a traveling auditor — was common 60 to 80 years ago in manufacturing, transportation, and retailing organizations. These individuals focused largely on examining operational practices and controls.

Typically, the traveling auditors acted as the eyes and ears of senior executives in a decentralized organization. (Usually they reported directly to a general manager or an executive vice-president, rather than to an organization's financial executive.) The main task of the traveling auditors was to evaluate the effectiveness and efficiency of local managers and to determine the degree of their adherence to organizational policies and their compliance with the controls that these practices were designed to enforce. Doing this might take the form, say, of verifying the accuracy of the local fixed asset records or of the accounts for local purchases of motor fuel and other supplies. Or, the auditor might be called up to observe actually how the manager dealt with particular employees, customers, and types of transactions.

One other thing distinguished both types of internal auditors from the external auditors. Neither the accounts auditor nor the traveling auditor considered that they had embarked upon an auditing career when they were assigned to such a position. Rather, they viewed the assignment — usually for two to four years — as another step in their move up through the organization. The accounts auditor next might become the supervisor, say, of the organization's accounts payable unit. And, the traveling auditor next might become, say, a supervisor in one of the offices that had been the subject of earlier examinations.

Organizational Issues in "Outsourcing Internal Auditing"

The outsourcing of internal auditing can be expected to change auditing generally in many different ways. These include:

1. The Entry of New Organizations Into This Field. At present, most of those offering internal audit outsourcing services are existing so-called Big Six external audit organizations. (Outsourcing internal auditing apparently is considered in this setting to be an additional line of business — comparable to such things as tax return preparation, conventional external auditing, consulting, and financial planning.) There is every reason to believe that some of the larger regional external audit organizations will enter this field in the near future. More significantly, there is equal reason to expect that those law firms that already are providing audit-like investigative services — largely in bankruptcy and fraud cases — to expand into offering internal auditing outsourcing arrangements. And, there is even more reason to believe that independent entrepreneurial organizations will enter this field as well. (Both the lawyers and the entrepreneurs can be expected to engage prominent holders of the CIA and the CISA for their ventures.)

2. A Different Career Orientation. Many internal and auditors do not identify themselves as pure auditors. Rather, they associate their future career with the future of the larger industrial grouping in which their employer's organization functions. That is, for example, they consider themselves primarily as part of the banking or insurance field, rather than basically as auditors. Yet, for those auditors who elect to work in an outsourced environment, their future will lie with the organization that employs them, not the one in which they do their work. This will lead, most likely, to conflict and

confusion over such things as training, promotion, and the continuity of assignments.

3. Changes in Audit Practices. The internal auditing service provider will be under strong pressure to extend the amount of work that can be performed by its employees. This should result in greater emphasis on following standard questionnaire-based audit work routines, employing the audit mechanisms that exist already in such things as telecommunication network management applications, applying advanced automated audit tools, and using artificial intelligence driven continuous monitoring of essentially uninterrupted data streams and transaction processes. All four of these audit approaches will increase the uniformity of the audit process, its results, and the costs associated with it. However, all four of them will reduce to some degree both the individual judgment and the knowledge of the environment in which an examination is being made that may be required of the human auditor.

4. Contention Over Liability and Responsibility. Among the concerns that could arise are:

   For whom is the internal audit vendor working — the stockholders, the public, the regulatory agencies, the organization's audit committee, or its senior executives? (This will be a particular issue when conflicts arise over the significance of potentially sensitive audit findings.)

   Who is accountable — the vendor or the responsible audit executive — for any errors or omissions in the audit process, or disputes over follow-up and resolution of audit findings? (Where this responsibility is shared, the issue then becomes how is it to be apportioned?) Whomever the internal auditing vendor is working with will be wise to remember that the ultimate responsibility for audit, security, and control outcomes cannot be contracted away. It remains with those — regardless of their positions or titles — who are directing the affairs of the organization that is being audited.

How is the erosion of audit independence to be avoided — especially when the same organization is acting as both the external and the internal auditor? (This also may be an issue where there is pressure to compete to maintain the audit service contract.)

How are vendor initiated changes in the personnel it has assigned as internal auditors to be resolved? (This may be an issue either when the individual's performance is not deemed to be suitable by the outsourcing organization, or when the individual is reassigned to another contract.)

How are such things as the confidentiality of sensitive organizational data and the protection of trade secrets to be handled? (This will be a particular issue when the outsourcing vendor is providing internal audit services to several competing organizations.

Developing A Fresh Career Strategy

The information systems auditor who wants to succeed in this new environment may find it useful to:

1. Emphasize maintaining continuous professional skills development and technical training. (Eventually those organizations certifying auditors can be expected to offer additional specialized certifications or to provide for concentrations within the existing offerings.) Some of this learning may have to occur after work hours and on weekends — possibly through programs offered through computer and telecommunication prod-

uct vendors or sponsored by community colleges or universities.

2. Stress working with specific types of software — such as a particular operating system or telecommunication environment. Also, consider specializing in examining particular types of information processing applications — such as, say, electronic data interchange or just-in-time manufacturing.

3. Invoke the entrepreneurial spirit and create innovative audit, control, and security products and services that can be marketed to this new environment.

Enhanced creativity is the best strategy for dealing effectively with the significant change that will be associated with the outsourcing of internal auditing.

The author wishes to thank Belden Menkus, CISA, CSP, CCP, CRM, the Editor of *EDPACS*, for his timely contribution not only to this text by way of this End Note, but to the auditing profession as a whole.

Appendix I Trends in Technology and Management Information Systems

- Intense competition in mid-range and low-end systems is leading to dramatic improvements in the areas of price/performance, communications, and user productivity.

- Increased use of distributed processing systems is resulting in greater flexibility and control at lower organization levels and heightened feelings of "ownership" of systems in user departments.

- More and more organizations are using the purchase of software packages to provide fast relief for specific application needs. The availability and capabilities of packaged software continue to improve.

- End-user involvement throughout the application system development cycle is increasing.

- Emphasis on computer-to-computer communications is increasing in the form of local area networks (LANs) at the department level, wide area networks (WANs) connecting remote locations, and electronic data interchange (EDI) between organizations.

- Telecommunications is the fastest growing element of management information systems (MIS) budgets. Links to remote operating locations and links to customers and suppliers are involved.

- Just-in-time (JIT) concepts are increasingly affecting business relationships in both manufacturing and wholesale distribution.

- There is rapid growth in the use of automated purchasing systems to process nondurable goods orders. Computers are increasingly performing routine buying functions, with purchasers managing exceptions.

- Automated manufacturing technologies such as computer-aided design and manufacturing (CAD-CAM) systems, process monitor/process control systems, automated material handling systems, automated data collection systems, and robotics increasingly are used to improve performance with respect to cost, quality, flexibility, and customer service.

Appendix II
Outsourcing Makes Sense When . . .

1. There is little opportunity for the organization to distinguish itself competitively through the quality of its information technology processing operations.

2. There is limited opportunity for the organization to distinguish itself competitively through the quality of its applications.

3. The predictability of uninterrupted information technology service is not of great importance (i.e., your organization will not be dependent upon — or face financial loss from — a delay in receiving critical information from the organization's computer systems).

4. It does not strip the organization of critical technical know-how that is key to future IS innovation.

5. Existing information technology capabilities are limited and ineffective.

Appendix III
What Outsourcing Buys You

Many organizations choose the outsourcing option because it improves their:

- **Economy**: Scale and specialization can enable vendors to deliver the same value for less money than the cost of maintaining an internal organization. For example, IBM and Electronic Data Systems Corp. claim that their experience and economies of scale can reduce a client's information technology costs by 20 percent to 40 percent.

- **Service quality**: Organizations often have more effective and more easily exercised leverage over vendors than over their own employees.

- **Predictability**: A fixed-price contract with service-level guarantees eliminates a lot of uncertainty.

- **Flexibility**: Business growth can be accommodated without having to make quantum changes in the IS infrastructure.

- **Making fixed costs variable**: Some agreements, such as running payroll, are based on price per unit of work done.

- **Freeing up human capital**: Scarce and costly talent can be refocused on higher value activity than managing and operating a technology factory.

- **Freeing up financial capital**: Some agreements include the sale for cash of technology capital assets to the vendor.

Appendix IV
To Outsource or Not to Outsource — An Outsourcing Plan of Attack

1. **Perform a Corporate Self-Analysis:**
   Any effort to assess outsourcing prospects must begin with a thorough evaluation of your organization's needs, goals, and current capabilities.

2. **Establish Baselines:**
   Baseline parameters spell out exactly the performance levels required by the organization for a given service which is to be outsourced. Any outsourcer that agrees to take responsibility for that service must agree to meet these minimum goals.

3. **Set Goals:**
   Establish performance and service goals beyond the minimum.

4. **Determine Costs:**
   Analyze and establish the current cost of all equipment and personnel involved in a given operation which is to be outsourced. This provides a baseline for use in determining the cost savings to be derived by outsourcing the operation.

5. **Define Billing Methods:**
   It is the responsibility of the user to come up with a suitable billing method. Whichever method is finally selected, the billing method should ensure that services will be provided in a timely manner, and that no surprise changes are levied against the client by the outsourcing vendor.

6. **Identify Specific Issues:**
   In addition to the basic issues concerning any outsourcing proposal, there are a variety of other issues to be worked out with the outsourcing vendor before a successful outsourcing agreement can be finalized (i.e., requisitioning additional DP services, PC purchases, telephone and date transmission services, migration of client personnel to the outsource vendor's staff, etc.).

Appendix V
Organizations Involved in Outsourcing as a Basic Organizational Strategy

American Cyanamid Co.
Amoco
Amtrak
Anchor Savings Bank
Anchor Savings Bank FSB
Armco Advanced Materials Co.
Balbacom (Belgium's state-owned phone company)
BancBoston Mortgage Corp.
Bank South
Blue Cross & Blue Shield of Massachusetts
BMW of North America
Boeing Company, The
Boston Five Bank
British Aerospace
British Petroleum Inc.
British Telecommunications PLC
Calgary General Hospital, The
California Federal Bank
California Republic Bank
Chase Manhattan Bank
Chevron
Comdata Holdings Corp.
Commerce Bankshares, Inc.
Continental Airlines Corp.
Continental Bank
Corporation for Regional & Enterprise Networking (The Internet Purchasing Consortium)
Cullum Companies
Del Monte Foods

Dollar Dry Dock Bank
Earle M. Jorgensen Co.
Eastman Kodak
Englehard Corp.
Enron Corp.
Equifax
Espsit de Corp.
Federal Home Loan Bank of San Francisco
Fireman's Fund of New Jersey
First American Bankshares Inc.
First City Bank Corp.
First Fidelity Bancorporation
Fluor Daniel Inc.
Ford Motor Co.
Ford of Europe
Freeport - McMoRan Inc.
General Dynamics Corp.
Gillette Company, The
Greenwich (Conn.) Hospital
Greyhound Lines of Canada Ltd.
H. J. Heinz Corp.
Harvest Foods
Hertz Corp.
Hibernia Bank
Honeywell, Inc.
Inland Revenue Department (UK)
J. P. Morgan
Kaiser Permanente
Kendall Motor Products
LaBarge Inc.
Libbey-Owens Ford
Matson Navigation Co.
Maxus Energy Corporation
Meritor Savings Bank
Merrill Lynch
Microsed Corp.
National Car Rental Systems, Inc.

NCNB Corp.
Neodata Corp.
Nolan, Norton & Co.
Pan American World Airways
Princeton Packaging Inc.
RAET (a Dutch IS service company)
Revlon Inc.
RMI Titanium
Royal Automobile Club
SCI Systems
Signet Banking Corp.
Southland Corp., The
Sun Oil
Sun Refining and Marketing Company
Supermarkets General Corp.
Top Network Associated Optical
Trane Co., The
Ultramar
United Technologies Corp.
Washington National Insurance
Xerox Corp.
Yankee Gas Co.

Appendix VI Organizations Involved in Downsizing as a Basic Organizational Strategy

Alaska Airlines
American Airlines
American Drug Stores
Andrew Jergens Co.
Arvin Industries, Inc.
Banc One
Batesville Casket Co.
Bendix/King
Black & Decker Corp.
Blue Cross & Blue Shield of Maine
Breuners Home Furniture
Brush Wellman Inc.
Burlington Coat Factory Warehouse, Inc.
Christian Broadcasting Network
Citibank NA
Coal Services Corp.
Colonial Williams Foundation, The
Comcar Industries, Inc.
Concord Group Insurance Co.
Consolidated International Insurance Group
Corporate Software
Cotter Canada
Dunkin Donuts, Inc.
Dyncorp.
E.I. du Pont de Nemours & Co.
Echlin, Inc.
Federal Guaranty Insurance Corp.
First Boston Group Corp., The
FirstLine Trust

Fish Engineering and Construction
Foxboro Co.
Fred Hutchinson Cancer Research Center, The
Fuller Co.
G. Heileman Brewing Co.
Gates McDonald & Co.
Gates Rubber Co.
General Electric Capital Corp.
General Electric Co.
Harley-Davidson, Inc.
Home Mutual Life Insurance Co.
Indian Head Industries, Inc.
Industrial Bank of Japan (LA branch)
Intel Corp.
J. M. Huber Corp.
Jet Propulsion Laboratory
JFK Medical Center
Kash-N-Karry, Inc.
Keyport Life Insurance Co.
Lever Brothers Company
Libbey-Owens-Ford Co.
Loma Linda University and Medical Center
McKesson Water Products Co.
Mead Data Central, Inc.
Millipore Corp.
NASA
NCR
Northrup King Co.
Pacific Gas & Electric Co.
Peat Marwick
Pennsylvania Blue Shield
Pepperidge Farms
Rockwell International
Rogers Group, Inc., The
San Diego Gas & Electric Co.
San Diego Housing Committee
Sara Lee Corp.

Sargent & Lundy
Scott Paper
Sequel Inc.
State of Mississippi
Sun Life of Canada
Travelers Corp.
Tremark Investment Management
TRW, Inc.
U.S. Army of Veterans Affairs
Union Bank (Los Angeles)
United Parcel Service of America, Inc.
University of Texas Medical School
Unum Life Insurance Co.
William B. Reilly & Co.
Wisconsin Electric Power Co.
World Corp.

Appendix VII
Downsizing Tips

- Decide on hardware after it is clear that software is available or can be developed on schedule at an acceptable cost.

- Start by downsizing part of an application or all of a non-mission-critical, read-only application.

- Pay close attention to EDP audit control requirements.

- Use stable hardware and software.

- Use secure operating systems and application development software.

- Provide a secure environment for hardware, including the network.

- Make very frequent backups and regularly test restore capability.

- Assure adequate personnel to support the application.

- Be sure that hardware and software can grow with the application.

Appendix VIII
Cost Considerations in Migrating to a Downsizing Strategy

Many CIOs who have downsized systems warn that the costs involved in downsizing often prove to be higher than anticipated. Here is a list of costs to consider:

- The cost of capital equipment, such as PCs and communications products, software, wiring, backup solutions, etc.

- The cost of running parallel systems during migration.

- Conversion expenses, including those incurred in hiring new staff.

- Increased administration expenses during the migration.

- Consultant fees.

- The price of new software tools for writing distributed applications.

- The cost of retraining both IS staff and end users (most organizations underestimate this item).

- Maintenance fees for multiple software packages in a distributed environment (these are often underestimated as well).

Appendix IX
Seven Approaches to Downsizing

1. **The Wallpaper Approach:**
   This option's name is derived from the fact that it changes your system's look without significantly changing its structure. An example would be having a PC-based program written which controls a mainframe-based application.

2. **Modified Wallpaper Approach:**
   Under this approach, the mainframe applications are preceded (front-ended) with a graphical user interface (GUI). However, this option beats the basic Wallpaper Approach by automatically executing PC-based software like electronic mail, word processing packages, groupware products and other PC tools, enhancing mainframe functionality.

3. **Mainframe Download and Display Approach:**
   The mainframe periodically downloads a data file of detail and/or summary information to the PC or LAN server. Once downloaded, PC-based applications read, summarize, display, analyze, and print this data.

4. **The Dynamic Download and Display Approach:**
   This method downloads specific pieces of information at the time they are requested rather than entire files.

5. **Mainframe Read/Server Write Approach:**
   This technique uses mainframe data as input to server-based applications. In this instance, however, the "official" copy of certain corporate data is being stored on a platform other than the mainframe.

6. **The Server-Only Approach:**
   Here, all data and stored procedures associated with data are stored on the server, and the application is stored on the PC (client).

7. **The Multiplatform Database Approach:**
   The multiplatform technique enables your application to read, manipulate, and update databases on both mainframe and the server.

Appendix X
How Not to Downsize — 10 Ways to Guarantee Trouble

1. **Start with a time-sensitive project:**
   Few projects worth doing lack any form of deadline, but the value of some projects depends heavily on meeting a particular date in the near future. These sorts of projects have a misguided popularity among downsizing proponents, who want to demonstrate how rapidly a downsized environment can respond to user needs.

2. **Support multiple microcomputer operating systems:**
   This is a mistake most computing professionals never make willingly and submit to only after hierarchical pressure caused by loud user demands. Nonetheless, it is a serious error in any organization too lean to have in-depth technical knowledge for each system.

3. **Support more than one network Operating System (OS):**
   Most downsizing projects require a strong network for data and resource sharing. To implement this, network services staff generally resist supporting more than one network OS.

4. **Rely on untested software products:**
   Successful downsizing efforts often depend on using new software. Such products can give important marketplace advantages, but they should be tested with the same thoroughness as any mainframe software that is tested.

5. **Ignore desktop-data security issues:**
   On-line mainframe systems have developed reasonably good security in the past two decades. Password identification is one form, use of systems like CICS can re-

strict certain commands to terminals in particular locations, and audit trails can allow an organization to reconstruct employees' on-line activities in greater detail than most imagine. Downsized operations rarely reproduce all of these protections.

6. **Create jealousy by training only select employees:** Downsizing is almost as big a change as automation was in the 1970s and raises the same problem of selective training. One popular method for providing immediate local support for newly downsized systems is to train one workgroup staff member to solve the most basic level of technical problems which frees the professional staff to deal with real problems. However, it often creates jealousies within the workgroups. The person with the extra training has a clearly superior, if not actually supervisory, position. That person may also grow to regret the burden if productivity expectations are not adjusted to allow for time spent helping others or if training is inadequate to answer many questions.

7. **Expect users to buy their own manuals and train themselves:**
Departments that want to train all staff members are often hampered in doing so.

8. **Expect users to do backups or production control tasks:** Behind-the-scenes jobs such as scheduling, production control, and backups are standard parts of mainframe computing. Without them, there would be a chaos of updates done in the wrong order, output routed to the wrong people, and data exposed to software and hardware disasters. No data center manager would consider abolishing them, but many user department managers fail to think about them.

One advantage of downsizing is that departments can run their own reports as often as they want. This does not, however, always work for reports that use information from another department. One staff member's vacations can disrupt several departments' schedules if key network-accessible files are not updated in the person's absence.

9. **Expect users to ensure the integrity of corporate data:** One of the biggest downsizing problems is data that has meaning and integrity in a departmental setting, but not when viewed from a corporate perspective. Many departments view downsizing as giving them greater autonomy, but that autonomy does not extend to altering shared corporate data unilaterally. In a downsized environment, shared data remains a corporate responsibility, and the database administrator (DBA) (or someone with similar duties) has responsibilities on workstations throughout the organization.

10. **Expect to save money in the short run:** Downsizing is expensive. Departments need new equipment, upgrades to old machines, network connections, software licenses, training programs, and help coordinating shared data. Virtually no one succeeds in rolling their mainframes out the door completely. A more common scenario is for downsizing merely to allow mainframe upgrades to be deferred. Downsizing can, however, have a disruptive effect on budgets if an organization is not prepared to spend extra funds to cover the hidden costs. (Seadle, 1994)

Appendix XI Evaluation of a Management Strategy — Downsizing: 11 of the Toughest Questions Management Must Answer

There are a number of additional factors that may be included in a discussion of the procedures associated with an organization's downsizing.

However, let's project our thoughts five or six years into the future and analyze one specific organization. We can ask a number of questions:

1. Was the downsizing successful?

2. Was the downsizing appropriate for this organization?

3. Did we accomplish what we had in mind during the process?

4. Were we able to maintain our costs within the estimated budgets?

5. Were we forced to continue the process for longer than hindsight tells us would have been appropriate?

6. Were we forced to undergo a second (or perhaps third) reorganization or downsizing since the initial efforts?

7. Was the organization subsequently sold to a third party (or perhaps a leveraged takeover by management) or merged with another organization? Did a failure of the

reorganization, a change in market structure, a loss of financial resources, or a loss of managerial ability or desire cause the organization to be subsequently sold or closed?

8. If the organization was sold, was a reasonable profit made on the investment and risk? Who benefited from this profit?

9. Were the results worth the risk in personnel, assets, and continuing resources?

10. Was there a more effective way in which we could have accomplished the same objectives?

11. Were we able to accurately define and satisfy the overall objectives or purposes for the reorganization, or were we just attempting to solve the puzzle and not the overall problem? (Morris, 1989)

Appendix XII Six Steps to Successful Rightsizing and the Questions to Ask to Get You There

1. **Identify business goals and relate them to information systems projects:**
   - How does your organizational structure support your business functions?
   - How do your current activities support your business goals?
   - What are the vital relationships among staff as they work to achieve IS goals?
   - How fast is the organization growing?

2. **Profile and analyze your current and future applications:**
   - How would you describe each of your major existing applications in terms of a general overview, implementation characteristics, technical architecture, organization dynamics, expectations concerning the application, and application data profile?
   - How would you describe each of your major current and future development projects in terms of the application's business function, the type of project, and development time required?

3. **Analyze data resources:**
   - How is the data accessed?
   - What applications use it?
   - Is the data static or dynamic? How often is it updated?
   - What backup, recovery, and security is in place for the data?

4. **Analyze applications and data interfaces for degree of dependency:**
   - What impact will each current and future development project have on existing applications? On data?
   - Does the application use redundant data? If so, how does it keep data synchronized?
   - How accessible is the data to the user? Are data structures simple or complex?
   - How is the data returned to the users (ad hoc reports, on-request reports)?

5. **Analyze your current and planned IS infrastructure:**
   - What software and hardware are currently used by the department?
   - What communications hardware and software is in place?
   - What methodology experience does your department have, including design, tuning, transition planning, and project management?

6. **Evaluate rightsizing opportunities relative to goals and feasibility:**
   - Will rightsizing help the organization achieve its strategic goals?
   - What are the costs involved? The risks?
   - What are the benefits?
   - Will distributing an application meet the requirement for new functionality?

Appendix XIII
Factors for Successful Reengineering

- A vision of the reengineered environment.
- A reengineered methodology.
- Participation from all levels, including senior management.
- Flexible, temporary teams.
- Continued quality improvement.
- Team training.
- Systemic thinking.
- Visible, active leadership (Gantz, 1993).

Appendix XIV Rapid Reengineering Five-Stage Program

Stage 1 Preparation
Mobilize, organize, and emerge the people who will perform the reengineering project.

Stage 2 Identification
Develop a customer-oriented process model of the business.

Stage 3 Vision
Select processes to reengineer that are capable of achieving breakthrough performance.

Stage 4 Solution
Define the technical and organization requirements for the new process and develop detailed implementation plans.

Stage 5 Implement your reengineering plans.

(Manganelli, 1992)

Appendix XV
Is Reengineering Right for You? Three Keys to Determine if Reengineering is Right for Your Firm

Why: If an organization cannot easily make a business case for establishing a reengineering case or program, they do not have the necessary rationale. The business case can be based on performance level or on product outcome, but usually revolves around cost, quality, service, and cycle time.

Where: Organizations need to know where they will start the reengineering process and how it will impact other areas. That focus should include an analytical look at the business — for instance, if an organization improves the time it takes to complete Process A by 10 percent, will it improve the outcome of Process B by 50 percent?

How: Create a simplified, logical look at the process of the business. That helps organizations focus on the most critical aspects of their business. (King, 1993)

Appendix XVI
Who Should Reengineer?

Despite its current popularity, reengineering is better suited to certain types of organizations:

- Nonmanufacturing and high-technological firms facing tough foreign competition.
- Organizations in recently deregulated industries, especially insurance and banking.
- Firms recently involved in mergers and acquisitions.
- Organizations in need of radical product breakthroughs.
- Organizations in highly competitive service industries.
- Organizations that do not have a deeply entrenched corporate culture.
- Organizations under fire from heavy end-user demands.
- Organizations facing financial crisis (i.e., several consecutive bad quarters).

Appendix XVII Reengineering: Tips to Success

Reengineering cannot be planned meticulously and carried out in cautious steps. It is a tumultuous task that, once started, usually leads to unexpected discoveries and uncharted territories within the organization. However, it has evolved from its earliest attempts — which were basically hit or miss — into a more organized discipline with definable and repeatable patterns of success. These patterns of success can act as a primer to other organizations trying to find new ways of working.

- **Task integration and compression of the process:** Traditional division-of-labor principles do not apply. "Divide up a process and assign tasks to different people" results in numerous hand-offs, errors, and delays. Under the new model, one person is given responsibility for an entire process whenever possible. Indeed, that person's job is designed around an outcome or objective — a completed task, a finished component of product — instead of a single task. This also decreases the need for coordination between tasks.

- **Decision making as part of the job:** The old model says, "A manager makes decisions. Another employee does the work." Under the new approach, many decisions are made by the person doing the work. This person is, after all, the "expert" on that particular job. This results in faster response to any problems that might arise during a task; it raises the level of quality and helps to "flatten" an organization. When those closest to the work are empowered to make decisions and fix problems, there is little need to "manage" the process — it is largely self-managing.

- **A hybrid of centralized and decentralized approaches:** Traditionally, centralization has been the key to economics of scale and eliminating redundant resources; decentralization has been the key to providing better customer service — and the two have often been in conflict. Now, common pools of information that are accessible to all far-flung operations of an organization combine economics of scale and hands-on expertise with customers. Purchasing is another area that benefits from this type of reengineering — each purchasing unit at widely dispersed organizational locations can respond quickly to local needs by having access to a shared vendor database that offers rates negotiated for the entire organization.

- **Concurrent performance of tasks:** The assembly-line approach is not for reengineered businesses. "You do your work, and when you are done, pass it along and I will do my work" is a thing of the past. Many processes, such as product development, become much more efficient when work is done collaboratively and concurrently. "Let me see what you are doing so I can make sure that what I am doing fits your specifications" is a new model. This cuts down on rework and streamlines operations. Communications networks, shared databases, and teleconferencing can keep coordination ongoing.

- **Capture information once, at the source:** A simple, but important, point. Information used to be difficult to transmit, so it made sense to collect it repeatedly in various departments and business units on distinct forms and with differing reporting requirements. But today it is entered into an on-line database once, through connected, integrated systems, and used over and over again. Bar coding, relational databases, and electronic data interchange (EDI) are the technologies that are key to eliminating errors and delays and reducing clerical overhead.

Appendix XVIII
Reengineering Rules

Rules are made to be broken. Technology can be the means by which organizations smash their old, constraining business processes and transform their operations.

Old Rule: Information can appear in only one location at one time.

Disruptive Technology: Shared databases.

New Rule: Information can appear simultaneously in as many places as needed.

Old Rule: Only experts can perform complex work.

Disruptive Technology: Expert systems.

New Rule: A generalist can do the work of the expert.

Old Rule: Businesses must choose between centralization and decentralization.

Disruptive Technology: Telecommunications networks.

New Rule: Businesses can simultaneously reap the benefits of centralization and decentralization.

Old Rule: Managers make all decisions.

Disruptive Technology: Decision-support tools (database access, modeling software).

New Rule: Decision-making is part of everyone's job.

Old Rule: Field personnel need offices where they can receive, store, retrieve, and transmit information.

Disruptive Technology: Wireless data communications and portable computers.

New Rule: Field personnel can send and receive information wherever they are.

Old Rule: The best contact with a potential buyer is personal contact.

Disruptive Technology: Interactive videodisc.

New Rule: The best contact with a potential buyer is effective contact.

Old Rule: You have to find out where things are.

Disruptive Technology: Automatic identification and tracking technology.

New Rule: Things tell you where they are.

Appendix XIX
Six Pointers to Help Maximize the Benefits of Application Reengineering

1. Keep records of all your activities, especially your early efforts. Document what worked and what didn't, and how you made improvements.

2. Involve the program "maintenance" staff in planning. Ask them what irritates them about the system and why, which programs are hard to work on or run slower than they should, and which modules take several tries to run correctly after a maintenance change.

3. Use a mixed reengineering team. Assign primary responsibility to a person who is *not* immersed in maintaining the current code, since an "outsider" is more likely to challenge existing assumptions and discover opportunities for improvement. Also, include technicians who know the system well and are adept at spotting design or logic defects.

4. Use automated tools as much as possible. They can provide better assurance that standards have been followed, and the reports they produce help prove the value of reengineering.

5. Involve senior IT and customer managers, keeping them informed of the benefits as they accrue. When opportunities for further improvements are discovered, consult with managers on the best way to sell them.

6. Temper your enthusiasm with a dose of reality. Your reengineering effort may give you lots of bright ideas for additional fixes, but curb that gung-ho attitude with an awareness of the resources available and the relative worth of alternative efforts. (Raynor and Cohen, 1994)

Appendix XX
Doing the Right Things: 11 Keys to Global Reengineering

1. **Assign** process owners for every major initiative from both the user and systems organization, with equal responsibility for the effort's success.

2. **Give** each major division responsibility for leading the implementation of a key application so that all buy into the global strategy and have an equal stake in its success.

3. **Select** lead sites for specific business functions with an eye to local business priorities.

4. **Form** cross-functional project teams that include representatives from key user and systems groups within each division. This will ensure that the lead location considers all requirements and agrees to global business definitions and data structures.

5. **Establish** common performance metrics wherever possible so that groups can learn from one another.

6. **Use** technology to facilitate communication among locations.

7. **Evaluate** business practices across locations so that the best ideas can come into play when reengineering a specific business process.

8. **Establish** a cross-functional review committee representing systems and user senior management.

9. **Expect** that cultural differences will initially complicate communication. As the teams become comfortable with one another, the common goal will transcend their differences.

10. **Establish** an issues database where teams record issues and solutions.

11. **Ensure** that a local owner is responsible for the success of the local installation. (Buchanan, 1994)

Appendix XXI Translating the Best of Intentions Into the Best of Plans: Reengineering Lessons from Charles Schwab & Company

- Be aware that, despite everyone's best intentions, the urge is very strong to focus on the shortcomings of existing systems, rather than on entirely new ways to deliver services to customers.

- Monitor how your team members are approaching their task. Many of the people on the team will be chosen because they are highly focused, task-oriented people who can meet deadlines. Yet those same qualities may need to be tempered if you're going to see and change the big picture.

- Make sure you have all of the data you need before you start. That means benchmarking against competitors and getting detailed information about your customers and their needs.

- Work hard at building a consensus of purpose and an identity for the business process reengineering team. Members should not see themselves as representative of different functional organizations brought together to protect their interests. They are there to benefit the business.

- Insist on direct, active upper management participation. That way, the team will have the clout to actually reengineer. And it will know the moment the strategic winds have changed. (Moad, 1994)

Appendix XXII
Reengineering Do's and Don'ts

If your organization is in the midst of — or is considering — a process redesign effort, consider the following list of reengineering do's and don'ts:

- Set "stretch" goals.

  Shoot for the sky at the start, then find acceptable "ceilings" as you go.

- Develop and manage to firm targets.

  Otherwise, a massive reengineering effort can quickly lose focus and wander.

- Beware "scope creep."

  As reengineering fever sweeps an organization, people are quick to want to apply the same principles to other processes or systems.

- Prepare for the FUD factor.

  Fear, uncertainty, and doubt (FUD) inevitably crop up when employees are not sure where they'll be sitting next week, or even if they'll have a desk at which to sit. By the same token, many employees are afraid of the new styles of thinking and working that go with reengineering.

  Communication, understanding, and encouragement — particularly from the executive level manager — is essential in helping people work through unavoidable anxieties.

- Add "yeast" to your recipe.

  As employee teams go about analyzing and redesigning internal processes, it helps to have outsiders (people from other work groups in the department, other departments in the firm, even from outside the firm entirely) involved. They are called "yeast" because they'll sit there and say, "Why do you do it that way?"

- Move ahead in parallel.

  To make meaningful progress, individual planning and implementation steps within an overall reengineering effort must occur simultaneously, not sequentially. Reengineering makes you do it all at one time. You can't say, "First I'm going to redesign the jobs, then we'll rework the processes." They're all interrelated.

- Plan-Do-Check-Act...but mostly Act.

  Because so many changes are being contemplated and implemented at once, reengineering can feel as though change is occurring faster than it really is. You have to be comfortable with ambiguity and 90 percent solutions at times. The key is to fail fast and go on. (Tschida, 1993)

Appendix XXIII Organizations Involved in Reengineering as a Basic Organizational Strategy

Abbott Laboratories
Agway
Alamo Rent A Car, Inc.
American Express Company
American Management Systems, Inc.
American Telephone & Telegraph
Banc One
Baxter Healthcare
Bayou Steel Corporation
Borden, Inc.
Bristol-Meyers Squibb Company
California State Automobile Association
Canadian National Railways
Citicorp
Connecticut Mutual Life Insurance Company
Corning Asahi Video Products Co.
CSX Technology, Inc.
Datacard Corporation
Digital Equipment Corporation
Dow Chemical
Eastman Kodak Company
Elf Atochem North America, Inc.
Equitable Resources, Inc.
Federal National Mortgage Association
Fleet Bank (Fleet Financial Groups, Inc.)
Ford Motor Company
GTE Telephone Operations
Hallmark Cards, Inc.
Health Care Service Corporation

Heller International Corporation
Home Depot, Inc., The
Household Finance Corp.
Hyatt Corporation
Inland Steel Industries, Inc.
J. M. Huber
Key Corporation
Kimberly-Clark
Levi Strauss & Co.
Moog Automotive, Inc.
Mutual Benefit Life Insurance
Nolan, Norton & Company
Ontario Ministry of Revenue
Pacific Bell
Pepsi-Cola General Bottlers, Inc.
Phillips Petroleum Corporation
Progressive Corporation, The
Ryder Systems, Inc.
Spalding Sports Worldwide
Spartan Stores, Inc.
Sprint
State of Oregon
Texas Instruments, Inc.
TRW - high reliability electronic products group
UCAR Carbon Company
Union Camp Corporation
Unisys Corporation
U.S. Shoe Corp.
Westinghouse Electric Corporation

Appendix XXIV Organizations Involved in Partnering as a Basic Organizational Strategy

Alcoa
Andersen Consulting
Applied Intelligent Systems
Baxter Healthcare Corp.
C. E. Smith Company
Epic Data, Inc.
Federal Express Business Logistics Services
Glen Raven Mills
High Point Chemicals
Intermec Corp.
J. D. Edwards
Leaseway Transportation
Macfield Texturing Company
Milliken Company
Motorola's Semiconductor Sector
Premenos Corp.
Soft-Switch
Sonoco Fibre Drum Division
Sterling Software
Texas Instruments
Travelers Insurance

Appendix XXV
The Six "I's" to Successful Partnering Relationships

1. Importance

- The relationship is important enough to both parties that each provides the resources and organizational experts necessary to make the partnership work.

2. Interdependence <u>AND</u> **3. Investment**

- The partners agree that the long-term nature of the relationship justifies such investment in the project and they recognize their interdependence.

4. Integration <u>AND</u> **5. Information**

- To keep the partnering process working, the organizations integrate their communications and activities, and keep each other informed.

6. Institutionalization

- The partnering process activities committed to by each institution is ingrained into the very fabric of each organization through such mechanisms as diverse as contracts and social ties (Moore, 1992).

Appendix XXVI
Six Steps Toward Determining Which Market Segments and Individual Customer Firms to Target for Close, Collaborative Relationships

1. Segment the market by product application and customer capabilities.

2. Assess the value of the product to customers in each segment.

3. Target segments, and customer firms within segments, for various kinds of relationships.

4. Develop and implement relationships — specific product offerings.

5. Evaluate relationship outcomes and reassign accounts.

6. Periodically update the value of the relationship offering. (Anderson, 1991)

Appendix XXVII
10 Steps Toward Developing a Partnering Strategy

Develop a partnering strategy. Make sure you understand what it is that you are trying to get out of each of your partnering efforts.

1. Beware of backing into partnering arrangements. Situations can come up where a customer is the driving force behind a partnering arrangement.

   Don't do it simply to gratify the customer. Make sure to examine such proposals in the context of your organization's overall partnering strategy.

2. Emphasize the importance of understanding and having access to each others' people. The closer the planned relationship between the two organizations, the greater the importance of the linkages between them. That is critical.

   The key people could include anyone from logistics, to MIS, to accounting, to R&D, to engineering. In major partnering relationships, the involvement will go all the way up to the CEO.

3. Realize that the partnering effort is a mutually dependent relationship. Buyers often don't fully recognize that, in order to make these things work, they have to invest as much effort as the supplier does.

   If the partnering effort is going to involve, for example, cooperative product design and development, both parties need to understand what is driving each of the businesses, and what its strategies and problems are.

4. Develop a clear agreement on what your goals are — and make sure they are measurable. Without this, there is significant risk that there will never be any agreement that anything was actually done. Just as with any other strategy, you need to have means for evaluating it.

   At the beginning, think through what the particular relationship strategy is. Then devise some form of evaluation that will measure how well that has been implemented. The measures are likely to vary from customer to customer.

   If, for example, the account serves the role of a lead-user of your product, you should not be as concerned about profits as you are about measuring the number of product modifications or new product ideas being generated.

5. Have an agreed-upon set of procedures in place that will help resolve the issues that arise. Veterans of partnering efforts point out that joint projects like these are extremely difficult to manage.

   The circumstances surrounding them are dynamic: the personnel involved change; the organizational strategies change; and business conditions change. Inevitably, there will be a need for a mechanism to handle things like price increase discussions and dispute resolutions.

6. Make sure to keep the personal relationships between key people open and constantly alive. Have the CEO and COO visit major customers and confer at trade meetings. Keep communications channels open and free; no one wants to have to call the lawyers when a problem arises.

7. Try to make sure that all levels of both organizations share the partnering attitude. Some organizations are set up so that you cannot work with them on partnership arrangements.

   On the buyer side, for example, there is a significant danger that the purchasing operation might continue to operate under the philosophy that success is measured by squeezing the best possible deal out of suppliers. Avoid the too-familiar situation where the vice president puts his arm around the supplier and says they are going to be partners — and the purchasing agent beats the heck out of the same supplier.

8. Examine the partner's internal reward structures — they need to be coordinated. For example, buyers traditionally have been rewarded for wringing out concessions from the seller and by showing that their efforts had achieved cost reductions.

   Sellers, on the other hand, have gotten their rewards on the basis of their sales performance. Each of these must be modified in a partnering arrangement.

9. Partner selection. Partners should be chosen with care. The questions of whom to choose as a partner and how to partner with them are of strategic importance.

10. Regularly review your partnering efforts. Periodically sit down with the partner and evaluate whether the relationship should be upgraded, maintained, or downgraded. (Yovovich, 1992)

Appendix XXVIII 10 Ways to Augment the Product Offering for Collaborative Relationships

1. **"Pull" promotional programs** can be directed at the customer firm's customers. This might involve trade journal advertisements touting the value of products made from or with the supplier firm's components.

2. **Warranty, maintenance, and repair agreements** can be offered to customer firms to reduce the risk associated with usage of a supplier's products.

3. **Cooperative advertising and promotional allowances** can serve the dual purposes of enabling smaller customer firms to advertise regularly and coordinating customer and supplier market communication efforts.

4. **Joint sales calls** can be utilized to assist customer firms in developing new markets or to deal with problem accounts.

5. **Coordinated cost-reduction programs** can be implemented to dramatically pare the customer firm's real costs of doing business. Joint material requirements planning (MRP) systems, computer-to-computer order entry systems, just-in-time inventory programs, and statistical process control are some examples.

6. **Technical assistance** can be provided to augment customer firms' technical product and application knowledge. Supplier firm technical and production experts can make suggestions on how the customer firm could gain

cost savings through substitute materials and alternative production processes.

7. **Logistics and delivery systems** can be used to create value. For instance, a manufacturer of paint pigments discovered through its customer relationships that offering the pigment in "slurry form" rather than in "dry bag" form created greater value for the customer. This enabled customer firms to reduce costs in the production process because they no longer had to emulsify the pigment before use. As a side benefit, the manufacturer was able to gain logistical cost savings because greater quantities of pigment were ordered at a time and the slurry could be delivered more economically.

8. **Computer networking capabilities** can be used to troubleshoot customer problems from a remote location. For instance, a manufacturer of scientific testing equipment uses its network to solve customer problems more quickly. Data and computer software can be down-loaded from the equipment on-site and transferred to the manufacturer's simulation computers via telephone interlink. The supplier can troubleshoot the software and make corrections in the case of problems. The corrected software can then be sent back to the customer firm via telephone interlink.

9. **Shared expertise programs** in which information is more openly shared between supplier and customer firms is another option. In the marketing area, one manufacturer of chemicals and plastics not only shares information on economic trends with customer firms but also performs market research studies for those customers who lack in-house research expertise. On the technical side, one manufacturing company has a "scientist exchange program" in which its own scientists spend time working in the research and development labs of customer firms.

10. **Value-enhancement and co-design programs** can be put in place to upgrade the value of present customer firm products as well as to jointly design new products. Considerable value can be added to the product offering at times simply by a reallocation upstream of processing and production functions. For instance, many steel service centers now perform the functions of stamping doors and window panels for the auto makers, resulting in lower overall cost. The assembly of electronic components into modules or boards by electronic component manufacturers is another example of this process. (Anderson, 1992)

Appendix XXIX Specifics to Include in a Right-to-Audit Clause

1. References to specific records, such as original estimate files, change order estimate files, and detailed worksheets; subcontract and supplier proposals for both successful and unsuccessful bidders; all project-related correspondence; subcontractor and supplier change order files (including detailed documentation covering negotiated settlements); back-charge logs and supporting documentation; any records detailing cash, trade, or volume discounts earned; and insurance proceeds, rebates, or dividends received.

2. A specific requirement for the contractor to provide the owner with copies of records in computer-readable format as well as hard copy.

3. A general reference providing the right to audit any other supporting evidence necessary to substantiate charges related to the contract (both direct and indirect costs, including overhead allocations as they may apply to costs associated with the contract).

4. A general reference providing the right to audit any records necessary to permit evaluation and verification of (a) contractor compliance with contract requirements, (b) compliance with the owner's business ethics policies, and (c) compliance with provisions for pricing change orders, payments, or claims submitted by the contractor or any of his payees.

5. A general description of the length of time the contractor's records shall be subject to audit, such as "throughout the term of this contract and for a period of three years after final payment, or longer if required by law."

6. A specific "flow-down" right of audit provision that requires the contractor to include the right of audit provisions in the contracts (including those of a lump sum nature) of all subcontractors, insurance agents, material suppliers, or any other business entity providing goods and services (specifically providing the right of the owner's representatives to examine their records).

7. A specific provision that allows the owner to interview any of the contractor's current and former employees during the audit.

8. A specific provision that the contractor will provide the owner with adequate and appropriate work space, with access to photocopy machines.

9. (Optional) A specific proviso that the owner will recoup the cost of the audit if the audit detected overcharges that reach or exceed a certain percentage of the total contract billings (for example, overcharges greater than 0.5 percent).

10. (Optional) A specific proviso that the contractor will not only repay the owner within a specific period of time, but will also pay an additional percentage of the overcharges (for example 1.5 times the amount overcharged) to the owner as liquidated damages. (Townsend, 1993)

Appendix XXX
Before You Sign, Have You Considered the Following?

- **Services to be performed:** Have detailed functional specifications been set? What facilities are provided?

- **Scheduling:** Has a date been set for delivery or initiation of service? What is the duration of the contract?

- **Costs:** What is the contract price? What happens if there are cost overruns? Is there a clear distinction between enhancements and bug fixes?

- **Quality standards:** Does the contract spell out performance standards? System hours of availability? Service/support hours of availability and response time? Acceptable downtime? Time allowed to rectify problems?

- **Vendor warranties:** What is the acceptable software error rate?

- **Risk management:** What provisions are there for preventing unauthorized access? For disaster recovery? Is there a backup facility? System redundancy? Under what conditions would you have access to operating-system source code?

- **Confidentiality:** Is there a clause detailing the confidentiality of your proprietary information?

- **Intellectual property rights:** Does the contract put restrictions on the use of codes or routines? Under what circumstances?

- **Remedies:** If something goes wrong, will the outsourcer pay damages? Penalties? Is there any provision for conflict resolution?

- **Personnel issues:** Does the contract restrict attempts to hire away the other party's staff? If some transfer of staff is agreed to, will the employer's contractual obligations be honored?

- **Termination:** Does the contract define procedures for the transfer of property/responsibility if performance is unsatisfactory? If the business is terminated by either party? (Williamson, 1993)

Appendix XXXI Top 10 Criteria to Remember When Forming Customer/Vendor Relationships

1. Don't be afraid to bring in experts when you need them; it will prevent painful problems later.

2. Unless you have a taste for risk, avoid vendors that are selling beta versions of products. Opt instead for vendors whose products have been generally available for at least six months.

3. Consider using bonuses when you write contracts to encourage vendor performance, as well as penalty clauses to discourage nonperformance.

4. Look for vendors that are willing to offer you performance guarantees.

5. Check out claims of previous successful client/server installations by visiting those sites.

6. Look for a vendor that has the same strategic thinking that you have.

7. Decide whether the vendor's product development direction fits where you're headed.

8. Make sure you clearly understand your needs before you expect a vendor to understand them.

9. Find vendors that can work together, especially vendors with strategic corporate partnerships among themselves.

10. Realize that developing a good partnership with a vendor may be more important than seeking the lowest possible vendor bid. (Alexander, 1994)

Appendix XXXII The IIA's Perspective on Outsourcing Internal Auditing

A Professional Briefing for Chief Audit Executives

Although the term can be defined in several ways, *outsourcing* essentially means to engage an external party to provide services or products previously provided by an internal source. Partly as a result of reengineering, downsizing, rightsizing, and other forms of organizational change, the outsourcing of many non-core functions has become prevalent in many business environments.

For several reasons, including the fact that outside organizations have recognized the value of internal auditing and the revenue potential in contracting for the internal auditing function, outsourcing has become a significant professional issue for internal auditors around the world. Contractors have been particularly aggressive in the United States, the United Kingdom, Australia, Brazil, and Germany.

The internal auditing function, or a part of it, has been outsourced in a number of different types of organizations, including, for example, some *Fortune* companies, large financial and retail organizations, and educational institutions. Other organizations have considered outsourcing, then rejected the idea.

In instances where the internal auditing function has been outsourced, management has not always simply eliminated the internal staff and replaced it with employees of a contracted service. Some managements have outsourced only part of the internal auditing function, perhaps retaining a director-level employee and a complement of in-house staff. This arrangement offers the projected benefits of an outside resource and the benefits of an existing internal auditing function.

Some internal auditing directors have outsourced part of their own function. This usually occurs when outside sources are better equipped, perhaps technologically or geographically, to conduct a more thorough or cost-effective audit of a particular site or function of the organization.

Regardless of whether internal auditors believe their departments are susceptible to outsourcing, it is important to examine The IIA's perspective on outsourcing, to consider why some managements would agree to outsource the internal auditing function, and to identify actions and strategies that will provide management with a balanced view of outsourcing and its consequences.

The IIA's Perspective on Outsourcing

The IIA's perspective is that internal auditing is best performed by an independent entity that is an integral part of the management structure of an organization. The IIA states unequivocally that a competent *internal auditing* department that is properly organized with trained staff can perform the internal auditing function more efficiently and effectively than a contracted audit service.

Internal auditing *by definition* should be internal and integral to the organization, and the internal auditing department should be staffed with professional internal auditors who adhere to the *Standards for the Professional Practice of Internal Auditing* and the related *Code of Ethics.* One of the best evidences of internal auditing competence is the Certified Internal Auditor (CIA) designation.

Most internal auditors are degreed professionals. In fact, many hold advanced degrees and have acquired specialized skills related to the organization for which they work. These professionals are aware of their responsibilities with regard to the organization and the *Standards*.

The key proficiency of internal auditors is internal control in its broadest sense. Internal auditors provide management and the board of directors with competent evaluations of an organization's system of internal control and the quality of performance of assigned responsibilities regarding the reliability and integrity of information, compliance with laws and regulations, the safeguarding of assets, the economical and efficient use of resources, and accomplishment of goals and objectives.

Several common themes recur in control models such as the Committee of Sponsoring Organizations of the Treadway Commission, the Criteria of Control Committee of the Canadian Institute of Chartered Accountants, and the Cadbury Committee: "Internal control is management's responsibility; tone from the top is important; controls must be built *in,* not *on;* and internal communication and people development are critical elements of the control framework." Internal auditors' value and effectiveness are linked not only to their attunement to management's philosophy and direction, but to their understanding of internal control and their direct knowledge of operating systems that are often in flux.

Internal auditors are in touch with governance issues and are intimately acquainted with their organization's policies, procedures, operating practices, and personnel. They are able to devote their full attention and loyalty to the organization and to identify subtle changes and ambiguities that may signal trouble. Internal auditors can respond immediately to the concerns of senior management because they are familiar with their organizations' culture and processes, and their status as employees ensures confidentiality and loyalty.

As long as internal auditing staffs are highly skilled, efficient, and responsive to management, organizations are best served by keeping the internal auditing function internal.

Why Outsourcing has Occurred

One of the reasons that outsourcing has occurred in certain venues is simply that outside contractors have convinced management that they can provide internal auditing services more effectively. Managements may have been influenced by promises of:

1. Lower cost and/or better quality auditing products.
2. Improved coordination with management.
3. Reduced fixed staff salary levels.
4. Shifted liability to an external organization when attestation is required.
5. Improved access to specialization.
6. A shift in management's focus to core business issues, with an attendant reduction in resources for recruiting, training, and other employment issues.

Different managements are likely to respond differently to selling tactics, of course. Some contractors focus on intangibles such as "comfort level." They sell a professed ability to understand and accommodate management's goals and objectives more completely and effectively.

An emphasis on economy appears to be the most common strategy, however. Contractors may provide "critiques" and "reviews" of internal auditing plans and processes and then offer what seem to be cost-efficient solutions and more effective practices. These offers are sometimes discussed between members of senior management and their executive counterparts from outside consulting firms. Internal auditors, who may not be privy to these communications, are unaware of the situation and, therefore, not involved in discussion or debate of the issues raised.

Responding to Outsourcing: A Short-Term Approach

Internal auditors who face the immediate possibility of losing their jobs to an outside contractor must be certain that they themselves have a clear-eyed perspective of their unique role and the value they bring to their organizations. In situations where outsourcing the internal auditing function is already under consideration by management, the internal auditing director's wisest response is to approach the decision-making process like any other organizational decision, with dispassion and a results-oriented perspective. The analytical model for make or buy decisions will work as well in a potential outsourcing environment as it will in any other situation.

Forward-thinking internal auditors will want to take advantage of the opportunity to compete with outside contractors by supplying their own proposals. To make sure the playing field is level, internal auditors should:

- Ask for or create the specifications against which all bidding parties are to be evaluated. Ensure that all explicit and implicit assumptions such as who provides office space, communications, and computers, are known and priced.
- Develop a *creative* bid. Be willing to make necessary changes in the auditing organization, its cost structure, workforce, and any areas that may need a fresh evaluation.
- Be prepared to present and reinforce the value of an internal auditing function as well as the advantages of purchasing specialized skills or expertise to complete short-term or one-of-a-kind assignments.
- Prepare a highly polished and professional sales presentation that will get the bid noticed and accepted by senior management.
- Avoid negative comparisons between internal and external auditing. Such *we/they* comparisons are often

meaningless to executive management, who may feel that auditing is auditing no matter who performs the function.

- Remember that outsourcing is a management *business* decision. The in-house response must be positive and demonstrate organizational rather than personal interests.

Internal auditors should provide management and the audit committee with key questions and issues that should be raised when they consider the possibility of outsourcing the internal auditing function:

1. What will management and the organization gain from outsourcing, and where has the existing auditing organization fallen short?
2. Can the contracted audit service provide:
   - In-depth knowledge of the business operations?
   - Experienced, knowledgeable, and certified staff? *The game plan of some outside contractors may be to staff the job with junior-level personnel during off-season months.*
   - Loyalty to the organization? *Outside auditing staff may have loyalties divided between their own firm and the client organization; in such cases, it isn't likely that the client organization will receive first priority.*
   - Continuous availability — to begin an investigation or a special study at a moment's notice, for example, and at no additional cost? *While internal auditors may need to divert resources to accommodate special projects, many contractors may increase their fees as soon as the audit schedule deviates from the contracted audit plan.*
   - The ability to assess controls in any area of the organization? *Many external auditors are trained to do substantive work, but they may not be experienced in other varieties of control assessment. The outsourced firm may have specialized staff, but usually these services are charged at premiums to the basic fee.*

- Continuous monitoring of controls at a level that will satisfy regulatory requirements?

3. Will the organization lose an important source of personnel development?
4. Are *all* the costs being considered? *Costs such as contract monitoring, staff occupancy, and possible price increases for unscheduled projects are often overlooked.*
5. Is the cost of a learning curve being considered? *Outsourcing carries a tremendous start-up cost to the provider and a substantial downtime cost to the organization when staff members unfamiliar with operations and systems begin their internal auditing work. This situation is exacerbated when non-dedicated personnel are used by a contracted audit service.*
6. Will the provider ensure adequate independence as prescribed by The IIA *Standards*?
7. Will an outside contractor subscribe to The IIA *Standards* and provide the scope of work that they dictate?
8. To limit the external contractors' liability, will members of management be compelled to do more themselves, so that they can reach and be confident about assertions regarding the adequacy of internal control?

It is not inconceivable that the potential of outsourcing can be turned to advantage by an efficient and effective internal auditing staff that clearly understands the issues and knows how to present them to management. A considered, businesslike approach to outsourcing may actually underscore internal auditing's contributions to the organization.

Responding to Outsourcing: A Long-Term Approach

Even in situations where the benefits and value of internal auditing are understood and appreciated by the management and board, and where outsourcing the internal auditing function is not an immediate consideration, internal auditors need to achieve the highest levels of internal auditing excellence. Internal auditors should evaluate their mission and strategies on an ongoing basis, and they should ensure that management is aware of the unique and critical contributions of the internal auditing department. The internal auditing function is measured by the benefits it provides, as well as by audit customers' awareness of those benefits.

Strong internal auditing departments are interwoven into the fabric of their organizations. The work of these departments is integral to the efforts of management, which helps to reduce the likelihood that these internal auditing departments will be confronted with the possibility of outsourcing.

The effectiveness of internal auditing departments begins with a vision statement, which is based on and linked to the overall organizational vision, and is implemented through a strategic plan. An internal auditing department with vision is:

Proactive. The proactive internal auditing department establishes itself as a change agent throughout the organization. It sets its own objectives in line with organizational goals and finds new ways to contribute.

Innovative. The innovative internal auditing department searches out the most valuable use of its resources, questioning the value of routine audits and creating opportunities to increase the value of the internal auditing function.

Focused. Decisions must be consistent with predetermined objectives. This applies to decisions made by auditing management as well as individuals.

Integrated. To be efficient, internal auditing information systems should be integrated and designed to support auditing and management processes.

Motivated. A motivated auditing staff has a sense of mission, teamwork, and organizational pride. Internal auditors find personal reward in the success of their organizations and work cooperatively to meet management goals.

Other key success indicators for strong internal auditing departments are likely to include:

- A clear image of who the most important internal auditing customers are, what they need from the internal auditing department, and what would *exceed* their expectations.
- A definition of the role and services that the internal auditing function must provide.
- An enhanced planning process that may include altering the audit universe, optimizing audit coverage, and adopting a more proactive approach.
- An enhanced methodology that provides selective, risk-based coverage and increased management involvement in the audit process.
- Expertise in the use, control, and auditability of the organization's technology.
- A means of measuring and improving customer satisfaction.
- A means of measuring continuous internal auditing improvement.
- Strong communication skills, including tailored internal auditing reports, regular meetings with audit customers, and overview report summaries for management.
- Enhanced organizational and staff development. This means acquiring a cadre of highly qualified and motivated professional internal auditors. It also means effective career planning and a greater emphasis on internal auditing and organizational knowledge.

In Conclusion

Keeping the internal auditing function as an integral part of the organization offers clear advantages. Through day-to-day experience in the business, internal auditors acquire — and operate from — an intimate knowledge of an organization's culture, processes, risks, and mitigating controls. The insight and expertise of internal auditors enable them to provide management with unique services, especially in the areas of internal control risk analysis and system assessments. Internal auditing professionals know and understand the organization to a degree that outsiders cannot, and their loyalty and confidentiality are ensured by the *internal* nature of their function.

Internal auditors are continually aware of management's goals and are in touch with important governance issues. Because their function is internal, internal auditors can, on a daily basis, view subtle changes that may indicate a need for increased focus.

Senior managements that recognize the benefits of an internal auditing function and identify it as an integral part of the management team will not view outsourcing as an attractive option. By marketing professionalism and demonstrating value-added qualities to management, internal auditing will further increase its stature within the environment of corporate governance and reduce its vulnerability to outside contractors.

Glossary of Key Terms

Acceptance Test
A test of a system or program in as close to operating conditions as possible in order to determine whether the system or program is ready for implementation. Sometimes referred to as user acceptance or user testing.

Application Software
Software written to perform certain tasks, such as payroll or accounts receivable.

Application Support Software
A general term for a variety of programmed routines, normally supplied by the equipment manufacturer, to perform standard recurring functions. The main categories of application support software are source language compilers/interpreters, general utility programs, on-line support software, and file organization and data management utilities.

Application System
An information system designed to perform a specific task, e.g., human resource management.

Asset Comparison Controls
Controls to compare assets on hand as shown in the books with a source that is independent from the accounting records.

Audit Asset Protection Controls
Controls to protect assets against theft or loss.

Audit Trail
Synonym for management trail.

Backup
Relates to information systems resources that are available for use in the event of service interruptions.

Backup Copy
A duplicate of data or software that can be used if the original is damaged or destroyed.

Balance Controls
Controls to provide an independent check over the completeness and integrity of accounting records.

Batch Control
A procedure whereby all transactions are added up prior to recording. That total is then compared with a control total produced by the computer system.

Batch System
A system whereby similar items are collected into groups (batches) for processing by a computer.

Business Process Reengineering (BPR)
Attempts to redesign the fundamental flow of business processes, rather than attempting to find small, incremental improvements in efficiency of business procedures developed long ago. The goal of BPR is to dramatically streamline workflow, thereby reducing the time and effort required to take appropriate action.

Central Processing Unit
The component of a computer system where the arithmetic, logic, and data transfer control is carried out.

CEO
Chief Executive Officer.

Check Digit
A digit determined by performing a calculation on the digits of a number according to a specified formula and then appended to that number. Check digits are used to provide protection against transposition, transcription, and random errors.

CIO
Chief Information Officer.

Client
The system that initiates requests to the server or engine and then uses its intelligence to further process the results.

Client/Server
An architecture that distributes computing responsibility between a front-end and a back-end program. Prior to "client/server," all the burden of data processing was placed on either the client (as in a typical Xbase environment) or the server (as in a typical mainframe). When two or more machines are involved, client/server can dramatically reduce network traffic and increase performance.

Client/Server Computing
(A) In a client/server system, the centralized computer, called a server, holds data, while PC workstations, called clients, use the data to do work on-line, real time. The two are connected by a network and share processing power. (B) Any application in which the requester of action is on one system and the supplier of action is potentially on another. (C) Can be referred to as a network-based systems architecture in which databases are stored on powerful file servers and accessed via applications running on distributed "client" computers — typically PCs and workstations. The server is the "back-end," where the database processing takes place, while the client is the "front-end," where most of the application processing occurs.

Computation Controls
Controls over computations performed by the computer system consisting of verification of correct logic in the application software.

Contract Logistics
The use of an outside distribution company — a transportation carrier, warehouse, or third-party freight manager — to perform all or part of an organization's material management or product distribution functions.

Control Report
A report generated by a computer program whose purpose is to aid in balancing or checking input or stored data.

Control Total
A sum of numbers which is computed prior to the start of a process being checked. This total is then compared to the equivalent total recomputed by the process and any difference between them indicates an error which needs to be identified and corrected in a timely manner.

Conversion Audit
An examination of changeover procedures, new accounting procedures, and files which takes place when there has been a significant change in the accounting system (e.g., a change from a manual to a computerized system, a change of computers, or switching to a new application).

Cooperative Processing
An environment where a smaller system might calculate new values for variables stored on larger systems. In cooperative processing, client/server databases can help to ensure a stable, secure operating environment.

Custom Software
Programs written specially for a particular user.

Database
A collection of related information stored together in computerized form that is shared and used by different users for different purposes.

Database Management System
Generalized software programs used to handle the physical storage and manipulation of databases.

Detective Controls
Internal controls designed to identify or maximize the chance of isolating errors and other irregularities.

Distributed Processing
Processing in a complex computer information network in which data relevant only to individual locations is processed locally, while information required elsewhere is transmitted either to the central computer or to another local computer for further processing.

Distributing
Any way of separating currently monolithic applications and databases, such as client/server.

Documentation
The collection of narratives records, reports, workpapers, and other documents that describe the information system and the procedures for performing data processing tasks.

Downsizing
A methodology; a management direction resulting in the moving or transferring of all or part of applications running on large systems, such as mainframes, to smaller, often lower-cost computer systems (i.e., PCs on LANs).

Electronic Data Interchange (EDI)
Intercompany, computer-to-computer transmission of business information in a standard format. For EDI purists, "computer-to-computer" means direct transmission from the originating application program to the receiving, or processing, application program, and an EDI transmission consists only of business data, not any accompanying verbiage or free-form messages. Purists might also contend that a standard format is one that is approved by a national or international standards organization, as opposed to formats developed by industry groups or organizations.

Engine
Sometimes referred to as the "back-end," engines are the server-based applications that provide access to and control modifications of data.

Error Message
A message produced by the program to describe or designate an error encountered during execution of the computer program.

Exception Report
A report from an information system, produced upon request or in response to certain specified conditions, which highlights exceptions from the normal or anticipated situation.

General and Environmental Controls
Controls which apply to all applications systems within an organization and thus are not unique to any individual application such as payroll, inventory, or accounts payable.

GUI
Use of icons or pictures to represent written commands.

Hardware
The physical equipment or devices in an information system, consisting of mechanical, magnetic, electrical, and electronic devices such as central processing unit, tape drives, disk files, etc.

Hash Total
A control used to establish accuracy of processing whereby a total of a data element is made by adding the values together (e.g., the sum of a list of part numbers) and subsequently comparing the answer to a computer-generated total of the same values.

In-house
Within the entity.

Integrated System
An information system in which data entered for one application is shared with a number of applications without having to reenter the data for each application.

Integrating
Any activity that links or combines currently separate applications and databases.

Internal Control
The plan of an organization and all coordinated systems established by the management of the enterprise to assist in achieving management's objectives of ensuring, as far as practicable, the orderly and efficient conduct of its business, including the timely preparation of reliable information.

IPX/SPX
The transport protocol found in most NetWare environments. In client/server environments, where the server engine is an NLM (NetWare Loadable Module), communication between the client and server usually is conducted over IPX/SPX.

IT
Information Technology.

Legacy Systems
IBM 3090 Model 200 class machines and like "systems." Large "iron," heavy-duty number-crunching machines designed for massive data processing operations — replaced by mid-range (AS 400 and equivalent client-server systems under the downsizing frenzy).

Local Area Network
(A) A communication network which directly links a number of computers, allowing them to communicate with each other and share data and peripherals such as a printer. (B) Connects computer terminals or PCs together, generally within a range of less than 2000 feet.

Management Trail
The predetermined route by which the processing of data can be traced either forward or backward through the application system.

MDNS
Managed data network service. Combines the best elements of private management and outsourcing, allowing users to unload day-to-day management tasks to an outsider while still retaining some control over the network.

Middleware
Any set of routines or functions that allows two dissimilar programs to interoperate.

Migrating
Any movement of an application or database from one platform to another.

Monolithic Application
A single program or a group of interrelated programs that performs all the data interpretation and presentation as a single unit, and always runs on a single platform.

Multiprocessing
The simultaneous execution of more than one computer program.

Named Pipes
An interprocess protocol used by OS/2, LAN Manager, and LAN Server to communicate between the back-end server and the client in client/server applications. It acts independently of the underlying network protocol.

NLM (NetWare Loadable Module)
An application that can be dynamically loaded and unloaded on a NetWare 3.x or 4.x server. Examples of engines available as NLMs are Sybase Inc.'s SQL Server and Oracle Corp.'s Oracle Server. Lotus Development Corp. is rumored to be releasing the NLM version of Notes shortly.

Non-processing Controls
Organizational controls that provide an appropriate segregation of duties and controls to ensure that applications systems and operating systems are properly maintained and used.

On-line System
An information system which maintains files of information in a form which is immediately accessible for either the acceptance of input transactions or the reporting of information through a device which is connected to the computer system.

Operating Software
A general term for operating system software and application support software.

Operating System
A set of programs designed to provide a facility for controlling the allocation and use of computer resources.

Operating System Software
A programmed set of routines provided by the equipment manufacturer to control all operations of the computer hardware.

Output Controls
Controls over the output produced by the system which determine the accuracy and completeness of output before it is accepted.

Outsourcing
When an organization contracts out its non-strategic operations to a third party.

Parallel Run
Concurrent data processing using the new system and the system to be replaced.

Parallel Testing
Concurrent data processing using a new system and the system to be replaced, with subsequent comparison of the output from both systems.

Partnering
A long-term commitment between two or more organizations with the goal of achieving specific business objectives by maximizing the effectiveness of each participant's resources.

Password
The unique set of digits or characters by which a user logging on is identified and granted access to authorized data. Password is also used to identify a user when submitting a program for execution.

Point-of-Sale (POS)
A national network of merchant terminals, at which customers can use client cards and personal security codes to make purchases. Transactions are directed against client deposit accounts. POS terminals are sophisticated cryptographic devices with complex key management processes. POS standards draw on ABM network experiences and possess extremely stringent security requirements.

Preliminary Survey
An initial investigation to gather and organize pertinent information about the business, its activities, and its information system, and identify future business and information requirements.

Preventive Controls
Internal controls designed to prevent, or minimize the chance of the occurrence of, errors and other irregularities.

Processing Controls
Controls over the processing of transactions through the computer system.

Programmed Controls
Automated control procedures contained within the computer programs.

Re-architecting
Means changing your applications to take advantage of new hardware and software technologies. It may be as simple as implementing a graphical user interface (GUI), or you could rewrite the entire application to take advantage of client/server technologies.

Reengineering
(A) The fundamental rethinking and radical redesign of business processes to achieve dramatic improvements in critical, contemporary measures of performance, such as cost, quality, service, and speed (Messers, Hammer and Champy). (B) A new (or revitalized) management philosophy of questioning the status quo. The formal name for the process of asking why is "business process reengineering."

Referential integrity
The rules governing data consistency by maintaining foreign-key-to-primary-key consistency and eliminating orphan foreign-key rows. This is done by cascading key changes from the primary to the foreign, by blocking changes to the primary key, but replacing the foreign key with a null value, or by deleting orphaned rows.

Rehosting
Moving applications off the mainframe and onto less expensive and a more easily supported host. Rehosting can still save bundles of money without having to retrain your staff, hire new people, or encounter the risk associated with a radically different environment such as Unix or PC-LANs.

Renovating
Any revamping or modernizing — such as going to a 4GL or adding interoperability — that does not specifically add new functionality.

Request For Proposal
A document specifying the attributes of a computer or computer programs required which is sent to potential suppliers who, in turn, use it as a basis for hardware or software proposed by them and price quotations for their proposals.

Rightsizing
(A) Redistributing the organization's electronic workload so that each computer handles the work it does best; (B) The right tools at the right time, at the right price, for the job at hand; (C) A strategy to deploy the best possible technology to deliver the best possible application solutions for particular business needs. Alternatives defined as:

A	Tuning	Cleanup activities that don't add functionality or alter the application or data.
B	Renovating	Modernizing, such as going to a fourth-generation language or adding interoperability that does not specifically add new business functionality.
C	Protecting	Actions such as improving recovery and security.
D	Integrating	Activities that link or combine currently separate applications and databases.
E	Distributing	Any way of separating currently monolithic applications and databases, such as client/server.
F	Migrating	Movement of an application or database from one platform to another.

Security Software
A generic term for the security features available with various types of access control software.

Selective Outsourcing
The act of strategically farming out pieces of an organization's operations to a third-party service provider.

Server
The server is typically a back-end application that services data and maintains data consistency. Server can be used either to refer to the software engine or the underlying hardware on which the engine runs.

Service Bureau
Refers to a company or organization which is in the business of providing computer and related facilities for the performance of data processing to different users.

SQL (Structured Query Language)
Unified language designed for defining, modifying, and controlling the data in a relational database. SQL is sometimes used to access data stored in other types of formats as well.

TCP/IP
A connectionless transport protocol often found in client/server environments. In some instances, the engine-specific protocol, such as Oracle's SQL*Net, must be compatible with the vendor-specific implementation of the transport protocol to work properly.

Test Pack
A set of test files and input data which is created to test a computer system.

Third Party(ies)
Vendors and suppliers that provide products and services to an organization, either for the organization's use or for the organization's customers' use.

Trailer Record
A file record that follows a group of records and contains summary information on the group.

Transaction Data
Information relating to individual transactions flowing from day-to-day activities with third parties or employees.

Transaction List
A printout of all transactions recorded, with the details on the listing being subsequently agreed to the original source documents.

Transaction Log
A record of the transaction initiated and transmitted to the main computer system. The log may be a by-product of a remote terminal input process, or may be prepared manually with control totals for verifying that all the information sent was correctly received by the system.

Tuning
Any clean-up activity such as recompilation or reconfiguration that does not add functionality or alter the application or data.

Two-phase Commit
A strategy of writing data that is physically located on two separate machines, which ensures that each statement within a transaction either succeeds or fails. When all statements succeed, the transaction is committed. When any of the statements fails, all the statements within the transaction roll back to their original states.

Utilities/Utility Programs
Programs used for standard routines such as sorting, adding, printing, copying, and tracing.

Value
The perceived worth in monetary terms of the economic, technical, service, and social benefits received by a customer firm in exchange for the price paid for a product offering.

Recommended Readings

Outsourcing

Adhikari, R. "The Security Risks of Outsourcing." *Info Security News, 3* (6), (November/December 1992), pp. 1, 9-10.

Alexander, M. "Users Get Serious About Growing Security Risk." *Computerworld,* (August 5, 1991), pp. 1, 10.

Ambrosio, J. "Outsourcing at Southland: Best of Times, Worst of Times." *Computerworld,* (March 25, 1991), p. 61.

Ambrosio, J. "Paine Webber Takes on New Outsourcing Role." *Computerworld,* (October 26, 1992), p. 4.

Ambrosio, J. "Soul-Searching: Four Case Studies." *Computerworld,* (December 3, 1990), pp. 69, 73.

Anonymous. "New Study Tracks Response to Third-Party Logistics." *Traffic Management, 31* (2), (February 1992), pp. 38-45.

Anonymous. "Outsourcing Produces a Merger Made in Heaven." *Bankers Monthly, 108* (11), (November 1991), p. 22.

Anonymous. "Technology Survey '91: Is Outsourcing About to Make the Big Time?" *Bank Systems & Technology, 28* (9), (September 1991), pp. 49-52.

Anonymous. "Technology Survey '91: Who is Spending What — and Where?" *Bank Systems & Technology, 28* (9), (September 1991), pp. 46, 48.

Anthes, G.H. "HUD Set to Outsource IS." *Computerworld,* (December 3, 1990), pp. 1, 119.

Anthes, G.H. "Outsourcing May Be Only Answer for Many." *Computerworld,* (March 25, 1991), pp. 51, 54.

Bers, J.S. "Outsourcing: A Deal or Dilemma for FMs?" *Facilities Design & Management, 11* (3), (March 1992), pp. 54-57.

Berst, J. "Outsourcing Your GUI Support." *Computerworld, 25* (50), (December 16, 1991), p. 54.

Bettis, R.A.; Bradley, S.P.; and Hamel, G. "Outsourcing and Industrial Decline." *Academy of Management Executive, 6* (1), (February 1992), pp. 7-22.

Betts, M. "Making the Mexican Connection." *Computerworld,* (December 13, 1993), pp. 91-94.

Betts, M. "Study: Outsourcing Big in Banks' Future." *Computerworld,* (October 7, 1991), p. 8.

Bingham, S. "When You Care Enough to Need the Best." *Communications Week Advertising Supplement,* pp. 28-29.

Bluemer, C. "Using Outsourcing to Realize the Corporate Mission." (October 11-14, 1992), CIO Perspectives Series. *The Process of IT: Organizing for Success,* Boca Raton Resort & Club, Boca Raton, Florida.

Blumenthal, M. Letter From the Editor. *CIO,* (December 1, 1993), p. 10.

Booker, E. "BT Targets Multinational Outsourcing." *Computerworld,* (September 23, 1991), p. 95.

Booker, E. "How IS Beat the Outsourcers at Amoco." *Computerworld,* (January 10, 1994), p. 77.

Booker, E. "Outsourcing Personnel Pays Off." *Computerworld,* (February 28, 1994), p. 74.

Booker, E. "Sun R&M Opts for Outsourcing." *Computerworld,* (May 1992), p. 67.

Bozman, J. "Esprit Outsources Legacy, Refocuses IS." *Computerworld,* (May 9, 1994), p. 30.

Braiotta, L. "A Local Practitioner's Guide to Internal Audit Services." *The CPA Journal,* (May 1992), pp. 54-58.

Brandel, W. "Vendors Seek Aid: More Software Suppliers Outsource Support." *Computerworld,* (June 6, 1994), pp. 39-41.

Brenner, L. "Outsourcing Redux." *CFO,* (July 1994), p. 54.

Brown, D. "Outsourcing: How Corporations Take Their Business Elsewhere." *Management Review, 81* (2), (February 1992), pp. 16-19.

Burch, B. "Xerox Turns Nets Over to EDS in $3.26 Deal." *Network World,* (June 27, 1994).

Burger, K. "To Outsource or Not to Outsource?" *Bank Systems and Technology,* p. 32.

Bush, V. "Managers Face Facts: It's Survival of the Trimmest." *Savings Institutions, 112* (11), (November 1991), pp. 30-35.

Caron, J. "Outsourcing LAN Management." *LAN Times,* (April 11, 1994), p. 65.

Carreker, J.D. "Strides in Electronic Checking Transforming Payment System." *Bank Management, 68* (3), (March 1992), pp. 18-30.

Chaplin, H. "Big Outsourcers Not Always Better." *Network World*, (February 17, 1992), pp. 36.

Cimino, D. "Delta Likes to Fly — Outsources to AT&T." *Software Magazine*, (October 1994), p. 30.

Clermont, P. "Outsourcing Without Guilt." *Computerworld*, (September 9, 1991), pp. 67-68.

Coale, K. "British Petroleum Outsources I.S." *Infoworld*, (February 3, 1992), p. 47.

Condon, R. "CA, EDS Embroiled in Outsourcing Dispute." *Computerworld*, (April 11, 1994), p. 14.

Constanzo, C. "To Outsource or Not to Outsource? The Question Continues to Rankle Industry." *Bank Technology News*, (February 1994), p. 1.

Cooney, M. "Memorex-Telex Steps Into Outsourcing Arena." *Network World*, (July 18, 1994), p. 13.

Courtemanche, G. "Outsourcing the Internal Audit Function." *Internal Auditor*, (August 1991), pp. 34-35.

Crenshaw, D. "Outsourcing: To be? Or Not to Be?" *Computerworld*, (March 8, 1993), p. 120.

Crockett, B. "Critics Assail Global Outsource Ventures." *Network World*, (November 4, 1991), pp. 31, 33.

Crone, R.K. "Negotiating an Outsourcing Agreement." *Bank Management, 68* (3), (March 1992), pp. 59-62.

Crone, R.K. "Negotiating With Outsources: A 'How-to' Guide." *Banking Software Review, 16* (4), (Winter 1991), pp. 21-25.

Crowley, A. "Passing the Buck: Hiring Outside Service Providers Can Help Overburdened IT Departments Focus Their Energy." *PC Week,* (October 17, 1994), pp. 25-32.

Cummings, J. "Bank Off-loads Data Center, Network Upgrade to Unisys." *Network World,* (October 12, 1992), pp. 51, 59.

Cummings, J. "Network Outsourcing: Second Time's a Charm." *Computerworld,* (September 19, 1994), p. 110.

Davidson, W.H. and Davis, S.M. "Management and Organization Principles for the Information Economy." *Human Resource Management, 29* (4), (Winter 1990), pp. 365-383.

DeBow, Y. and Meade, P. "Technology Priorities for the 1990s." *Insurance & Technology, 16* (1), (April 1994), pp. 17-24.

Deckleva, S. "CFO's, CIO's and Outsourcing." *Computerworld,* (May 16, 1994), p. 96.

Diamond, S. "An Inside-Out Alternative to Outsourcing." *Chief Information Officer Journal,* (May/June, 1993), p. 61.

Diamond, S. "Survey Reveals the Top Strategies for Reducing IS Costs." *Chief Information Officer Journal, 4* (3), (Winter 1992), pp. 55-57.

Dickson, G.W. and Wetherbe, J.C. *The Management of Information Systems,* (1985), McGraw-Hill.

Downer, C.B. "More Companies Opting to 'Rent' Technology." *National Underwriter, 96* (6) 9, (February 10, 1992), pp. 18-19.

Drtina, R. "The Outsourcing Decision." *Management Accounting,* (March 1994), pp. 56-62.

Due, R.T. "The Real Costs of Outsourcing." *Information Systems Management, 9* (1), (Winter 1992), pp. 78-81.

Duffy, C.A. "Hidden Costs Can Undermine Savings From Outsourcing." *Computerworld, 25* (46), (November 18, 1991), p. 109.

Dykeman, J.B. "Farming It Out: A Viable Alternative." *Modern Office Technology,* (October 1991), p. 10.

Eckerson, W. "CIOs Eagerly Embracing Open Systems, Survey Finds." *Network World, 9* (9), (March 2, 1992), pp. 27-28.

Eckerson, W. "CSC Grabs Up Giant Outsource Contract." *Network World,* (September 30, 1991), pp. 9, 47.

Eckerson, W. "IBM Forms Business Unit to Focus Outsourcing Efforts." *Network World,* (May 20, 1991), p. 4.

Eckerson, W. "Outsourcing: Tending to the People Issues." *Network World, 9* (12), (March 23, 1992), pp. 23, 26.

Eckerson, W. "Outsourcing Unlikely to Offer Big Savings." *Network World, 8* (40), (October 7, 1991), pp. 27, 30.

Eckerson, W. "Regaining Control After Outsourcing." *Network World,* (August 5, 1991), pp. 15-16.

Eckerson, W. "Users Creating New Twists to Outsourcing." *Network World, 9* (8), (February 24, 1992), pp. 21-22.

Eckerson, W. "Workers Wage War Against Outsourcing by Filing Suit." *Network World,* (December 3, 1990), pp. 4, 70.

Evagora, A. "IBM Outsource Unit — New Company to Manage Computers & Data Nets." *Communications Week*, (March 23, 1992), p. 26.

Fisher, S. "Study: Outsourcing Use to Decline." *Communications Week*, (March 15, 1993), p. 35.

Fitzgerald, M. "System Odyssey Leads to Outsourcing." *Computerworld, 26* (7), (February 17, 1992), pp. 73, 76.

Frank, H. "Outsource Now or Pay Later." *Networking Management, 9* (14), (December 1991), pp. 57-58.

Frank, H. "Planning Your Outsourcing Strategy." *Networking Management, 9* (11), (October 1991), pp. 42-45.

Fried, L. "Outsourcing: One to Do Job, Another to Check It." *Computerworld*, (August 31, 1992), p. 33.

Friedberg, A.H. and Harberry, W.A. Jr. "Audit Rights in an Outsource Environment." *Internal Auditor*, (August 1991), pp. 53-57.

Friedman, Rick. "Outsourcing as a Way to Reduce Major Costs." *The Office, 114* (4), (October, 1991), pp. 70-72.

Gantz, J. "Outsourcing: The Scam May Be On You." *Computerworld*, (April 18, 1994), p. 41.

Gillin, P. "Outsourcers: Get Close, But Not Too Close." *Computerworld*, (December 21, 1992), p. 54.

Gillooly, C. "Firms Retain Control of LAN Management." *Network World*, (June 24, 1991), pp. 19, 70.

Gilman, J. "Certification and Outsourcing Strategic Software." *AICCP Newsletter*, (July 1992), p. 5.

Goodenbury, G. "Design Service Bureaus: Friend or Foe?" *Printed Circuit Design, 9* (3), (March 1992), pp. 11-16.

Goodwin, C. "Outsourcing On the Increase." *Accountancy, 108* (1179) (November 1991), pp. 112-113.

Guimaraes, T. and Wells, S. "Outsourcing for Novices." *Computerworld,* (June 8, 1992), pp. 89-91.

Haavind, R. "The Outsourcing Option." *CFO: The Magazine for Senior Financial Executives, 7* (11), (November 1991), pp. 52, 54.

Halper, M. "EDS Rival Bids Low, Lands General Motors Contract." *Computerworld,* (September 6, 1993), p. 73.

Halper, M. "EDS Wins Fight with One Texas Bank, Faces Another." *Computerworld,* (July 4, 1994), p. 32.

Halper, M. "Ford Drives Exclusive Outsourcing Deal." *Computerworld,* (February 21, 1994), p. 59.

Halper, M. "Hertz Talks with Outsourcer." *Computerworld,* (November 9, 1992), p. 12.

Halper, M. "HP to Enter Outsourcing." *Computerworld,* (December 27, 1993/January 3, 1994), pp. 1-2.

Halper, M. "IBM Pilot Reduces Outsourcing Costs." *Computerworld,* (October 26, 1992), pp. 1, 16.

Halper, M. "ISSC Grabs Another Railway in Amtrak Outsourcing Deal." *Computerworld,* (May 9, 1994), p. 68.

Halper, M. "Outsourcers Assess IBM Tactics." *Computerworld,* (November 30, 1992), p. 109.

Halper, M. "Outsourcers: Black Magic or White?" *Computerworld*, (July 12, 1993), p. 97.

Halper, M. "Outsourcers in Need of Telecom Experience." *Computerworld*, (June 13, 1994), pp. 85-89.

Halper, M. "Outsourcers: Saviors or Charlatans?" *Computerworld*, (August 2, 1993), p. 63.

Halper, M. "Outsourcing's Pricing Conundrum." *Computerworld*, (August 2, 1993), p. 1.

Halper, M. "Texas Bank Sues EDS." *Computerworld*, (May 30, 1994), p. 8.

Halper, M. "Trane Again Chooses Outsourcing Track." *Computerworld*, (January 17, 1994), p. 70.

Halper, M. "UK Royal Automobile Club Makes Outsourcing Switch." *Computerworld*, (March 21, 1994), p. 83.

Halper, M. "UK Tax Agency Will Outsource to EDS." *Computerworld*, (November 29, 1993), p. 16.

Halper, M. "Utilities Plug In to Outsourcing." *Computerworld*, (November 28, 1994), p. 1.

Halper, M. "Xerox Signs Up EDS." *Computerworld*, (March 28, 1994), p. 1.

Halper, M. "Xerox Splits IS Duties with EDS." *Computerworld*, (June 20, 1994), p. 12.

Harbison, T.O. "Seize the Customer Day." *Computerworld*, (November 30, 1992), pp. 77-79.

Heywood, P. "Global Outsourcing: What Works, What Doesn't." *Data Communications,* (November 21, 1994), pp. 75-80.

Hoewing, M. W. "The Outsource Option." *Association Management, 44* (2), (February 1992), pp. 37-40.

Hoffman, T. "End Users Won't Wait." *Computerworld,* (January 27, 1993/January 3, 1994), pp. 28-29.

Hoffman, T. "Outsourcing Deal Proves Costly." *Computerworld,* (January 10, 1994), p. 14.

Hopper, M. "Tiptoeing Through the Outsourcing Minefield." *Computerworld,* (February 1, 1993), p. 29.

Horwitt, E. "J.P. Morgan on Outsource Bandwagon." *Computerworld,* (February 17, 1992), p. 50.

Hudson, K. "Kodak Exec Relates Outsourcing Lessons." *Network World,* (December 17, 1990), pp. 27-28.

Iacobuzio, T. "Pioneers of Outsourcing." *Insurance & Technology, 16* (7) (September 1991), pp. 22-29.

Jathanna, V. "Outsourcing." *CMA Magazine, 65* (10), (December 1991/January 1992), pp. 25-27.

Jathanna, V. "Outsourcing — Taking Stock of New Opportunities to Contract Out Non-strategic Business Activities." *CMA Magazine,* (December/January 1992), pp. 25-27.

Johnsen, J.L. and Tyniec, J.W. "Automation Choices for Policy Administration." *National Underwriter, 96* (13), (March 30, 1992), pp. 10, 14.

Johnson, D. and Johnson, N. "Bottom Line and Beyond: A Recession is the Right Time to Take Advantage of Contract Manufacturers." *Industrial Management & Data Systems, 91* (7), (1991), pp. 12-13.

Johnson, M. "Outsourcing Win for DEC." *Computerworld,* (August 26, 1991), pp. 1, 6.

Kiely, T. "The Shape of Excellence." *CIO,* (August 1992), pp. 26-32.

Kiely, T. "The Wrong Goodbye." *CIO,* (September 1, 1992), pp. 34-43.

King, J.L. and Nolan, R.L. "The Nolan Stage Model: A Debate." *Twelfth International Conference on Information Systems New York,* (December 16-18, 1991).

Kirvan, P. "Outsourcing: Is It a Boon or Boondoggle?" *Communications News, 29* (3), (March 1992), p. 46.

Knight, R. "New Technologies Open Doors to Outsourcing Partnerships." *Software Magazine,* (November 1994), pp. 71-76.

Korzeniowski, P. "To Downsize or To Outsource?" *Communications Week,* (October 15, 1990), p. 21.

LaPlante, A. "PC Expo Panel Will Highlight Importance of Writing a Good RFP." *Infoworld,* (June 15, 1992), p. 66.

Leinfuss, E. "How Outsourcing Impacts IS Managers." *Computerworld, 25* (37) (September 16, 1991), p. 113.

Leinfuss, E. "Outsourcers Have Limited Liability." *Computerworld, 26* (13) (March 30, 1992), p. 88.

Livingston, D. "Outsourcing: Look Beyond the Price Tag." *Datamation*, (November 15, 1992), pp. 93-97.

Llana, A. "Managemcnt Strategy for a Mixed Computer Environment." *Communications News, 28* (10), (October 1991), p. 30.

Llana, A. "The Ups and Downs of Outsourcing." *Data Communications*, (January 21, 1993), pp. 69-71.

Lyzs, M. "Outsourcing's Fallout: Vendors Must be Diligent in Seeking Partners." *Crain's New York Business*, (April 4, 1994), p. 21.

Maglitta, J. "Mr. Fixit." *Computerworld*, (October 26, 1992), pp. 133-135.

Margolis, N. "Anchor Bank Outsources IS." *Computerworld*, (April 13, 1992), p. 4.

Margolis, N. "Bank IS Fights Outsourcing Challenge." *Computerworld*, (June 1, 1992), p. 12.

Margolis, N. "Bank Outsourcing: Not Dead Yet." *Computerworld*, (June 8, 1992), p. 93.

Margolis, N. "IBM Unit Bags Bank Outsourcing bucks." *Computerworld*, (September 23, 1991), p. 16.

Margolis, N. "Insurance Eyes Outsourcing." *Computerworld*, (November 23, 1992), p. 6.

Margolis, N. "Outsourcing Boom Over? You Ain't Seen Nothin'." *Computerworld, 26* (2), (January 13, 1992), p. 8.

Margolis, N. "Outsourcing Could Be a $21B Niche by 1996." *Computerworld*, (September 30, 1991), p. 72.

Margolis, N. "Outsourcing Is It at Diesel Technology." *Computerworld*, (May 27, 1991), p. 61.

Margolis, N. "Recession Alters Market, Triggers Comdisco Revamp." *Computerworld, 26* (10), (March 9, 1992), p. 12.

Margolis, N. "UT Taps IBM for Outsourcing Project." *Computerworld*, (November 11, 1991), p. 10.

Margolis, N. and Wilder, C. "Inside Outsourcing — Early Adopters Give Qualified Approval, But Urge IS to Keep Its Hands on the Reins." *Computerworld*, (May 4, 1992), pp. 1, 20.

May, T. "Outward Bound." *CIO*, (March 1, 1994), pp. 26-28

McClelland, S. "Outsourcing: The Trend Continues." *Telecommunications*, (August 1992), pp. 31-32.

McCusker, T. "There is Life After Outsourcing?" *Datamation*, (April 1, 1991), pp. 62-65.

McKeon, J.E. "Outsourcing Begins In-house." *Transportation & Distribution, 32* (9), (September 1991), pp. 24-28.

McQuillan, J. "Consolidation and Outsourcing: Stepping Stones to Broadband." *Business Communications Review, 21* (11), (November 1991), pp. 19-20.

Mead, T. "Will Your Job Be Outsourced?" *Datamation*, (December 15, 1990), p. 104.

Mehling, H. "Options for Outsourcing Network Management Vary." *Client/Server Computing*, (February 1994), pp. 77-79.

Melymuka, K. "Is There Life After Outsourcing?" *Computerworld*, (May 16, 1994), pp. 89-93.

Messmer, E. "Internet Group Plans to Outsource U.S. Backbone." *Network World*, (March 14, 1994), p. 1.

Messmer, E. "Outsourcing the Way to Go?" *Network World*, (October 12, 1992), p. 44.

Moad, J. "Cover Story — Management." *Datamation*, (February 15, 1993), pp. 21-26.

Moad, J. "Shock Therapy Cures Fossilitis." *Datamation*, (June 1, 1994), pp. 57-59.

Molloy, M. "CMA '91 Survey Spotlights Technology, Mgmt. Issues." *Network World, 8* (41), (October 14, 1991), pp. 27, 29.

Moore, S. "Unocal's Outsourcing Decision Stirs Up Networking Operations." *Computerworld*, (November 14, 1994), p. 8.

Morken, C. "Outsourcing: Worst Nightmare or Useful Idea?" *Communications News*, (February 1993), p. 38.

Morris, A.M. "Trends Toward Integrating IS Technology." *Capacity Management Review, 20* (3), (March 1992), pp. 1-3.

Mulqueen, J.T. "BT Scales Back on Outsourcing Service." *Communications Week*, (September, 23, 1991), p. 5.

Nash, K.S. "Del Monte Feeds EDS its IS Operations." *Computerworld*, (November 9, 1992), p. 12.

Pastore, R. "One Cost Center, Slightly Used." *CIO,* (July 1992), pp. 31-34.

Pastore, R. "Pan Am to Go Outsourcing Route." *Computerworld,* (April 8, 1991), pp. 1, 96.

Pastore, R. "Short Terms of Agreement." *CIO,* (December 1, 1993), pp. 54-60.

Polilli, S. "Is Outsourcing a Bargain?" *Software Magazine,* (March 1993), pp. 36, 40.

Pounsett, D. "Outsourcing Battle." *Computing Canada, 18* (6), (March 16, 1992), p. 11.

Powell, D. "To Outsource or Not to Outsource?" *Networking Management,* (February 1993), pp. 56, 58, 60, 61.

Quinn, J., Doorley, T.L., and Paquette, P.C. "Beyond Products: Services-based Strategy." *Harvard Business Review,* (March-April 1990), pp. 58-60, 64-67.

Radding, A. "The Economics of Outsourcing." *Bank Management, 67* (9), (September 1991), pp. 20-27.

Randall, H.L. "Contract Logistics: Should Your Company Outsource?" *Corporate Controller, 3* (6), (July/August 1991), pp. 7-11, 30.

Randall, H.L. "Outsourcing Logistics in Europe." *Journal of European Business, 3* (2), (November/December 1991), pp. 21-26.

Recciuti, M. "Outsourcing as a Survival Tactic." *Datamation,* (April 15, 1994), pp. 48-51.

Rinaldi, D. "Go Outside? Why Should We? Outsourcing Can Be a Tough Sell to an IT Staff." *Client/Server Computing,* (July 1994), p. 26.

Robinson, M.A. "Decentralize and Outsource: Dial's Approach to MIS Improvement." *Management Accounting,* (September 1991), pp. 27-31.

Roussel, A.M. "MDNS: In-House Management of Outsourced Networks." *Data Communications,* (July 1992), pp. 78-80, 84-85.

Sandy S. "Smaller Staffs and Budgets Boost FM Outsourcing." *The Office,* (August 1993), p. 28.

Schatz, W. "Get Ready for Bail Out Sourcing." *Computerworld,* (January 25, 1993), pp. 57-58.

Schreider, T. "The Effect of Outsourcing on Disaster Recovery." *Enterprise Systems Journal,* (February 1993), pp. 82-83.

Schwartz, J. "Ordering Out for IS." *CIO, 5* (7), (February 1992), p. 18.

Schwartz, J. "Outsource Fallout." *Communications Week,* (August 13, 1990), p. 1.

Scrupski, S. "Boston Rocks Outsourcing." *Datamation,* (June 1, 1994), p. 34.

Scrupski, S. "Outsourcing: It Could Be Good." *Datamation,* (June 15, 1994), p. 32.

Semilof, M. "Brokerages Go Out of House." *Communications Week,* (June 10, 1991), p. 38.

Semilof, M. "Outsourcing Rule: Know Your Customers." *Communications Week*, (February 3, 1992), p. 25.

Sharp, B. "Outsourcing Branches Out." *CFO*, (December 1993), pp. 55-57.

Sharpe, A. "Some Legal Aspects of Outsourcing." *Australian Accountant, 61* (9), (October 1991), pp. 70-73.

Sherizen, S. "Protecting Information in a Changing Corporate Environment: Downsizing, Outsourcing and Mergers." The 12th Annual Conference on Control, Audit & Security of Information Systems: Meeting the Challenge of Multi-Platform Environments, Session G33.

Shulman, R.E. "DP Outsourcing: A Resource in Your Company's Future?" *Supermarket Business, 46* (10), (October 1991), pp. 25-26.

Sinensky, A. and Wasch, R. S. "Understanding Outsourcing: A Strategy for Insurance Companies." *Journal of Systems Management, 43* (1), (January 1992), pp. 32-33, 36.

Stewart, A. "How to Get the Most Out of Outsourcing." *Communications News*, (February 1993), p. 39.

Suh, R. "Guaranteeing That Outsourcing Serves Your Business Strategy." *Information Strategy: The Executive's Journal, 8* (3), (Spring 1992), pp. 39-42.

Sullivan, D. "Systematics Grows by 'Outsourcing'." *Financier, 15* (8), (August 1991), pp. 47-49.

Systematics Outsourcing IS Deal in the Bank. "Management shorts." *Computerworld*, (August 26, 1991), p. 49.

Thomas, S.D. "Outsourcing: Solution for the 1990s or Just Another Buzzword?" *Financial Managers' Statement, 13* (6), (November/December 1991), pp. 10-12, 35.

Turner, M.J. "The First Step to Outsourcing: Look Within." *Data Communications, 21* (1), (January 1992), pp. 23-23.

Turner, M. and Juneau, L. "Crafting a Net Outsourcing Strategy." *Network World, 9* (7) ,(February 17, 1992), pp. 1, 31-36.

Valovic, T., Wang, G., Mandela, A., and Clark, C. "Telecommunications Trends: A Yankee Group Roundtable." *Telecommunications*, (April 1990), pp. 31-36.

Verschoor, C.C. "Evaluating Outsourcing of Internal Auditing." *Management Accounting, 73* (8), (February 1992), pp. 27-30.

Wagner, J. "Factors in the Outsourcing Decision." *Journal of End User Computing*, 6(2), (Spring 1994), pp. 27-31.

Walter, U. "Outsourcing Offers Obvious Benefits, But Beware of 'Subtle Disadvantages'." *Networking Management*, (March 3, 1993), p. 8.

Welch, J.A. and Nayak, P.R. "Strategic Sourcing: A Progressive Approach to the Make-or-Buy Decision." *Academy of Management Executive, 6* (1), (February, 1992), pp. 23-31.

Wexler, J. "Outsourcing is Everywhere." *CFO*, (December 1994), p. 23.

Wexler, J. "Smartsourcing: Get the Most from Service Vendors." *Datamation*, (December 1, 1994), pp. 38-44.

Wexler, J. "Users Warm to Outsourcing." *Network World,* (November 28, 1994), p. 31.

Wilder, C. "Aerospace CIOs Differ on Outsourcing." *Computerworld,* (October 14, 1991), p. 71

Wilder, C. "An Ounce of Outsourcing and a Dash of Downsizing." *Computerworld,* (August 20, 1990), p. 10.

Wilder, C. "Banking Giant Buys Into Outsourcing." *Computerworld,* (November 11, 1991), pp. 1, 108.

Wilder, C. "80% Satisfied with Outsourcing, Survey Says." *Computerworld,* (January 27, 1992), p. 77.

Wilder, C. "Giant Firms Join Outsourcing Parade." *Computerworld,* (September 30, 1991), pp. 1, 91.

Wilder, C. "IBM Users Get Outsource Itch." *Computerworld,* (March 4, 1991), pp. 1, 83.

Wilder, C. "IBM's Outsourcing Unit Scores." *Computerworld,* (August 12, 1991), p. 87.

Wilder, C. "Mellon Reviews Outsourcing Role." *Computerworld,* (March 2, 1992), p. 20.

Wilder, C. "Survey Uncovers Resistance to Outsourcing." *Computerworld,* (June 10, 1991), p. 55.

Wilder, C. and Hildebrand, C. "Faster! Better! Cheaper! Now!" *Computerworld, 25* (51), (December 23, 1991/January 2, 1992), pp. 2-6.

Wilder, C. and Margolis, N. "Outsourcing's Hidden Cost Bite." *Computerworld,* (September 24, 1990), pp. 1, 12.

Williamson, M. "Outsourcing: The Decision." *CIO, 5* (2), (October 15, 1991), pp. 24-35.

Williamson, M. "Outsourcing: The Vendors." *CIO, 5* (2), (October 15, 1991), pp. 38-40.

Zahler, R. "Clear Performance Rules Ease Outsourcing Hassles." *Network World,* (April 6, 1992), pp. 29, 32.

Zahler, R. "Identifying the Key Issues for Assessing Outsourcing (Part 1)." *Network World, 9* (13), (March 30, 1992), pp. 21, 23.

Downsizing

Alzua, R. "Downsizing Means More Work." *ISSA Access, Inc., 5* (2) , (2nd quarter, 1992), pp. 16-17.

Anthes, G. "Downsizing NASA Plans Data Megacenter." *Computerworld,* (April 11, 1994), p. 6.

Anthes, G. "Feds to Downsize with IT." *Computerworld,* (September 13, 1993), p. 1.

Anthes, G. "Message to Federal IS Execs: Time to Think Downsizing." *Computerworld,* (September 2, 1991), p. 1.

Asbrand, D. "Downsizing Poses a Delicate Staffing Question: Should Corporations Retrain or Replace Their Mainframe Support Employees?" *Infoworld,* (March 1, 1993), p. 47.

Bloom, E.P. "Getting Down." *Computerworld,* (August 10, 1992), pp. 69-72.

Bolles, G.A. "Less Bandwidth Can Greatly Reduce Your Wide Area Communications Costs." *Network Computing,* (September 1991), pp. 56-59.

Booker, E. "IS Managers Admit Downsizing Fears." *Computerworld*, (March 23, 1992), pp. 59-60.

Bozman, J.S. "Downsizing on Slow Road Until 1996." *Computerworld*, (February 14, 1994), p. 8.

Bozman, J.S. "Downsizing, Rightsizing, Somethingsizing." *Computerworld*, (December 28, 1992/January 4, 1993), pp. 6-7.

Bozman, J.S. "Giving Downsizing the Hard Sell." *Computerworld*, (March 23, 1992), pp. 105-106.

Buerger, D. "A Critical Look at Downsizing Applications." *Communications Week*, (January 18, 1993), p. 40.

Campbell, J.E. and Mohan, N. "The Impact of Corporate Downsizing on Internal Auditing." *Internal Auditing*, (Spring 1992), pp. 3-9.

Chivis, A. and Geyer, J. "Think Again." *Corporate Computing*, (August 1994), p. 43.

Currid, C. "Downsizing Some Egos in MIS May be the First Step to Change." *InfoWorld*, (October 28, 1991), p. 54.

Cusack, S. "Downsizing Brings Unexpected Bonus." *Computerworld*, (January 6, 1992), p. 31.

DeBalko, J. "Peer to Peer." *Infoworld*, (July 13, 1992), p. 45.

"DoD's Strassmann: The Politics of Downsizing." *Datamation*, (October 15, 1992), pp. 107-110.

Dostert, M. "Users Bring Downsizing Demands to Exposition." *Computerworld*, (February 22, 1993), p. 16.

Eckerson, W. "Hidden Costs May Come With Downsizing Savings." *Network World*, (June 29, 1992), pp. 41-43.

Eckerson, W. "Personnel Concerns Need Attention When Downsizing." *Network World*, (January 13, 1992), pp. 23-24.

Eckerson, W. "Survey: Downsizing Taking Root in Corporate America." *Network World*, (March 9, 1992), pp. 1, 43.

Faegre, D. "Lessons From a Seasoned Downsizer." *Network World*, (November 16, 1992), p. 74.

Francett, B. "Downsized Financial APPS Challenge DBMS." *Software Magazine*, (December, 1993), pp. 77-83, 88.

Frank, H. "The Downside of Downsizing." *Networking Management*, (December 1992), pp. 82-84.

Gantz, J. "The Cooperative Computing Fire Ignites." *Networking Management*, (June 1992), pp. 74, 73.

Gantz, J. "Dinosaurs Should Beware: The Future is in Downsizing." *Infoworld*, (September 23, 1991), p. 101.

Gerber, B. "The Upside and Downside of Downsizing." *Network Computing*, (January 1991), pp. 39, 42, 44-46.

Gerber, B., Schlesinger, L., Lutz, D., and Bing, G. "Stability, Security, The Key to Downsizing." *Network Computing*, (January 1991), pp. 47-50, 52-53, 56.

Glass, B. "Technology is Not a Downsizing Cure-All." *Infoworld*, Vol: 14, Iss: 6, (February 10, 1992), p. 73.

Glassman, H. "Think Twice Before You Topple the Control Tower." *Computerworld*, (November 2, 1992), p. 33.

Greenberg, E.R. "The Latest AMA Survey on Downsizing." *Personnel,* (October 1989), pp. 38-44.

Greenstein, I. "The Sinking Mainframe Succumbs to Downsizing." *Networking Management,* (February 1992), pp. 21, 22, 24, 25.

Gruhn, M. "How Vendors Can Die From Downsizing." *Computerworld,* (January 25, 1993), p. 29.

Haight, T. "Daring to Downsize." *Network Computing,* (January 1991), pp. 59-69.

Huff, S.L. "You and the Computer — Information Technology and the Future Organization." *Business Quarterly,* (Summer 1989), pp. 94-96.

"Inside Job: A Look at Vendor Vision." *Computerworld,* (March 15, 1993), p. 109.

Jaben, J. "Downsizing Shapes Corporate Real Estate." *National Real Estate Investor,* Vol: 34, Iss: 3, (March 1992), pp. 77-84.

Kelly, D. "Breaking the News: How to Tell Your Staff About a Corporate Downsize." *Computerworld,* (November 28, 1994), p. 125.

Kiely, T. "Keeping up With the Ins and Outs." *CIO,* (April 15, 1992), pp. 34, 38, 39, 42.

Kiely, T. "Nuts and Bolts." *CIO,* (April 15, 1992), pp. 48-49.

King, S. "After Downsizing: Overcoming Client-Server Chaos." *Data Communications,* (May 21, 1994), pp. 52-60.

Klein, T.P. "How to Avoid the Five Biggest Downsizing Errors." *Computerworld,* (June 11, 1990), pp. 91-93.

LaPlante, A. "Decentralizing Systems is not the Best Solution for Everyone." *Infoworld*, (March 9, 1992), p. 57.

Leinfuss, E. "IS Managers Explain Benefits of Downsizing." *Computerworld*, (July 29, 1991), p. 73.

Leinfuss, E. "Training in the Age of Downsizing." *Computerworld*, (January 25, 1993), p. 77.

Letendre, A. "Honey, I Shrunk the Employees Today — Welcome to the Age of Downsizing." *Hartford Courant*, (May 22, 1994), Section C.

Louderback, J. "I've Been Downsizing So Long that it Looks Like Upsizing to Me." *PC Week*, (April 4, 1994), p. 110.

Lyons, D. "In, Out or Both?" *Computerworld*, (July 13, 1992), pp. 69-71.

Molloy, M. "Diversification Can Protect Managers From Downsizing." *Network World*, (February 10, 1992), p. 3.

Molloy, M. "Downsizing to LANs Not Easy, Users Say." *Network World*, (July 8, 1991), pp. 21-22.

Molloy, M. "Dunkin' Donuts Wins Through Downsizing." *Network World*, (July 15, 1991), pp. 27, 30.

Molloy, M. "Leaner Cost Structure Drives Downsizing." *Client/Server Computing*, (February 1994), p. 24.

Morris, R.M. "Corporate Downsizing From a Management Planning Perspective." *IM*, (September/October 1989), p. 2-5.

Nash, J. "Downsizing Focus Shifts to Impact IS Function." *Computerworld*, (September 16, 1991), p. 4.

Nash, K.S. "Del Monte Reaps Fruits of IS Overhaul." *Computerworld*, (October 19, 1992), pp. 1, 12.

O'Leary, J. Computer Security Institute. "Securing the Downsize Platform." 19th Annual Computer Security Conference & National Exhibition, Chicago, IL, (November 16-18, 1992), pp. 2-35.

O'Leary, M. "Hearts and Minds." *CIO*, (April 15, 1992), pp. 44, 46.

O'Leary, M. "Means to an End." *CIO*, (April 15, 1992), pp. 54-56.

Pastore, R. "The Power of Positive." *CIO*, (October 1, 1992), pp. 30-36.

Peltier, T.R. "Hard Times: Infosecurity and Downsizing." *ISPNews*, (July/August 1992), p. 25.

Peri, R.[a] "Big 3 Adapt to 'Small' Trend." *Communications Week*, (February 1, 1993), p. 19.

Peri, R. [b] "Tuning the Team for a New Game." *Communications Week*, (February 1, 1993), pp. 21-23.

Peri, R. [c] "Which Path is Best?" *Communications Week*, (February 1, 1993), pp. 11-18.

Peri, R. [d] "Down to Savings." *Communications Week*, (February 1, 1993), pp. 5-8.

Peri, R. [e] "Filling the Gaps." *Communications Week*, (February 1, 1993), pp. 27-32.

Radding, A. "Dirty Downsizing." *Computerworld*, (August 10, 1992), pp. 65-67.

Radding, A. "Downsizing Without the Fuss." *Computerworld,* (November 30, 1992), pp. 81-82.

Rinaldi, D. and Desmond J. "Exploring Downsizing's Hidden Costs." *Software Magazine,* (March 1993), pp. 62-66.

Savage, J.A. "Failed Merger Spawns Downsizing Plan." *Computerworld,* (September 16, 1991), p. 50.

Scannell, E. "IBM Hosts Dounsize Via Objects." *Computerworld,* (July 11, 1994), pp. 1, 12.

Schwartz, J. "Downsizing: Users Exercise Patience." *Communications Week,* (October 19, 1992), pp. 1, 70.

Scott, K. "NetWare on Downsizing Fast Track." *Infoworld,* (February 10, 1992), pp. 61, 63-64.

Scott, M.E. "A Downside of Downsizing." *Computerworld,* (September 30, 1991), p. 62.

Seadle, M. "How Not to Downsize." *Enterprise Systems Journal,* (March 1994), pp. 10-16.

Semilof, M. "People Issues in Downsizing." *Communications Week,* (October 14, 1991), p. 18.

Sharp, B. "Where to Find Expert Help for Downsizing." *Datamation,* (September 1, 1992), pp. 61, 62, 64.

Sirkin, B. "Few Account for Hidden Costs of Downsizing." *PC Week,* (June 3, 1991), p. 65.

Slater, D. "Mainframe Firms Feel Downsizing Heat." *Computerworld,* (October 26, 1992), p. 153.

Thayer, W. "20 Do's and Don'ts of Cost Cutting." *Progressive Grocer,* (May 1991), pp. 67-70.

Thress, S.C. and Pegolo, S.R. "Auditing in a Microcomputer Environment." *Internal Auditing,* (Fall 1991), pp. 82-87.

Van C. "Downsizing Creates Need For Upscaling Security." *Bank Technology News,* (October 1992), pp. 5-7.

Wagner, J. "The Temporary in an Era of Downsizing." *Office,* Vol: 115, Iss: 1, (January 1992), p. 38.

Walbert, L. "Tales From the Survivors." *Treasury & Risk Management,* (May-June 1994), pp. 20-27.

Wexler, J.M. and Klett, S.P. Jr. "Sun Life Walks Down/Upsizing Line." *Computerworld,* (December 6, 1993), pp. 61, 63.

Whitman, R. "Puzzled by Computer Downsizing?" *Digital Update,* (January 1993), Special Advertising Section.

Wilder, C. "CIOs Say Downsizing Is In the Cards." *Computerworld,* (May 13, 1991), p. 65.

Wilder, C. "Users: Downsizing Gain is Worth the Pain." *Computerworld,* (October 14, 1991), p. 4.

Willett, S. "Vendors Seek Third-party Support for Downsizing." *Infoworld,* (July 26, 1993), p. 24.

Yarborough, W. J. "Emerging Network Strategies for Corporate Downsizing." *INTE NET,* (February 1993), pp. 49-50, 58.

Reengineering

Alter, A. "Japan, Inc. Embraces Change." *Computerworld*, (March 7, 1994), pp. 24-25.

Alter, A. "Reengineering Tops the List Again." *Computerworld*, (January 31, 1994), p. 8.

Anthes, G. "Pentagon Wields IS Strategic Weapon." *Computerworld*, (June 8, 1992), pp. 1, 20.

Ballou, M.C. "Market for Reengineering Tools Burgeons." *Computerworld*, (February 7, 1994), p. 95.

Barber, N. "EDI II and Reengineering: A Design Approach." *EDI World*, (May 1994), pp. 20-22.

Barr, S. "Elizabeth Arden Gets a Makeover." *CFO*, (December 1994), pp. 73-75.

Barr, S. "When System Change Means Process Change." *CFO*, (August 1993), pp. 37-45.

Barrett, J. "Process Visualization: Getting the Vision Right is Key." *Information Systems Management*, (Spring 1994), pp. 14-23.

Bashein, B., Markus, L., and Riley, P. "Preconditions for BPR Success and How to Prevent Failures." *Information Systems Management*, (Spring 1994), pp. 7-13.

Booker, E. "Bank Launches Major Client/Server Overhaul." *Computerworld*, (February 7, 1994), p. 1.

Booker, E. "White-Collar Workflow: Beyond the Factory Floor." *Computerworld*, (March 1994), pp. 28-32.

Buchanan, L. "A Process-Change All-Star Team." *CIO*, (March 15, 1994), pp. 46-52.

Cafasso, R. "Rethinking Reengineering." *Computerworld*, (March 15, 1993), p. 102.

Canton, A. "BPR: The Arguments Every CIO Hears." *Information Systems Management*, (Spring 1994), pp. 87-89.

Champy, J. "Reengineering: An Ambitious Agenda." *CIO*, (February 1, 1994), pp. 24-26.

Champy, J.A. "Grand Designs — Reengineering Will be More Important Than Ever Next Year — and Harder to Do." *CIO*, (January 1993), pp. 26.

Connolly, D. "Software Reengineering." *Enterprise Systems Journal*, (March 1994), pp. 44-51.

Couger, J.D., Flynn, P., and Hellyer, D. "Enhancing the Creativity of Reengineering." *Information Systems Management*, (Spring 1994), pp. 24-29.

Cypress, H.L. "Reengineering." *OR/MS Today*, (February 1994), pp. 18-20 & 22-29.

Dailey, L. "Reengineering: Cliche` or Concept?" *EDI World*, (May 1994), p. 6.

Dejong, J. "Reengineering the Workplace: Marketing." *Computerworld*, (February 7, 1994), pp. 113-119.

Donovan, M. "10 Tips for Reengineering Manufacturing." *Management Accounting*, (July 1994), pp. 12, 13.

Drucker, P.F. "Restructuring Middle Management." *Modern Office Technology*, (January 1993), p. 8.

Eliot, L. "Don't Get Caught with Your Pants Down." *Computerworld,* (March 28, 1994), p. 92.

Eskow, D. "Make More Money." *Corporate Computing,* (July 1992), p. 41.

Francis, B. "Getting Ready for PC RAID." *Datamation,* (May 15, 1992), pp. 53-56.

Frye, C. "Imaging Proves Catalyst for Reengineering." *Client/Server Computing,* (November 1994), pp. 53-59.

Gantz, J. "Surviving the Reengineering Revolution." *Network Management,* (January 1993), pp. 17-24.

Hallberg, C. and DeFiore, R. "Reengineering the Information Services function." *SIM Network,* VIIII(III), 1, (1994), 3-4.

Halper, M. "Microsoft May Fit Levi Strauss Reengineering Scheme." *Computerworld,* (April 18, 1994), p. 26.

Halper, M. "Outsources Sharpen Reengineering Skills." *Computerworld,* (April 11, 1994), p. 30.

Hammer, J. and J. Champy. *Reengineering the Corporation: A Manifesto for Business Revolution.* New York: Harper Collins, (1993).

Hammer, M. "Making the Quantum Leap." *Beyond Computing,* (March/April 1992), pp. 11-14.

Hanna, M. "Reengineering Aims for Legacy Salvation." *Software Magazine,* (September 1993), pp. 41-50.

Harris, L.R. and Aikins, J. "KBS as Automated Edge." *Software Magazine,* (February 1993), p. 8.

Hoffman, T. "Reengineering Begins at Home." *Computerworld,* (September 5, 1994), p. 40.

Hoffman, T. "Ryder Reengineers for the Road." *Computerworld,* (March 21, 1994), p. 12.

Horton, A. "Reengineering Means Change, Success, and Change." *Computerworld,* (April 4, 1994), p. 33.

Jebber, E. "Getting Started: Why Not Reengineer the IS Process Itself?" CIO Perspectives Series The Process of IT: Organizing for Success, Boca Raton Resort & Club, Boca Raton, Florida, (October 11-14, 1992).

Kalthoff, R. "Reengineering: Just Fad or Benchmarking a New Era?" *Imaging World,* (February 1994), p. 1.

Kendall, J. "End-user Reengineering: Breaking the Rules Systems Developers Wrote." *Journal of End User Computing,* 6(2), (Spring 1994), pp. 24-26.

King, J. [a] "Rip it Up!" *Computerworld,* (July 15, 1991), pp. 55-56.

King, J. [b] "Reengineering Puts Progressive on the Spot." *Computerworld,* (July 15, 1991), p. 58.

King, J. [c] "Do You Really Need a Reengineering Consultant?" *Computerworld,* (July 15, 1991), p. 56.

King, J. "Firm Gets Mixed Results in Reengineering Project." *Computerworld,* (November 28, 1994), p. 93.

King, J. "Reengineering Slammed." *Computerworld,* (June 13, 1994), p. 1.

King, W. "Process Reengineering: The Strategic Dimensions." *Information Systems Management,* (Spring 1994), pp. 71-73.

Kirvan, P. "Should You Reengineer Telecommunications?" *Communications News,* (May 1994), p. 56.

Klein, M. "Captains Courageous." *CIO,* (October 15, 1994), pp. 24-26.

Klein, M. "Reengineering Methodologies and Tools." *Information Systems Management,* (Spring 1994), pp. 30-35.

Klott-Dempsey, P. and Noyes, E. "Reengineering the Army Procurement Process." *EDI World,* (October 1994), pp. 38-39.

LaPlante, A. "Insurance Firm's Pen Computing Project Prompts Reengineering." *Infoworld,* (January 18, 1993), p. 53.

Lindquist, C. "Touchdown!" *Computerworld,* (June 8, 1992), pp. 93-94.

Louderback, J. "The CSIRD Methodology." *DBMS,* (June 1991), pp. 46-65.

Maglitta, J. "American Express Claims Reengineering Saves $1.8B." *Computerworld,* (September 26, 1994), p. 12.

Maglitta, J. "Glass Act." *Computerworld,* (January 17, 1994), pp. 80-84, 88.

Maglitta, J. "One On One: Michael Hammer." *Computerworld,* (January 24, 1994), pp. 84-86.

Maglitta, J. "Reengineering the Workplace: Best Face Forward." *Computerworld,* (May 16, 1994), pp. 100-107.

Maglitta, J. "Tool Time: Reengineering the Workplace." *Computerworld*, (November 21, 1994), pp. 96-105.

Mallach, E. "Reengineering: Read Before Investing." *Computerworld*, (March 14, 1994), p. 84.

Margolis, N. "Reengineering Gets Real." *Computerworld*, (January 18, 1993), p. 69.

Margolis, N. "Reengineering: It's Great, Whatever It Is." *Computerworld*, (June 29, 1992), p. 87.

Margolis, N. "Voices of Experience." *Computerworld*, (December 28, 1992/January 4, 1993), pp. 16-17.

McCusker, T. "EDI II To The Rescue." *Datamation*, (May 15, 1992), pp. 60, 62, 64.

Menagh, M. "Crossfire." *Computerworld*, (February 28, 1994), pp. 87-90.

Mentz, S. L. "The Reengineers: A Guide for the Perplexed." *CFO*, (October 1994), pp. 43-54.

Middlebrook, W. "Reengineering the Procurement Process." *EDI World*, (May 1994), pp. 46-48.

Moad, J. "Reengineering: Report From the Trenches." *Datamation*, (March 15, 1994), pp. 36-40.

Monteleone, F. "Reengineering: Don't Miss the Train." *Computerworld*, (January 31, 1994), p. 35.

Morris, J. "Brave New Bank." *CFO*, (March 1994), pp. 26-34.

Musthaler, L. "Reengineering Tools." *Network World*, (April 4, 1994), p. 47.

Pastore, R. "Designing a Brand New Shoe." *CIO*, (March 1, 1994), pp. 42-50.

Pleroa, J. "The Distribution Dilemma: Annual CIO Survey — Reengineering." *CIO*, (May 1, 1994), pp. 30-34.

Ray, G. "Just How Do You Spell Reengineering." *Computerworld*, (March 15, 1993), p. 98.

Reynolds, B. "The Rap on Reengineering." *Computerworld*, (September 26, 1994), pp. 118-121.

Ryan, A.J. "Is Reengineering Right For You?" *Computerworld*, (July 15, 1991), p. 57.

Ryan, H. "Reinventing the Business." *Information Systems Management*, (Spring, 1994), pp. 77-79.

Santosus, M. "Pursuing the Perfect Pitch." *CIO*, (June 1, 1994), pp. 30-37.

Santosus, M. "Rethinking the Distributive Principle." *CIO*, (December 1, 1993), pp. 32-40.

Schatz, W. "What is Reengineering, Anyway?" *Computerworld*, (August 31, 1992), pp. 97-98.

Scheier, R.L. "Hold On to Your Hat: Surviving Yet Another IT Reorg." *PC Week*, (December 12, 1994), p. 21.

Snell, N. "Making IS Accessible." *Datamation*, (May 15, 1992), pp. 79-82.

Staff, "After Reengineering: Taking Care of Business." *Datamation*, (October 15, 1994), pp. 40-44.

Stockton, T. "Reengineering Begins with Revitalization." *EDI World*, (May, 1994), pp. 28-32.

Thomas, M.L. "Reengineering: The Frantic Discovery of the Obvious." *Modern Office Technology*, (January 1993), p. 48.

Tieman, L. "Reengineering Product Development for the '90s." CIO Perspectives Series The Process of it: Organizing for Success, Boca Raton Resort & Club, Boca Raton, Florida, (October 11-14, 1992).

Wang, S. "Object-Oriented Modeling of Business Processes." *Information Systems Management*, (Spring 1994), pp. 36-43.

Wexler, J. "Reengineering Report Cards." *Computerworld*, (July 6, 1992), p. 51.

Whitmore, S. "Reengineering: Pyrrhic Panacea or Ugly Necessity?" *PC Week*, (December 13, 1993), p. 81.

Wreden, N. "Business Reengineering: The Technology Imperative." *Datamation*, (March 1, 1994), pp. 52-58.

Wreden, N. "Reengineering: The Ultimate Test of Skill." *Beyond Computing*, (May - June, 1994), pp. 30-36.

Partnering

Anderson, J.C. and Narus, J.A. "Partnering as a Focused Market Strategy." *California Management Review*, (Spring 1991), pp. 95-113.

Baker, S.T. "Partnering: Contracting for the Future." *Cost Engineering*, Vol: 32, Iss: 4, (April 1990), pp. 7-12.

Davis, C. "Partnering in the 1990s." *Hospital Material Management Quarterly*, Vol: 12, No. 4, (August 1993), pp. 8-12.

Henricks, M. "The Power of Partnering." *Small Business Reports*, (June 1991), pp. 46-57.

Moore, C., Mosley, D., and Slagle, M. "Partnering: Guidelines for Win-Win Project Management." *Project Management Journal*, (March 1992), pp. 18-21.

Muhlestein, C.B. and Smith, J.D. "A Cost-effective Audit Partnership." *Internal Auditor*, (June 1991).

Yovovich, B.G. "Do's and Don'ts of Partnering." *Business Marketing*, (March 1992), pp. 38-39.

Yovovich, B.G. "Partnering at Its Best." *Business Marketing*, (March 1992), pp. 36-37.

Rightsizing

Bell, R. and Louis, Z. "Rightsizing Computer Output." *Enterprise Systems Journal*, (September 1993), pp. 90-92.

Carlini, J. "Wrong Management Style for Rightsizing." *Network World*, (February 7, 1994), p. 31.

Davenport, T.H., Hammer, M., and Metsisto, T.J. "How Executives Can Shape Their Company's Information Systems." *Harvard Business Review*, (March-April 1989), pp. 130-134.

Dillard, J. "Rightsize, Don't Wrongsize." *Treasury & Risk Management*, (May-June 1994), p. 6.

Ehrenreich, D. "Rightsizing: Redistributing the Electronic Workload." *INTE NET*, (June 1992), pp. 59-61.

Goldberg, J. "The Right Fit." *CIO*, (March 15, 1994), pp. 24-26.

Haight, T. "Rightsizing." *Network Computing*, (February 1993), pp. 87-97.

Herbert, S.M. "Rightsizing Information Systems in the Real Estate Industry." *Real Estate Accounting & Taxation*, Vol: 6, Iss: 4, (Winter 1992), pp. 76-79.

Kanin-Lovers, J. "Pay After Rightsizing." *Journal of Compensation & Benefits*, Vol: 7, Iss: 2, (September/October 1991), pp. 51-54.

Klasnic, J. "Rightsizing the In-Plant." *In-Plant Printer*, (December 1993), pp. 20, 24.

Koenig, K.K. "Rightsizing." *Bank Mgmt*, Vol: 66, Iss: 6, (June 1990), pp. 38-42.

Kolodziej, S. "Rightsizing Rewrites Rules for Managing Performance." *Software Magazine*, (February 1994), pp. 51-57.

Mansell-Lewis, E. "Reed Open to Rightsizing." *Accountancy*, Vol: 109, Iss: 1182, (February 1992), pp. 102-103.

Meyer, D. "Learning to Rightsize." *Computerworld*, (October 24, 1994), p. 37.

Morse, S. "Rightsizing — Tailoring the Applications and the Platforms." *Network Computing*, (February 1993), pp. 63-77.

Radding, A. "Those Temptation Eyes." *Midrange Systems*, (March 25, 1994), p. 1.

Sacks, D. "Rightsizing Perspectives." *Enterprise Systems Journal*, (March 1994), pp. 91-95.

Schneider, J.D. "It Pays to Get Your Hands Dirty Rightsizing." *PC Week*, (November 16, 1992), p. 97.

Sheridan, J.H. "A Tool for Rightsizing." *Industry Week*, Vol: 238, Iss: 9, (May 1, 1989), pp. 54-55.

VanDame, M. "Midrange Systems: Rightsizing." *Supplement to Midrange Systems*, (November 9, 1993), pp. 2-24.

VanDame, M. "The Right Platform for Rightsizing Legs." *PC Week*, (May 2, 1994), p. 24.

VanDame, M. and Catchings, B. "Getting Ready for Rightsizing." *Corporate Computing*, (June 1994), p. 141.

Videtich, J. "Responding to Demands for Change." *Networking Management*, (June 1992), p. 70.

Wilder, C. "Bend Me, Shape Me." *Computerworld*, Vol: 24, Iss: 52, 53, (December 24, 1990/January 1, 1991), p. 14.

Auditing

"Avoiding Managerial Liability: Developing Corporate Strategies for Information Protection, Ethics and Privacy." April 26-27, Center for Business Ethics, Bentley College, Waltham, Mass. 02154, (617) 891-2981.

Betts, M. "Do Laws Protect Wireless Nets?" *Computerworld*, (June 17, 1991).

Betts, M. "Plumbing the Soul of IS: 'Computers and Society' Proponents Question Social Consequences of New Technology." *Computerworld*, (Oct. 29, 1990).

Casatelli, C. "Electronic Mail: Setting Ground Rules for Privacy." *Computerworld,* (March 18, 1991).

Computer Law Reporter. Suite 200, 1519 Connecticut Ave. NW, Washington, D.C. 20036, (202) 462-5755, Monthly publication covering computer law, including patents, copyright, privacy and criminal, civil and contract law.

Computer Law Strategist Leader. Leader Publications, Suite 900, 111 8th Ave., New York, N.Y. 10011, (800) 888-8300, Monthly newsletter that examines trends and actions from top law firms regarding computer cases.

De Maio, H.B. "Information Protection and Other Unnatural Acts: Every Manager's Guide to Keeping Vital Computer Data Safe and Sound." Amacom Books, 1992 ($24.95).

Information Systems Integrity. Technology Investment, Strategies Corp., 5 Speen St., Framingham, Mass. 01701, (508) 872-8200, Three-part series of reports on roles and responsibilities of end users and management in the integrity of a distributed information system.

Jurimetrics, Journal of Law, Science and Technology. Published quarterly, Computer Law Division, American Bar Association, 750 North Lake Shore Drive, Chicago, IL 60611, (312) 988-5000

Mize, B.R. "Vendor Audits." *Internal Auditor,* (August 1992), pp. 47-52.

Rohan, J.E. "Auditing Third-Party Risk." *Internal Auditing,* (Spring 1991), pp. 69-73.

Works Cited

Part 1
Managing the "New" Organization

Bradley, L. C. "Market Focus: The Key to Success." *Enterprise Systems Journal,* 96, (August 1992).

Davenport, T. H., et al., "How Executives Can Shape Their Company's Information Systems." *Harvard Business Review,* (March-April 1992), pp. 130-134.

Devanna, M. A. and Collins, E. G. C. (eds.). *The Portable MBA.* New York: John Wiley & Sons, (1990).

Drucker, P. F. "The Coming of the New Organization." *Harvard Business Review,* Vol. 66, No. 1, (Jan.-Feb. 1988), pp. 43-45.

Drucker, P. F. *Managing for the Future: The 1990s and Beyond,* New York: Truman Tally Books-Dutton, (1992).

Huff, S. L. "Computer Impacts on Organizations — Unanswered Questions." *Business Quarterly,* Vol. 51, No. 2, (November 1986), pp. 16-17.

Huff, S. L. "Information Technology and the Future Organization." *Business Quarterly,* (Summer 1989), pp. 94-96.

Keen, P. *Shaping the Future: Business Design Through Information Technology.* Boston: Harvard Business School Press, (1991).

Morris, R. M. "Corporate Downsizing from a Management Planning Perspective," *Information Management,* (September/October 1989), pp. 2-5.

Quinn, J. B. et al. "Beyond Products: Services-Based Strategy." *Harvard Business Review*, (March-April 1990), pp. 58-67.

Toffler, A. *Power Shift*. New York: Bantam Books, (1990).

Part 2 — Audit and Control of the "New" Organization

Outsourcing

Ambrosio, J. "Outsourcing at Southland: Best of Times, Worst of Times." *ComputerWorld*, (March 25, 1991), pp. 61.

Ambrosio, J. "Soul-Searching: Four Case Studies." *ComputerWorld*, (December 3, 1990), pp. 69-73.

Ambrosio, J. "Paine Webber Takes on New Outsourcing Role." *ComputerWorld*, (October 26, 1992), p. 4.

Anthes, G.H. "U.S. Firms Go Offshore for Cheap DP." *ComputerWorld*, (August 26, 1991), p. 1.

Anthes, G.H. "Outsourcing May Be Only Answer for Many." *ComputerWorld*, (March 25, 1991), pp. 51-54.

Anthes, G.H. "Feds Take Ride on Outsourcing Express." *ComputerWorld*, (May 17, 1993), p. 86.

Anthes, G.H. "HUD Set to Outsource IS." *ComputerWorld*, (December 3, 1990), p. 1.

Betts, M. "Study: Outsourcing Big in Banks' Future." *ComputerWorld*, (October 7, 1991), p. 8.

Bingham, S. "When You Care Enough To Need The Best." *Communications Week*, (November 1990), pp. 28-29.

Blair, D. "I Survived Outsourcing." *CIO,* (July 1990), pp. 20-22.

Booker, E. "Sun R&M Opts for Outsourcing." *ComputerWorld,* (May 1992), p. 12.

Booker, E. "BT Targets Multinational Outsourcing." *ComputerWorld,* (September 23, 1991), p. 95.

Brown, B. "Kodak Turns Net Over to IBM and DEC." *Network World,* (January 15, 1990), p. 1.

Burger, K. "To Outsource or Not to Outsource?" *Bank Systems and Technology,* (May 1991), pp. 31-32.

Coale, K. "British Petroleum Outsources IS." *Infoworld,* (February 3, 1992), p. 47

Condon, R. "CA, EDS Embroiled in Outsourcing Dispute." *ComputerWorld,* (April 11, 1994), p. 14.

Crenshaw, D. "Outsourcing: To Be? Or Not to Be?" *ComputerWorld,* (March 8, 1993), p. 120.

Crockett, B. "Critics Assail Global Outsource Ventures." *Network World,* (November 4, 1991), pp. 31, 33.

Cummings, J. "Bank Off-loads Data Center, Network Upgrade to Unisys." *Network World,* (October 12, 1992), pp. 51, 59.

Dickson, G.W. and Wetherbe, J.C. *The Management of Information Systems,* McGraw-Hill, (1985).

Duffy, C.A. "Hidden Costs Can Undermine Savings from Outsourcing." *ComputerWorld,* (November 18, 1991), p. 109.

Dykeman, J.B. "Farming It Out: A Viable Alternative." *Modern Office Technology,* (October 1991), p. 10.

Eckerson, W. "Workers Wage War Against Outsourcing by Filing Suit." *Network World,* (December 3, 1990), pp. 4, 70.

Eckerson, W. "IBM Forms Business Unit to Focus Outsourcing Efforts." *Network World,* (May 20, 1991), p. 4.

Eckerson, W. "Users Creating New Twists to Outsourcing." *Network World,* (February 24, 1992), pp. 21-22.

Eckerson, W. "CSC Grabs Up Giant Outsource Contract." *Network World,* (September 30, 1991), pp. 9, 47.

Eckerson, W. "Regaining Control After Outsourcing." *Network World,* (August 5, 1991), pp. 15-16.

Eckerson, W. "Outsourcing: Tending to the People Issues." *Network World,* (March 23, 1992), pp. 23, 26.

Evagora, A. "IBM Outsource Unit." *Communications Week,* (March 23, 1992), p. 26.

Fisher, S. "Study: Outsourcing Use to Decline." *Communications Week,* (March 15, 1993), p. 35.

Fitzgerald, M. "System Odyssey Leads to Outsourcing." *ComputerWorld,* (February 17, 1992), pp. 73, 76.

Fox, J. "Outsourcing Your Network." *PCToday,* (March 1991), pp. 16-21.

Franchi, M. "Outsourcing Adds Jobs." *Datamation,* (March 15, 1993), p. 82.

Frank, H. "Planning Your Outsourcing Strategy." *Networking Management,* (October 1991), pp. 42, 44, 45.

Friedberg, A.J. and Yarberry, Jr., W.A. "Audit Rights in an Outsource Environment." *Internal Auditor*, (August 1991), pp. 53, 57.

Friedman, R. "Outsourcing as a Way to Reduce Major Costs." *The Office*, (October 1991), pp. 70-72.

Frost, N. "Outsourcing: The Right Move For Today's Virtual Organization." *The Office*, (May 1993), pp. 40-41.

Gillooly, C. "Firms Retain Control of LAN Management." *Network World*, (June 24, 1991), pp. 1, 70.

Gilman, J. "Certification and Outsourcing Strategic Software." *AICCP Newsletter*, (July 1992), p. 5.

Guimaraes, T. and Stuart W. "Outsourcing for Novices." *ComputerWorld*, (June 8, 1992), pp. 89-91.

Haavind, R. "The Outsourcing Option." *CFO*, (November 1991), pp. 52-54.

Halper, M. "Hertz Talks With Outsourcer." *ComputerWorld*, (November 9, 1992), p. 12.

Halper, M. "Outsourcers Assess IBM Tactics." *ComputerWorld*, (November 30, 1992), p. 109.

Halper, M. "Armco Outsources to Genix." *ComputerWorld*, (April 26, 1993), p. 58.

Halper, M. "Texas Bank Sues EDS." *ComputerWorld*, (May 30, 1994), p. 8.

Halper, M. "EDS Wins Fight with One Texas Bank, Faces Another." *ComputerWorld*, (July 4, 1994), p. 32.

Harbison, T. "Seize the Customer Day." *ComputerWorld,* (November 30, 1992), pp. 77-79.

Hoewing, M.W. "The Outsource Option." *Association Management,* (February, 1992), pp. 37-40.

Hoffman, T. "Outsourcing Deal Proves Costly." *ComputerWorld,* (January 10, 1994), p. 14.

Horwitt, E. "Banker Signs $80M Contract with MCI." *ComputerWorld,* (May 10, 1993), p. 2.

Horwitt, E. "J.P. Morgan on Outsource Bandwagon." *ComputerWorld,* (February 17, 1992), p. 50.

Hudson, K. "Kodak Exec Relates Outsourcing Lessons." *Network World,* (December 17, 1990), pp. 27-28.

Jathanna, V. "Outsourcing." *CMA Magazine,* (December/January 1992), pp. 25-27.

Johnson, M. "Outsourcing Win for DEC." *ComputerWorld,* (August 26, 1991), pp. 1, 6.

Kiely, T. "The Wrong Goodbye." *CIO,* (September 1, 1992), pp. 34-43.

Kiely, T. "The Shape of Excellence." *CIO,* (August 1992), pp. 26-32.

King, J.L. and Nolan, R.L. "The Nolan Stage Model: A Debate," Twelfth International Conference on Information Systems. New York, (December 16-18, 1991).

LaPlante, A. "Decentralizing Systems is Not the Best Solution for Everyone." *Infoworld,* (March 9, 1992), p. 57.

Leinfuss, E. "How Outsourcing Impacts IS Managers." *ComputerWorld,* (September 16, 1991), p. 113.

Maglitta, J. "Mr. Fixit." *ComputerWorld,* (October 26, 1992), pp. 133-135.

Mangan, T. "Perspective: Question of Control." *Communications Week,* (June 24, 1991), p. 14.

Margolis, N. "UT Taps IBM for Outsourcing Project." *ComputerWorld,* (November 11, 1991), p. 10.

Margolis, N. "Outsourcing ISSC, Equifax Sign $650M Deal." *ComputerWorld,* (May 3, 1993), p. 12.

Margolis, N. "Outsourcing Is It at Diesel Technology." *ComputerWorld,* (May 27, 1991), p. 61.

Margolis, N. "Bank IS Fights Outsourcing Challenge." *ComputerWorld,* (June 1, 1992), p. 12

Margolis, N. "Anchor Bank Outsources IS." *ComputerWorld,* (April 13, 1992), p. 4.

Margolis, N. "Insurance Eyes Outsourcing." *ComputerWorld,* (November 23, 1992), p. 6.

Margolis, N. "IBM Unit Bags Bank Outsourcing Bucks." *ComputerWorld,* (September 23, 1991), p. 16

Margolis, N. "Outsourcing Boom Over? You Ain't Seen Nothin.'" *ComputerWorld,* (September 1992), p. 15.

McClelland, S. "Outsourcing: The Trend Continues." *Telecommunications,* (August 1992), pp. 31-32.

McCusker, T. "There is Life After Outsourcing." *Datamation,* (April 1, 1991), pp. 62-65.

Mead, T. "Will Your Job Be Outsourced?" *Datamation,* (December 15, 1990), p. 104.

Medina, D. "Farming Out the Networks." *Information Week,* (February 25, 1991), pp. 12-13.

Messmer, E. "Outsourcing the Way to Go?" *Network World,* (October 12, 1992), p. 41.

Middleton, T. "It's Time to Duel for Dollars." *Corporate Computing,* (June 1993), pp. 27-28.

Moad, J. "Outsourcing at First Fidelity Bank." *Datamation,* (February 15, 1993), pp. 21-27.

Morken, C. "Outsourcing: Worst Nightmare or Useful Idea?" *Communications News,* (February 1993), p. 38.

Mulqueen, J.T. "BT Scales Back on Outsourcing Service." *Communications Week,* (September 23, 1991), p. 5.

Nash, K.S. "Del Monte Feeds EDS its IS Operations." *ComputerWorld,* (November 9, 1992), p. 12.

Pastore, R. "For Sale: One Cost Center, Slightly Used." *CIO,* (July 1992), pp. 31-34.

Pastore, R. "Pan Am to Go Outsourcing Route." *ComputerWorld,* (April 8, 1991), pp. 1, 96.

Polilli, S. "Is Outsourcing a Bargain?" *Software Magazine,* (March 1993), pp. 36, 40.

Quinn, J.B.; Doorley, T.L. and Penny, C.P. "Beyond Products: Services-Based Strategy." *Harvard Business Review,* (March-April 1990), pp. 58-60, 64-67.

Ricciuti, M. "Outsourcing as a Survival Tactic." *Datamation,* (April 15, 1994), pp. 51.

Rizzo, T. "Do You Really Know What It All Means?" *Network Computing.*

Roussel, A. "MDNS: In-House Management of Outsourced Networks." *Data Communications,* (July 1992), pp. 78-84.

Salamone, S. "Survey: Drawing a Bead On Net Managers' Top Concerns." *Network World,* (June 3, 1991), pp. 1, 46, 103, 107.

Schwartz, J. "Outsource Fallout." *Communications Week,* (August 13, 1990), pp. 1, 49.

Schwartz, J. "Ordering Out for IS." *CIO,* (February 1992), p. 18.

Scrupski, S. "Boston Rocks Outsourcing." *Datamation,* (June 1, 1994), p. 34.

Semilof, M. "Brokerages Go Out Of House." *Communications Week,* (June 10, 1991), p. 38.

Stewart, A. "How to Get the Most Out of Outsourcing." *Communications News,* (February 1993), p. 39.

Stewart, A. "Outsourcing Rule: Know Your Customers." *Communications Week,* (February 3, 1992), p. 25.

Valovic, T., Wang, G., Mandela, A., Clarke, C. "Telecommunications Trends: A Yankee Group Roundtable." *Telecommunications,* (April 1990), pp. 31-36.

Wagner, J. "Factors in the Outsourcing Decision." *Journal of End User Computing,* (Spring 1994), pp. 27-31.

Wilder, C. "An Ounce of Outsourcing and a Dash of Downsizing." *ComputerWorld,* (August 20, 1990), p. 10.

Wilder, C. "Banking Giant Buys into Outsourcing." *ComputerWorld,* (November 11, 1991), pp. 1, 108.

Wilder, C. "80% Satisfied with Outsourcing, Survey Says." *ComputerWorld,* (January 27, 1992), p. 77.

Wilder, C, and Margolis, N. "Outsourcing's Hidden Cost Bite." *ComputerWorld,* (September 24, 1990), pp. 1, 12.

Wilder, C. "IBM's Outsourcing Unit Scores." *ComputerWorld,* (August 12, 1991), p. 87.

Wilder, C. "Giant Firms Join Outsourcing Parade." *ComputerWorld,* (September 30, 1991), pp. 1, 91.

Wilder, C. "IBM Users Get Outsource Itch." *ComputerWorld,* (March 4, 1991), pp. 1, 83

Wilder, C. "Mellon Reviews Outsourcing Role." *ComputerWorld,* (March 2, 1992), p. 20.

Wilder, C. "Survey Uncovers Resistance to Outsourcing." *ComputerWorld,* (June 10, 1991), p. 55.

Xenakis, J.J. "The Uncertainty of Outsourcing." *CFO,* (October 1992), pp. 75-76.

Xenakis, J.J. "Outsourcing: Threat or Salvation for Today's Telecom Professional." *Network Management*, (October 1990), pp. 25, 40.

Part 2
Downsizing

Anthes, G.H. "Message to Federal IS Execs: Time to Think Downsizing." *ComputerWorld*, (September 2, 1991), pp. 1, 99.

Asbrand, D. "Downsizing Poses a Delicate Staffing Question: Should Corporations Retrain or Replace Their Mainframe Support Employees?" *Infoworld*, (March 1, 1993), p. 47.

Bloom, E.P. "Getting Down." *ComputerWorld*, (August 10, 1992), pp. 69- 72.

Booker, E. "IS Managers Admit Downsizing Fears." *ComputerWorld*, (March 23, 1992), pp. 59-60.

Bozman, J.S. "Downsizing, Rightsizing, Somethingsizing." *ComputerWorld*, (December 28, 1992/January 4, 1993), pp. 6, 7.

Bozman, J.S. "Giving Downsizing the Hard Sell." *ComputerWorld*, (March 23, 1992), pp. 105-106.

Bozman, J.S. "Software Makers Fear Downsizing Toll." *ComputerWorld*, (October 26, 1992), pp. 1, 15.

Bucken, M. and Desmond, J. "Downsizing Saves Insurance Company $3 Million." *Software Magazine*, (July 18, 1993).

Buerger, D. "A Critical Look at Downsizing Applications." *Communications Week*, (January 18, 1993), p. 40.

Currid, C. "Downsizing Some Egos in MIS May be the First Step to Change." *ComputerWorld,* (October 28, 1991), p. 54.

Cusack, S. "Downsizing Brings Unexpected Bonus." *ComputerWorld,* (January 6, 1992), p. 31.

DeBalko, J. "InfoWorld IS Learns the Lessons of Downsizing From First-Hand Experience." *Infoworld,* (July 13, 1992), p. 45.

Dostert, M. "Users Bring Downsizing Demands to Exposition." *ComputerWorld,* (February 22, 1993), p. 16.

Eckerson, W. "Hidden Costs May Come with Downsizing Savings." *Network World,* (June 29, 1992), pp. 41-43.

Eckerson, W. "Personnel Concerns Need Attention When Downsizing." *Network World,* (January 13, 1992), pp. 23-24.

Faegre, D. "Lessons From a Seasoned Downsizer." *Network World,* (November 16, 1992), p. 74.

Frank, H. "The Downside of Downsizing." *Networking Management,* (December 1992), pp. 84, 82.

Gantz, J. "Dinosaurs Should Beware: The Future Is In Downsizing." *Infoworld,* (September 23, 1991), p. 101.

Greenberg, E.R. *Personnel,* (October 1989), pp. 38-44.

Greenstein, I. "The Sinking Mainframe Succumbs to Downsizing." *Networking Management,* (February 1992), pp. 21-25.

Grensing, L. "Downsizing: How to Do it Right." *Office Systems,* (May 1993), pp. 62-65.

Gruhn, M. "How Vendors Can Die from Downsizing." *ComputerWorld,* (January 25, 1993), p. 29.

Haight, T. "Daring to Downsize." *Network Computing,* (January 1991), pp. 59-69.

Halper, M. "Hertz Mulls Outsourcing Rescue." *ComputerWorld,* (June 22, 1992), pp. 1, 10.

Halper, M. "IBM Pilot Reduces Outsourcing Costs." *ComputerWorld,* (October 26, 1992), pp. 1, 16.

Halper, M. "Sabre Eyes Downsizing." *ComputerWorld,* (March 29, 1993), pp. 1, 10.

"Inside Job." *ComputerWorld,* (March 15, 1993), pp. 109-113.

Kiely, T. "Keeping Up with the Ins and Outs." *CIO,* (April 15, 1992), pp. 34, 38-39.

Kiely, T. "Nuts and Bolts." *CIO,* (April 15, 1992), pp. 48-49.

King, S. "After Downsizing: Overcoming Client-Server Chaos." *Data Communications,* (May 21, 1994), p. 3.

Korzeniowski, P. "To Downsize or to Outsource?" *Computer Networking,* (October 15, 1990), p. 21.

Leinfuss, E. "IS Managers Explain Benefits of Downsizing." *ComputerWorld,* (July 29, 1991), p. 73.

Leinfuss, E. "Training in the Age of Downsizing." *ComputerWorld,* (January 25, 1993), p. 77.

Lyons, D. "In, Out or Both?" *ComputerWorld,* (July 13, 1992), pp. 69-71.

Miller, S. "The Downsides of Downsizing." *Chief Information Officer Journal,* (May/June 1993), pp. 25-29.

Molloy, M. "Diversification Can Protect Managers from Downsizing." *Network World,* (February 10, 1992), p. 33.

Molloy, M. "Downsizing to LANs Not Easy, Users Say." *Network World,* (July 8, 1991), pp. 21-22.

Molloy, M. "Dunkin' Donuts Wins Through Downsizing." *Network World,* (July 15, 1991), pp. 27, 30.

Morris, R. "Corporate Downsizing from a Management Planning Perspective." *Information Management,* (September/October 1989), pp. 2-5.

Nash, J. "Downsizing Focus Shifts to Impact IS Function." *ComputerWorld,* (September 16, 1991), p. 4.

Nash, K.S., "Del Monte Reaps Fruits of IS Overhaul." *ComputerWorld,* (October 19, 1992), pp. 1, 12.

Nash, K.S. "Server Makers Pushing Mainframers to Downsize." *ComputerWorld,* (May 31, 1993), p. 47.

O'Leary, J. "Securing the Downsize Platform." *19th Annual Computer Security Conference & National Exhibition* (November 16-18, 1992), pp. 2-35, Chicago, IL.

O'Leary, M. [a] "Hearts and Minds." *CIO,* (April 15, 1992), pp. 44-46.

O'Leary, M. [b] "Means to An End." *CIO,* (April 15, 1992), pp. 54-56.

O'Leary, M. "The Upshot of Downsizing." *CIO,* (June 1, 1993), pp. 42-47.

Pastore, R. "The Power of Positive SHRINKING." *CIO*, (October 1, 1992), pp. 30-36.

Peal, D. and Pike H. "Technology Phoenix: Unisys Slims Down, Refocuses." *Corporate Computing*, (June 1991), p. 38.

Peltier, T.R. "Hard Times: Infosecurity and Downsizing." *ISP News*, (July/August 1992), p. 25.

Peri, R. [a] "A New Order in the Enterprise." *Communications Week*, (February 1, 1993), pp. 13-18.

Peri, R. [b] "Big 3 Adapt to 'Small' Trend." *Communications Week*, (February 1, 1993), p. 19.

Peri, R. [c] "Down to Savings." *Communications Week*, (February 1, 1993), pp. 5-8.

Peri, R. [d] "Filling the Gaps." *Communications Week*, (February 1, 1993), pp. 27-32.

Peri, R. [e] "Tuning the Team for a New Game." *Communications Week*, (February 1, 1993), pp. 21-23.

Peri, R. [f] "Which Path is Best?" *Communications Week*, (February 1, 1993), p. 11.

Radding, A. "Dirty Downsizing." *ComputerWorld*, (August 10, 1992), pp. 65-67.

Radding, A. "Downsizing Without the Fuss." *ComputerWorld*, (November 30, 1992), pp. 81-82.

Rinaldi, D, and Desmond, J. "Exploring Downsizing's Hidden Costs." *Software Magazine*, (March, 1993), pp. 62-65.

Savage, J.A. "Failed Merger Spawns Downsizing Plan." *ComputerWorld*, (September 16, 1991), p. 50.

Schwartz, J. "Downsizing: Users Exercise Patience." *Communications Week*, (October 19, 1992), pp. 1, 70.

Scott, K. "Netware on Downsizing Fast Track." *Infoworld*, (February 10, 1992), pp. 1, 63-64.

Seadle, M. "How Not to Downsize." *Enterprise Systems Journal*, X, (March, 1994), pp. 10-16.

Semilof, M. "People Issues in Downsizing." *Communications Week*, (October 14, 1991), p. 18.

Sharp, B. "Where to Find Expert Help for Downsizing." *Datamation*, (September 1, 1992), pp. 61-64.

Slater, D. "Mainframe Firms Feel Downsizing Heat." *ComputerWorld*, (October 26, 1992), p. 153.

Strassmann, D. "The Politics of Downsizing." *Datamation*, (October 15, 1992), pp. 107-110.

"The Strategic Opportunities of Smartsizing." *Datamation*, (October 15, 1992), pp. 2-4.

Truman, T. "For Success in Downsizing Scott Paper Uses the Team Approach: Digital and Unidata." *Datamation*, (March, 1993).

Whitman, Rich. "Puzzled by Computer Downsizing?" *Digital Update*, (January 1993).

Wilder, C. "CIOs Say Downsizing is in the Cards." *ComputerWorld*, (May 13, 1991), p. 65.

Wilder, C. "Users: Downsizing Gain is Worth the Pain." *ComputerWorld*, (October 14, 1991), p. 4.

Yarborough, W.J. "Emerging Network Strategies for Corporate Downsizing." *INTE NET*, (February 1993), pp. 49-50, 58.

Part 2
Rightsizing

Anthes, G.H. "Software AG Aids Rightsizing." *ComputerWorld*, (June 28, 1993), p. 91.

Chivvis, A. and Geyer, J. "Think Again." *Corporate Computing*, (April 1992), p. 43.

Ehrenreich, D. "Rightsizing: Redistributing the Electronic Workload." *INTE NET*, (June 1992), pp. 59-61.

Haight, T. "Rightsizing." *Network Computing*, (February 1993), pp. 87-97.

Kanin-Lovers, J. "Pay After Rightsizing." *Journal of Compensation & Benefits*, 7(2), (September/October 1991), pp. 51-54.

Koenig, K.K. "Rightsizing." *Bank Mgmt*, 66(6), (June 1990), pp. 38-42.

Morse, S. "Sizing — Tailoring the Applications and the Platforms." *Network Computing*, (February 1993), pp. 63-77.

Robinson, M.A. "Decentralize and Outsource: Dial's Approach to MIS Improvement." *Management Accounting*, (September 1991), pp. 27-28.

Sacks, D. "Rightsizing." *Enterprise Systems Journal,* (March 1994), p. 91.

Schneider, J.D. "It Pays to Get Your Hands Dirty Rightsizing." *PC WEEK,* (November 16, 1992), p. 97.

Sheridan, J.H. "A Tool for Rightsizing." *Industry Week,* (May 1, 1989), pp. 54-55.

"Top Down Rightsizing." *Software AG of North America,* (1993), pp. 1-8.

VanDame, M.L. and Catchings, B. "Getting Ready for Rightsizing." *Corporate Computing,* (June 1991), p. 141.

Videtich, J.W. "Responding to Demands for Change." *Network Management,* (June 1992), p. 70.

Part 2
Reengineering

Ambrosio, J. and Cafasso, R. "Reengineering the Railroad: Canadian Operation Upgrades Host to Improve Customer Service." *ComputerWorld,* (June 7, 1993), p. 16.

Anthes, G.H. "Penagon Wields IS Strategic Weapon." *ComputerWorld,* (June 8, 1992), pp. 1 & 20.

Blumenthal, M. Editorial. *CIO,* (June 15, 1993), p. 8.

Booker, E. "Work Flow Emerges as Imaging Trend." *ComputerWorld,* (July 6, 1992), p. 50.

Brousell, D.R. "Anything But Predictable." Editorial. *Datamation,* (August 1993), p. 8.

Buchanan, L. "Doing the Right Thing — Eleven Keys to Global Reengineering." *CIO*, (March 15, 1994), p. 51.

Cafasso, R. "Payoffs Lag, But Number of Projects Doubles." *ComputerWorld*, (March 29, 1993), p. 92.

Cafasso, R. "Reengineering: Just First Step." *ComputerWorld*, (April 19, 1993), p. 94.

Cafasso, R. "Rethinking Reengineering." *ComputerWorld*, (March 15, 1993), pp. 102-105.

Champy, J.A. "Grand Designs: Reengineering Will be More Important Than Ever Next Year — and Harder to Do." *CIO*, (January 1993), p. 26.

Currid, C. "Asking Why Could Uncover More Efficient Ways to Do Things." *Enterise Computing/Management*, (June 1, 1992), p. 55.

Cypress, H.L. "Reengineering." *OR/MS Today*, (February 1994), pp. 18-20, & 22-29.

Eskow, D. "Make More Money." *Corporate Computing*, (July 1992), p. 41.

Gantz, J. "Surviving the Reengineering Revolution." *Networking Management*, (January 1993), pp. 17-24.

Halberg, C. and Defiore, R. "Reengineering the Information Services Function." *SIM Network*, VIIII(III), (1994), pp. 1, 3-4.

Hammer, M. and J. Champy. *Reengineering the Corporation: A Manifesto for Business Revolution*, New York: Harper Collins (1993).

Hammer, M. and Champy J. "Explosive Thinking." *ComputerWorld,* (May 3, 1993), pp. 123-125.

Hammer, M. "Making the Quantum Leap." *Beyond Computing,* (March/April 1992), pp. 10, 12-14.

Harris, L.R. and Aikins, J. "KBS as Automated Edge." *Software Magazine,* (February 8, 1993), p. 35.

Hayley, K. and Plewa, J. "Four CIOs Bring Their Frontline Perspectives to a Survey on the State of IS." *CIO,* (April 15, 1993), pp. 26, 30-34.

Hoggman, T. "Reengineering Pays Off Cigna." *ComputerWorld,* (August 9, 1993), p. 70.

King, J. [a] "Do You Really Need a Reengineering Consultant?" *ComputerWorld,* (July 15, 1991), p. 56.

King, J. [b] "Reengineering Puts Progressive on the Spot." *ComputerWorld,* (July 15, 1991), p. 58.

King, J. [c] "Rip it Up!" *ComputerWorld,* (July 15, 1991), pp. 55-56.

King, J. [d] "Reengineering Repercussions." *ComputerWorld,* (June 28, 1993), pp. 149-151.

LaPlante, A. "Insurance Firm's Pen Computing Project Prompts Reengineering." *Enterprise Computing/Management,* (January 18, 1993), p. 53.

Lauderback, J. "The CSIRD Methodology: Deliver LAN Systems Faster and at a Lesser Cost the Client-Server Iterative Rapid Development ("Scissored") Methodology." *DBMS,* (June 1991), pp. 46-52.

Lindquist, C. "Touchdown!" *ComputerWorld*, (June 8, 1992), pp. 93-94.

Maglitta, J. "In Depth: Michael Hammer." *ComputerWorld*, (January 24, 1994), pp. 84-86.

Manganelli, R.L. "Define 'Reengineer'." *ComputerWorld*, (June 1992), pp. 115 & 117.

Margolis, N. "Close Link to Rightsizing." *ComputerWorld*, (March 29, 1993), p. 92.

Margolis, N. "Reengineering: It's Great, Whatever It Is." *ComputerWorld*, (June 29, 1992), p. 87.

Margolis, N. "Reengineering Gets Real: IS is Gearing Up to Convert Concept into Action." *ComputerWorld*, (January 18, 1993), p. 69.

Margolis, N. "Voices of Experience." *ComputerWorld*, (December 28, 1992/January 4, 1993), pp. 16-17.

McCreary, L. "Deconstruction the Status Quo." *CIO*, (June 15, 1993), pp. 32-34.

Miller, K. "The Not-So-Hidden Costs of Client-Server Computing." *Data Communications*, (August 1993), pp. 25-26.

Moad, J. "Does Reengineering Really Work." *Datamation*, (August 1, 1993), pp. 22, 23-24, & 28.

Moad, J. "Reengineering: Report from the Trenches." *Datamation*, (March 15, 1994), p. 39.

O'Leary, M. "A New Life for Purchasing." *CIO*, (May 1, 1993), pp. 32-36, & 41.

Ray, G. "Just How Do You Spell 'Reengineering'?" *ComputerWorld,* (March 15, 1993).

Rochester, J.B., Douglas, D.P., and Chikofsky, E.J. "Reengineering Existing Systems: Commentary." *I/S Analyzer, 29(10),* (October 1991), p. 1-16.

Ryan, A. J. "Is Reengineering Right for You?" *ComputerWorld,* (July 15, 1991), p. 57.

Santosus, M. "Keeping Customers Connected." *CIO,* (June 15, 1993), pp. 36-38, & 43.

Schatz, W. "What is Reengineering, Anyway?" *ComputerWorld,* (August 31, 1992), p. 97.

Thomas, M.L. "Reengineering the Frantic Discovery of the Obvious." *Modern Office Technology,* (January 1993), p. 48.

Tschida, R.G. "Reengineering Do's and Don'ts." *Public Sector Quality Report,* (February 1993), p. 3. [downloaded from the InterNet]

Verity, J.W. and McWilliams, G. "Is it Time to Junk the Way You Use Computers?" *Business Week,* (July 22, 1991), pp. 66 & 69.

Wexler, J.M. "Reengineering Report Cards." *ComputerWorld,* (July 6, 1992), p. 51.

Williamson, M. "Coming Back from the Brink." *CIO,* (June 15, 1993), pp. 46-47, 50 & 52.

Williamson, M. "Getting Into the Game." *CIO,* (June 15, 1993), pp. 56-59.

Wreden, N. "Reengineering: The Ultimate Test of Skill." *Beyond Computing,* (May/June 1994), p. 36.

Part 2
Partnering

Anderson, J.C. & Narus, J.A. "Partnering as a Focused Market Strategy." *California Management Review,* (Spring 1991), pp. 95-113.

Henricks, M. "The Power of Partnering." *Small Business Reports,* (June 1991), pp. 46-57.

Moore, C., Mosley, D. and Slagle M. "Partnering: Guidelines for Win-Win Project Management." *Project Management Journal,* XXIII, (March 1992), pp. 18-21.

Yovovich, B.G. "Partnering at its Best." *Business Marketing,* (March 1992), pp. 36-37.

Yovovich, B.G. "Do's and Don'ts of Partnering." *Business Marketing,* (March 1992), pp. 38-39.

Part 3 — Third-Party Service Organizations: The Impact on In-House Operations

Auditing

Adhikari, R. "The Security Risks of Outsourcing." *Info Security,* (November/December 1992), pp. 1, 9-10.

Alexander, M. "Users Get Serious About Growing Security Risk." *ComputerWorld,* XXV(31), (August 5, 1991), pp. 1, 10.

Alexander, S. "Client/Server's New Deal." *ComputerWorld*, (April, 1994), p. 71.

Alzua, R. "Downsizing Means More Work." *92 Access*, (2nd quarter), pp. 16-17.

Bradley, L.C. "Outsourcing the Data Center." *Enterprise Systems Journal*, (September 1993), pp. 18-22.

Braiotta, L. "A Local Practitioner's Guide to Internal Audit Services." *The CPA Journal*, (May 1992), pp. 54-58.

Campbell, J.E. and Mohan, N. "The Impact of Corporate Downsizing on Internal Auditing." *Internal Auditing*, (Spring 1992), pp. 3-9.

Courtemanche, G. "Outsourcing the Internal Audit Function." *Internal Auditor*, (August 1991), pp. 34-39.

Crone, R.K. "Negotiating an Outsourcing Agreement." *Bank Management*, (March 1992), pp. 59-62.

Daly, J. "Insecurity Complex." *ComputerWorld*, (June 21, 1993), pp. 91, 94.

Daly, J. "Open Security." *ComputerWorld*, (August 11, 1993), pp. 22-26.

Eckerson, W. "Outsourcing Unlikely to Offer Big Savings." *Network World*, (October 7, 1991), pp. 27-30.

Fried, L. "Outsourcing: One to Do Job, Another to Check It." *ComputerWorld*, (August 31, 1992), p. 33.

Friedberg, A.H. and Yarberry, W.A. Jr. "Audit Rights in an Outsource Environment." *Internal Auditor*, (August 1991), pp. 53-59.

Gerber, B., Schlesinger, L., Lutz, D., and Bing, G. "Downsizing: Platform Alternatives." *Network Computing,* (January 1991), pp. 47-56.

Gerber, B., Schlesinger, L., Lutz, D., and Bing, G. "The Upside and Downside of Downsizing." *Network Computing,* (January 1991), pp. 39-46.

Gillin, P. "Outsourcers: Get Close But Not Too Close." *ComputerWorld,* (December 21, 1992), p. 54.

Glass, B. "Technology is Not a Downsizing Cure-All." *Infoworld,* (February 10, 1992), p. 73.

Glassman, H. "Think Twice Before You Topple the Control Tower." *ComputerWorld,* (November 2, 1992), p. 33.

Goldsten, L.M., "As Others See Us." *Internal Auditor,* (February 1991), pp. 22-29.

Halper, M. and Hoffman, T. "Ruling Hits Outsourcing." *ComputerWorld,* (April 19, 1993), p. 1.

Hopper, M.D. "Tiptoeing Through the Outsourcing Minefield." *ComputerWorld,* (February 1, 1993), p. 29.

Klein, T.P. "How to Avoid the Five Biggest Downsizing Errors." *ComputerWorld,* (June 11, 1990), pp. 91-93.

LaPlante, A. "PC Expo Panel Will Highlight Importance of Writing a Good RFP." *Infoworld,* (June 15, 1992), p. 66.

Leinfuss, E. "Outsourcers Have Limited Liability." *ComputerWorld,* (March 30, 1992), p. 88.

Livingston, D. "Outsourcing: Look Beyond the Price Tag." *Datamation,* (November 15, 1992), pp. 93-97.

Llana, A. "The Ups and Downs of Outsourcing." *Data Communications*, (January 21, 1993), pp. 69-71.

Margolis, N. and Wilder, C. "Early Adopters Give Qualified Approval, But Urge IS to Keep Its Hands on the Reins." *ComputerWorld*, XXVI(1), (May 4, 1992), p. 20.

Mautz, R.K., and Sharaf, H.A. *The Philosophy of Auditing. Sarasota: American Accounting Association*, (1961).

Mirlocca, N.C. and Hollander, N.D. "Don't Get Stung by Software Contracts." *ComputerWorld*, (June 7, 1993), p. 100.

Mitchell, R. "Third-Party Processors Continue to Grow." *Bank Processing Special Report*, (June 1993), p. 21.

Mize, B. "Vendor Audits." *Internal Auditor*, (August 1992), pp. 47-52.

Muhlestein, C.B. and Smith, J.D. "A Cost-Effective Audit Partnership." *Internal Auditor*, (June 1991), pp. 144-146.

"Outsourcing in the '90s." Information Technology Association of America, 1616 N. Fort Myer Drive, Suite 1300, Arlington, VA 22209

Peacock, E. and Pelfrey, S. "How Internal Auditors View the External Audit." *Internal Auditor*, (June 1989), pp. 49-54.

Powell, D. "Outsourcing Offers Obvious Benefits, But Beware of Subtle Disadvantages." *Networking Management*, (March 1993), p. 8

Powell, D. "To Outsource or Not to Outsource?" *Networking Management*, (February 1993), pp. 56-61.

Ricchute, D. *Auditing Concepts and Standards,* South-Western Publishing, Co., (1989).

Rohan, J.E. "Auditing Third Party Risk." *Internal Auditing,* (Spring 1991), pp. 69-73.

Schuetz, W.D. *SEC Accounting Update.* (November 1994.) Paper presented at the meeting of the AICPA's Nineteenth Annual Conference on Banking, Washington, DC.

Scott, Y. "Outsourcing: Audit and Control." *19th Annual Computer Security Conference & National Exhibition,* Chicago, IL , (November 16-18, 1992).

Sherizen, S. "Protecting Information in a Changing Corporate Environment: Downsizing, Outsourcing and Mergers." *The 12th Annual Conference on Control, Audit & Security of Information Systems: Meeting the Challenge of Multi-Platform Environments,* Session G33.

Sirkin, B. "Few Account for Hidden Costs of Downsizing." *PC Week,* (June 3, 1991), p. 65.

Thayer, W. "20 Do's and Don'ts of Cost Cutting." *Progressive Grocer,* (May 1991), pp. 67-70.

Thress, S.C. and Pegolo, S.R. "Auditing in a Microcomputer Environment." *Datamation,* (November 15, 1990), pp. 82-87.

Van Collie, S. "Downsizing Creates Need for Upscaling Security." *Bank Technology News,* (October 1992), pp. 5-7.

Verschoor, C.C. "Evaluating Outsourcing of Internal Auditing." *Management Accounting,* (February 1992), pp. 27-30.

Williamson, M. "Outsourcing Terms of Agreement." *CIO*, (June 1, 1993), pp. 31-36.

Wyatt, C. "Trusting Third Parties with Customer Relations." *Bank Processing Special Report*, (June 1993), pp. 19-20.

Xenakis, J.J. "The Uncertainty of Outsourcing." *CFO*, (October 1992), pp. 75-76.

Zahler, R. "Clear Performance Rules Ease Outsourcing Hassles." *Networld World*, (April 6, 1992), pp. 29, 32.

Zahler, R. "Identifying the Key Issues for Assessing Outsourcing." *Network World*, (March 30, 1992), pp. 21, 23.